THE ULTIMATE GUIDE
TO HOMESCHOOLING
TEENS

Debra Bell

The Ultimate Guide to Homeschooling Teens

Published by

Apologia Press

A division of Apologia Educational Ministries, Inc.

1106 Meridian Plaza, Suite 220/340

Anderson, Indiana 46016

www.apologia.com

Manufactured in the USA

First Printing: July 2010

ISBN: 978-1-932012-99-6

Cover and design by Doug Powell

Printed by Courier, Inc., Stoughton, MA

Unless otherwise indicated, Scripture quotations are from:
The Holy Bible, New International Version © 1973, 1984 by International Bible Society,
used by permission of Zondervan Publishing House.

Other Scripture quotations are from:
The Holy Bible, English Standard Version (esv) © 2001 by Crossway Bibles, a division
of Good News Publishers. Used by permission. All rights reserved.

For Gabe, Mike, Kayte and Kristen—
As you know I'm very available to help
homeschool the next generation.
Just sayin'.

And for Billy, who is kind of a big deal.

CONTENTS

ACKNOWLEDGMENTS

A very close second to the joy I found in home educating my own four children is the meaning I have found in being part of many families' high school programs as an English teacher at CHESS family school and online through PA Homeschoolers.

Over the years I have received many thoughtful notes from parents and students saying I had inspired them to achieve beyond their abilities. The truth is, the kids inspired me with their insight, their passion, their boundless curiosity, their seriousness of purpose, and their faith. I have always been humbled by their eagerness to learn and their willingness to tolerate my probing questions, my directness, my standards (rooted in a bygone era) and my fondness for revision.

The devotion of these children's parents and the sacrifices they've made have formed the bedrock underlying the character of the fascinating teens I have had the privilege of teaching. I thank you all for allowing me be a small part of the wonder of your children's passage into adulthood. I am most grateful.

In particular, I'd like to thank the students in my AP Literature and AP Language courses for 2007–08 and 2008–09 who discussed the content of this book with me and supplied many of the anecdotes and samples provided herein. (Please friend me on Facebook so I can keep track of you

7

all!) I'd also like to thank Scott Woodruff of HSLDA, whose kids are wonderful former students, for his thoughtful and timely e-mails that helped me clarify my thinking on this book and on working with teens in general.

I'd also like to give a shout out to my sounding boards: Zan Tyler, Vicki Dincher, Joanna Breault, Melanie Wasko, Jill Panyard, Kathy Teaman, Susan Richman, Colette Bailes, and Cindy McKeown. Your experiences and views on education have informed my own—and so I just went ahead and put them in my book. (I knew you'd be flattered.)

And then there's the terrific team at Apologia who came along just when I was having a bit of a pity party for myself (*What's a retired homeschooled mom to do with all these opinions? My life has no meaning anymore!*). Thank you, Davis, Rachel, Zan, and David. Wow, this cleaned up *purty* good! You made that happen.

Finally, I want to thank my husband, Kermit, the most faithful man I know on so many levels. He's unwavering in his support, patience, and understanding. Love you, Pal!

INTRODUCTION:
A JOURNEY OF FAITH

Welcome to this user-friendly guide to the high school years and beyond, written for homeschooling families from the perspective of one who has been to the edge and safely returned. I'm eager to pass along what I've learned about long-term home education while it is still fresh in my mind.

In retrospect, homeschooling through high school was a great opportunity for our family. Sure, there were plenty of moments when I cried, "Aren't we done yet?" And there were plenty of moments when my children asked the same. But they're grown now, and each can see clearly how God used our homeschool as a launch pad for their college years and their subsequent adult lives. Throughout this book I will tell you their stories, as well as the stories of other homeschooling families, in the hope that you can see your own situation in at least one of them.

In a nutshell, here's what happened with our four children (as of this writing) after they completed high school at home.

Mike and Gabe, identical twins now in their mid-twenties, graduated from an honors college program at a state university. One majored in international business; the other double-majored in economics and finance. College proved a great adventure for both of them. They spent almost as much time abroad as they did on campus. Mike studied in France, Thailand, and Bangladesh and volunteered one summer in South Africa. Gabe studied in England, Spain, and Bangladesh. They have also backpacked, together or individually, through North Africa, Europe, and Southeast Asia. Today, Mike lives overseas with his wife, where he's working on his MBA. Gabe is newly married and will soon be starting law school.

Kayte, 24, graduated from the University of Pittsburgh with degrees in mathematics and French and a minor in Arabic. She currently teaches in inner-city Philadelphia and has just finished her Masters in Education at the University of Pennsylvania. Also infected with the travel bug, she sailed around the world during college and studied in France and Cairo.

Kristen, 21, recently graduated with a degree in elementary education. She also plans to teach in an inner-city school. Although she did not read until age ten, she made the dean's list every semester and completed her degree in three-and-a-half years.

So academically, homeschooling through high school worked out just fine for our kids. However, the greatest joy in our lives is that all four have embraced our Christian faith and prioritized their lives around the spread of the gospel and the building of Christ's church.

STARTING FROM A FOUNDATION OF FAITH

This is a practical book. I have set out to provide you the nuts and bolts of high school homeschooling, to give you reliable inside information from someone who's been there, done that.

Yet if you don't gather your sources and resources from a foundation of faith, all the information I'm about to share can lead to your becoming overwhelmed, discouraged, and fearful of failure. There's a lot to do and keep track of. In an institutional setting, this responsibility is distributed among administrators, teachers, guidance counselors, and support staff. In homeschooling, it boils down to the parents, primarily Mom, and that's why a lot of naysayers suggest it cannot be adequately done. I agree—if you set out to do this in your own strength.

You can be sure there will be dropped balls, lots of gaps and holes, many missed deadlines, and a general struggle just to keep up. But here's the good news: This overwhelming responsibility is just the kind of situation in which we may tangibly experience the unmerited favor of God as He faithfully provides for our every need. That's what is really exciting about long-term homeschooling: You get to experience God's faithfulness in new and profound ways. We need to rest our confidence upon Him, certainly not on our own abilities and strength—that would only result in a lesson in humility (or humiliation).

You see, God not only *knows* your children's futures. He's *authoring* their lives—and yours as well. Homeschooling is merely the way He's chosen for your family to learn more keenly how the God of the universe personally involves Himself in your cares. Our role as parents is to put our confidence in Him so that He receives the glory for His kind provision.

Got that? Then onward.

PART 1
MAKING THE DECISION

1 SHOULD I HOMESCHOOL MY TEEN?

This is the first and, also, the last question you will answer while using this book. Part one of this guide is designed to provide you a framework for making a good decision. Should you decide to proceed, the rest of the book will equip you with the knowledge and resources necessary to complete your journey. Initially, you may feel overwhelmed by the breadth of information and all that's at stake. Hang in there! It's not as difficult as it may sound at first. The homeschool community is far more recognized and organized than it was just twenty years ago.

Remember, I'm writing from the perspective of one who has survived and completed the journey. In hindsight, I realize how unprepared and uninformed I was in the beginning. Hey, we made it through anyway. You will too. Your kids will survive and ultimately arrive where they need to be.

So take a deep breath, thank God for His faithful provision and care in your life, and trust Him with your child's future. Then read the following pages with eyes of faith, not fear.

So when should you begin thinking about homeschooling your teen through high school? About the time your child enters the seventh grade. Certainly you may want to be gathering information about the prospects of high school homeschooling before then, but prior to the middle school years you won't have a clear picture of your child's needs or your long-term family situation. Kids change a lot during this season of life, and you will want to assess the situation with that information in mind.

What factors should you consider when looking at high school at home? Let's break this down into three areas: spiritual, academic, and practical.

SPIRITUAL MATTERS TO CONSIDER

First things first. For Kermit and me, our greatest priority in parenting has always been our children's standing before God. We desired above all else to see them, as children and as adults, pressing upward and onward into the goodness of God. This was always the bottom line for us in making the choice to homeschool. We simply never saw another path that safeguarded this priority and gave our kids the best place for growing in the compelling grace of God.

Here are the essential questions I think we, as parents, should be asking.

Where is the best place for my child to experience the grace of God which leads to repentance?
Until you have confidence in your child's salvation, you should proceed cautiously in choosing a learning environment that isn't supporting that goal. And at least in our home, three of our children date their

> Until you have confidence in your child's salvation, you should proceed cautiously in choosing a learning environment that isn't supporting that goal.

conversion stories from age fourteen and not from earlier confessions of faith. We were not confident that true conversion had taken place until each of our kids demonstrated a consistent interest in spiritual things, evident in our home through a desire to be in church, reading books with spiritual themes, and eagerly attending events designed to foster their spiritual growth, such as youth camp.

Yes, there were ongoing discussions concerning thorny issues of interest to teenagers—dating, driving privileges, curfews, etc.—but the kids demonstrated a maturing faith by keeping these communications on the level of discussion, not arguments. Our teens had come to their own convictions about God's design for parental leadership, and they had faith in His capacity for changing our hearts if we were wrong.

So, conservatively, where would you assess your child in terms of his or her conversion? If you have confidence in your child's salvation, then you know that the Holy Spirit is in residence and you can rest in the assurance that God is at work within your child's heart both to will and to work for His good pleasure.

Where is the best place for my child to grow toward Christian maturity?

Be patient, we will talk about evangelism. But even if our children are converted from an early age, there is still a process through which they must grow to maturity in Christ. And in order for them to grow in grace, they need a time of equipping and seasoning.

Scripture implies this time should be strategic and intentional. Christ did not enter public ministry until age thirty. The disciples, Paul, and Timothy all received training before going into ministry. So let us likewise not gloss over the importance of a time of preparation. And don't assume it will happen without a focused effort. Christian maturity is not a guarantee—we are called to press on (Philippians 3:12), make every effort (2 Peter 1:5), throw off everything that hinders us (Hebrews 12:1), and undergo strict training to gain the crown that will last forever (1 Corinthians 9:25). Proverbs 22:6 assigns parents a role in this equation: "Train a child in the way he should go, and when he is old he will not turn from it." The best gift you can give your child, apart from the knowledge of his need for a Savior and the good news that God has provided One, is a robust understanding of the benefits of pursuing Christian maturity.

> The best gift you can give your child, apart from the knowledge of his need for a Savior and the good news that God has provided One, is a robust understanding of the benefits of pursuing Christian maturity.

Close your eyes a moment. Imagine the future you desire for your child. What are the basic things you long for him or her to have? A good marriage? Health? Happiness? Security? A successful career? The only certain path to any of these is the path of godliness:

His divine power has given us everything we need for life and godliness through our knowledge of him. . . . For this very reason, make every effort to add to your faith goodness; and to goodness, knowledge; and to knowledge, self-control; and to self-control, perseverance; and to perseverance, godliness; and to godliness, brotherly kindness; and to brotherly kindness, love. For if you possess these qualities in increasing measure, they will keep you from being ineffective and unproductive. (2 Peter 1:3–8, ESV)

17

Therefore, since we have been justified through faith, we have peace with God through our Lord Jesus Christ, through whom we have gained access by faith into this grace in which we now stand. And we rejoice in the hope of the glory of God. Not only so, but we also rejoice in our sufferings, because we know that suffering produces perseverance; perseverance, character; and character, hope. And hope does not disappoint us, because God has poured out his love into our hearts by the Holy Spirit, whom he has given us. (Romans 5:1–5)

Three things I want you to notice in these passages:

1. God gives us the power for this process through His redemptive grace. Yahoo for the assurances of salvation and the power it gives us!
2. The path to godliness is not the easy road. Suffering, tribulations, difficulties, challenges—these are indications you are headed in the right direction.
3. The outcome is joy—hope that never disappoints and love that endures. You want to be happy? Pursue godliness.

Do you want your children to be happy in the long run? Teach them to pursue godliness. Implied in all of this, of course, is the assumption that a child's teen years are primarily intended to prepare them for adulthood and not for pursuing leisure and ease.

So make an honest assessment of your child's spiritual health and the type of training provided by various educational choices. Will the environment you're considering help your child grow in godliness? Or will it place your child in danger of spiritual decline?

Where is the best place for my child to develop his gifts and talents with a view toward a future calling?

Now we come to the issue of evangelism and other endeavors that require interaction with others beyond the scope of the family. We want to increase our children's concern for those who do not know Christ, but it's impossible to cultivate true love and motivation for this if we don't know any unbelievers. We also want them to learn how to put the gospel on display in word and deed so others are attracted to the fragrance of Christ in their lives.

> We want to increase our children's concern for those who do not know Christ, but it's impossible to cultivate true love and motivation for this if we don't know any unbelievers.

If our children never transition from homeschooling into the larger society, it's difficult for me to see how this is effectively accomplished. Because of the evidence of conversion in our children's lives, we did strategically and intentionally increase their sphere of influence during their teen years. Our sons played scholastic sports and took a number of classes outside the home during their high school years. Kayte spent part of a summer at an academic camp mixing with kids from many ethnic and religious backgrounds. Kristen worked at a resort and for a restaurant. We hosted exchange students for several years, and our kids began traveling internationally. All four kids attended public universities and also lived in dormitories for a portion of their college years. So you see, I'm writing from a conviction that kids are eventually *launched* into a sphere of influence. Our motivation in homeschooling was to *prepare*, not protect.

What happens during this preparation? Well, we parents have some equipping to do. And part of that equipping is the development of our child's gifts and talents. Each of us has innate abilities, given to us at birth by the unmerited kindness of God—we like to call them talents and forget we didn't earn or deserve them (1 Corinthians 4:7). The purpose for these talents, though, is made clear in Scripture:

> But to each one of us grace has been given as Christ apportioned it. . . . From him the whole body, joined and held together by every supporting ligament, grows and builds itself up in love, as each part does its work. (Ephesians 4:7, 16)

We each have a responsibility to discern the work Christ has given to us in building His body. And the apportionment of grace in our lives is an indication of that specific calling. Does your child have innate musical talent? How potentially might that be used in corporate worship or in attracting others to the gospel? Is she relationally gifted? Do others quickly feel comfortable with her, and is she energized by a wide network of friends? What might God's eternal purposes be for this gifting?

Modern American parents seem to revel in their kids' abilities, no matter how slight; schedules packed with athletics, dance, drama, and music are the norm from preschool forward. I'm not talking about that kind of approach. I'm pressing for a more God-centered view of our children's gifts. Teens in particular need our help in this area:

* They need help identifying areas of Gods' grace in their lives.

Each of us has innate abilities, given to us at birth by the unmerited kindness of God.

20

* They need help cultivating their talents, not hiding them in the ground (Matthew 25:14).
* They need help recognizing that their talents are not for their own glorification but, rather, for the building up of the body of Christ in love.

So in considering your educational options, seriously consider how a particular environment will support the identification, development, and purpose of the gifts your child possesses.

At our house we found the teen years an exciting time. We tailored our program to strengthen each child's talents and gave them a vision for what the future might hold. One reason why I discuss the college years in this manual is to give you a vision too for what God may have in store for your teens as you prepare to send them out into the world.

ACADEMIC MATTERS TO CONSIDER

While academic matters are important yet subordinate to the larger picture of spiritual concerns, academics can play a vital role in meeting the goals we've just discussed. To advance the kingdom of God in a postmodern world, our teens need to expand their knowledge base, hone their skills, and learn to think critically. Academic rigor is one way of fostering this.

I've often said homeschooling would be relatively simple if we were preparing our children for life of simplicity and isolation among the Amish. But for most of us that's not the intent—we live in a complex society—they'll be entering a highly trained marketplace where skills are specialized and sophisticated. To have their opinions heard and considered, they must be articulate, engaging, and persuasive. Further, they have to be relevant—if they cannot make a cultural connection, they'll have as much influence as junk mail. How can we expect them

21

to enter the fray without adequate training?

And as we're all aware, the curriculum gets pretty daunting as we press forward into the high school years. I tapped out my math skills, for instance, when my kids hit junior high—and then three of them chose math-heavy majors in college. How did we make that work? Well, it wasn't easy. And once they got to college they all wished they had applied themselves more earnestly during high school. But God's grace was sufficient for them then too.

Here are a few questions to consider in this area:

Where will my child best acquire the knowledge and skills he needs for life after high school?
Let's break that question down. First, you have to find out what educational options are available. No sense working your way through to a logical conclusion that doesn't exist. Presumably, homeschooling is one option, and public school is another. But there may also be Christian schools, classical Christian schools, charter schools, cyber-charter schools, and vocational-technical schools available in your area.

Next, where is your child headed after high school? You may not know yet, but you have to know enough to make a logical decision about high school. What's the most competitive option you want to have opened for your child? Here's a list of possibilities to get you started:

> What's the most competitive option you want to have opened for your child after high school?

* Community college
* Four-year university at a state school

* Four-year university at an elite school
* Four-year university on a pre-professional track (engineering, medicine, law)
* Christian liberal arts school
* Bible college or seminary
* Trade or technical School
* Military
* Military academy
* The job marketplace
* Marriage

Make your list and then determine through research which options have the most stringent entrance requirements. On my list, that is going to be a military academy, an elite school, or an engineering or pre-med course of study. These are the toughest doors to get opened, and for your child to have a shot at gaining entrance, she needs to complete a rigorous course of study in high school and have a strong résumé of extracurricular activities. I know homeschool students who have made themselves even more appealing candidates because of their homeschooling experience, but this requires intentional planning.

For some of the options on the list above, your child will also need advocates to open doors. He or she will need recommendations and counsel from experienced individuals who know the ropes. Our daughter Kayte took a course at a local college specifically because she needed a recommendation from a qualified professor for a scholarship opportunity. As you are working toward the options you are shooting for, think about what kind of individuals will be needed to help your child along the way.

Which educational system will best support his academic goals?

It's one thing to have access to educational options you need; it's another thing to be surrounded by good teachers and like-minded peers. Even the most grounded kids find it hard to stay academically focused when those around them couldn't care less. They may also find it difficult to rise to their potential if they aren't testing their mettle against other talented individuals who set the bar just a bit higher. Some students need this competitive environment; others will be stressed and drained by it. In this book I'll give you a few tools for understanding how your teen learns best, then you should take this information into account as you make decisions.

Something to keep in mind: There is no replacement for a mentor who can inspire your teen. In searching for the right mentor, look no further than your local church or homeschool network. We found that retirees and hobbyists in our community were more than willing to take an eager student under wing. Who is available and willing among your network of friends and family? Don't be afraid to ask. I know plenty of stories of successful mentoring that began with a mom timidly asking someone to consider working with her homeschooled teen.

PRACTICAL MATTERS TO CONSIDER

Let's talk brass tacks. What practically needs to happen to make your choice of educational options a reality? Only public education is ostensibly free, but how much will it cost to homeschool through high school or send your child to a private school? Do you have faith that God will provide if homeschooling is the best choice for your child? What budgetary sacrifices may be required to send your child to private school? As you weigh the financial considerations, talk to some folks who are exercising the educational choice in question to get a clearer picture of the expenses you may be facing.

Besides finances, what other obligations must factor into your decision? Are there health issues in your family? Do any of your children have needs that would compete or conflict with exercising a particular option?

WHY WE CHOSE HOMESCHOOLING

It wasn't a laborious decision to choose homeschooling for my children when they were toddlers. I have a background in teaching and was something of a renegade while in school, both as a student and teacher. I love to learn, but I started questioning the system very early. The whole structure doesn't make sense to me in terms of setting up an environment that's conducive to learning.

John Holt's writings resonated with me (see, for example, *How Children Fail*). I attended my first homeschool meeting when my twins were two years old and found that's where all my hippie friends from the 1970s had gone! They were nursing babies they'd had at home, singing in family folk bands, grinding grain, and living counter to the culture. Their children were carefree, unscheduled, and happy. I was hooked. I could do this.

We were the first family in our school district to homeschool. That first year, we were active in the movement to legalize homeschooling in our state. Once it became legal to homeschool, people began leaving the public school system in droves.

We had a great experience during the elementary years, but when my twins reached

> We had a great experience during the elementary years, but when my twins reached seventh grade, fissures began to appear.

25

seventh grade, fissures began to appear. The boys began advocating for change. Four teens later, I know this is quite normal, but as they were my first, their complaints were alarming.

My sons had been playing organized sports since age five, and this had become a big part of their lives and identity. Well, their teammates all went to public school. My sons were naturally curious about public school and began wondering, *How long is she going to do this to us?*

At the same time, I was thinking (with a growing sense of foreboding) about what lay ahead. How was I going to teach high school physics? I had opted out of higher math and science very early in high school—I never got beyond algebra 2 and biology. I did take a chemistry class, but that was a joke. In college, I took biology again and a general mathematics course before diving into my major, English. I had never really planned to go this far with homeschooling. Initially I had thought I would teach the kids through third grade and then send them off to school. But as the homeschool movement grew in popularity and options, I just kept on going without a thought. We were really having a lot of fun. Then suddenly, I looked up and saw where all this was heading—*high school at home!* Whoa. I had never even dreamed of going this far.

> Suddenly, I looked up and saw where all this was heading—high school at home! Whoa. I had never even dreamed of going this far.

How would my kids get into college without a diploma? How would I teach the hard stuff? Was I finally going to have to learn math? And if the kids got to college, would the jig be up and their educational deficiencies come to light?

Things finally came to a head when in eighth grade the boys announced that *they* had decided to go to public school for high school. The fact they thought it was their decision was shocking enough, but we soon found out they had already told their friends and coaches that they'd be there in the fall. So the forces were marshaled against us.

What did we do? (I mean, after overreacting and yelling. We'll just skip that part of the story.) We went through a process of evaluating all our choices again and seeking wise counsel. And we allowed our sons to be a part of that process. They were welcomed to weigh in on the options, with the understanding that the decision was, in fact, ours to make, not theirs.

I admit to being a bit foggy in the beginning about who should make this call, but my husband was not. He knew it was our responsibility and, after getting together with our pastor and his wife to talk this through, I understood this more clearly too. Perhaps you are wavering in this area as well, so let me share our understanding of why parents still hold the reins during the teenage years. At age fourteen, our sons were living under our roof and were completely financially dependent upon us. It was clear that God still held my husband and me accountable for their well-being and spiritual growth; therefore, we were the ones to whom He would reveal His counsel. Certainly others, including our children, could be used by God to provide input that we would be wise to consider; but ultimately we had to have faith that God would confirm in our hearts the wisest course for our children through the teen years. From experience and from the Scriptures, I think it highly unlikely your financially dependent child will sense God leading him in a direction you don't also have the same inclination toward.

Do we ever let go of or transfer this responsibility? You bet—and with gladness. As our children take on added personal responsibility, especially financial responsibility, they certainly should be given the freedom to make their own decisions. All four of our kids assumed responsibility for paying for college,

27

so that is when the greatest transfer of "power" occurred in our home. Because their independence was not yet complete—we were still providing for a lot of their needs—we felt free to give our counsel and, on occasion, just say no, especially during the summer months when they were living under our roof and driving our cars.

If our older teens show evidence of conversion and are responding consistently to the grace of God in their lives, then it is wise for us as parents to progressively let them make decisions. After all, they need to learn to hear the voice of God for themselves. By having the freedom to decide what summer job to take, which friends to pursue, or where to volunteer

> If our older teens show evidence of conversion and are responding consistently to the grace of God in their lives, then it is wise for us as parents to progressively let them make decisions.

their time, they can learn from their decisions, even if their choice proves not to be the best one. Such decisions can easily be revoked, if necessary, but where to spend their high school years—at home or in school—that is a HUGE decision with many ramifications that you understand much better than your teenagers. In an ideal world, both parents and teen will agree on the best place for the child to spend these years. But in our world, that didn't happen.

My husband told me several times privately the boys simply were not going to public school. He felt their reasons for wanting to attend high school were immature and actually quite funny: hot lunches, girls, and popularity. When these reasons failed to impress us, they played the evangelism card: "But we can witness to our friends!" Kermit's leanings remained pretty consistent, but he did allow for an honest assessment of the options. Originally, he had been the more reluctant parent when it came to homeschooling, but at this juncture he was the more committed to pressing forward. Of course, there were still chinks in my own resolve:

* I didn't feel qualified to handle all the subject matter necessary for a college-preparatory program.
* We were living in tight quarters, with our growing boys still sharing a room, and there was a lot of conflict in the house during the day.
* I had bought into the boys' argument that they could be leaders and influencers at school.
* The boys said I was "feminizing" them. They wanted to get out into the world of men.
* My daughters often fended for themselves in school because I was consumed with addressing our sons' needs and their growing resistance.

I'm sharing these concerns with you because I think they are each worthy of consideration. And even though we chose to continue homeschooling, we had to realistically address each of these challenges.

We decided homeschooling was the best option because we realized our sons were spiritually and emotionally immature. They wanted to go to public school for understandable reasons— they desired a wider social experience, and they craved the recognition that comes with being jocks on campus. Of course, they had trouble seeing the potential pitfalls. While I thoroughly enjoyed my sons' athletic participation, I was grateful that they spent most of their time with homeschooled friends who cared little about such things. Although athletics might give them an open door for influencing others, the world's tendency to glorify athletes feeds self-centeredness and arrogance.

29

I did investigate the academic opportunities our district could provide. I met with a guidance counselor to discuss the various college-preparatory tracks they could follow. In doing so, I realized that as homeschoolers we actually had greater access to accelerated coursework in our community. Community colleges were allowing homeschooled kids to take classes early, and online Advanced Placement classes

> I realized that as homeschoolers we actually had greater access to accelerated coursework in our community.

were readily available. Our district didn't allow for acceleration until eleventh grade, and then only after all available classes offered at the high school level had been completed.

In addition, administrators strongly recommended my sons be tested by the school psychologist to determine placement. I actually felt this might prove interesting. Testing is a huge part of student evaluation in public education, and they would likely find it an eye-opening experience. Everyone was more than cordial and eager to make Mike and Gabe feel welcomed, but their experience with the "system" definitely cooled some of their ardor. They did not like the interview with the school psychologist, who they each felt summed them up rather quickly and erroneously. I told them to get used to it, because that's the way mass education works.

Our decision-making process spanned several months. We set a deadline for the end of May—the guidance department said if we waited much longer to enroll them, Mike and Gabe might not be able to get into the classes they wanted. Despite their negative experience with the school psychologist, my sons were now pushing forcefully for going to public school. We were planning to attend an annual conference held by our association of churches over Memorial Day weekend, and

Kermit and I felt that the opportunity to talk with some wise friends would enable us to make a clear decision.

During this weekend, we worshiped God with abandon and, without distractions, came to the realization our sons' spiritual growth superseded all other factors. At age fourteen, they simply were not ready to launch. I had no answers yet as to how we would provide for all their academic and social needs, but I had the assurance that God would provide as we responded in obedience to His direction.[3]

> I had no answers yet as to how we would provide for all their academic and social needs, but I had the assurance that God would provide as we responded in obedience to His direction.

The day after we arrived home from the conference, my husband called a meeting with Mike and Gabe and we told them they would be staying home for high school. Mike said bitterly, "I knew it," and Gabe responded with the full force of his emotions. We explained patiently why we felt this was the right decision, and we also made a commitment to get them together with their closest Christian friends more often. For me, this meant a commitment to drive them some distance. It had been easy to let them socialize with the friends on their sports teams and in the neighborhood, but we now realized our own laziness had contributed to the current impasse. Their closest friend in church lived a forty-minute round trip away. And the young man who was the best influence in their lives lived on the other side of the state. Fortunately, his parents were willing to have Mike and Gabe spend a week with their family during summer vacations, and we were able to have Stephen visit us as well.

I told them we would give them space to process this emotionally, and they could feel free to continue asking questions while they grappled with their disappointment. But forty-eight hours later, I'd had enough. I asked them if they felt that we hadn't done all we could to hear God in the situation? Was there someone else they thought we should seek counsel from? Did they doubt our dedication to praying about this decision? Had we not listened fully to their concerns? I honestly offered to do whatever they felt we still could do to hear the Lord. When they begrudgingly admitted that, no, they realized we had put our best effort into figuring this out, I told them soberly that they were not angry with us—they were angry with God and His will for their lives.

Mike still remembers that moment. When I pointed out that he was angry with God, he was pricked by the truth of this, and he quickly snapped out of his funk. Gabe took a bit longer to cease bemoaning his fate. But surprisingly, once they realized the decision had been made and we were not going to waffle, all the fight went out of them. And a few months into ninth grade, they were actually happy about being homeschooled. I believe this was a work of the Holy Spirit in their hearts, and while we still had many moments of conflict to work through in the years that followed, today none of us questions the wisdom of the decision.

Our sons continued to play scholastic sports for the public school teams, and they even took a couple of on-campus classes during their eleventh- and twelfth-grade years. By that point, they were more mature, and they actually did use these opportunities to share their faith without compromise. In

> By their eleventh and twelfth grade years, our sons were more mature, and they actually did use these opportunities to share their faith without compromise.

fact, during their junior year of high school, they began holding Bible studies in our home for their football buddies. When they got to college, they immediately started a Bible study in their dormitory which continues today.

In case you're wondering what happened with our daughters, neither of them ever seriously considered not continuing with homeschooling. Because they took advantage of athletic opportunities in our homeschool community—volleyball and girls' basketball—public school didn't hold the same draw for them. And unlike our sons, all their closest friends continued with homeschooling as well. But Kayte and her friends did leverage this spirit of cooperation and compliance: They called a meeting with the homeschool moms at our co-op the summer before they entered ninth grade. At this meeting, they told us they didn't mind remaining home for high school, except they regretted not having access to a drama program like they might find at a public school. We had been putting on parent-directed productions for years, but they honestly felt these were a bit embarrassing. So we negotiated a settlement: If they would help, we would direct our energies toward improving the quality of our annual production.

I had a "coincidental" conversation with a professional drama coach soon after this and discovered she had never considered offering acting classes to the homeschool community but was certainly interested. That fall, my new friend, Cory, began offering classes at our co-op, and that spring we put on our first full-length show. Things evolved, Cory trained one of our moms to direct, and we started raising money. We eventually secured non-profit status and Encore! Homeschool Productions was born. Since then, our annual full-scale musical has become a regular part of our community. As this book goes to press, our drama group is preparing to stage *Beauty and the Beast*—with all the bells and whistles you'd find at any local high school.

33

I think if you ask around you will find our story is not much different from the stories of long-term homeschoolers in your area. Taking the time to make a thoughtful decision about homeschooling through high school, coupled with prayer and wise counsel, will give you confidence in God's leading and provide staying power during the ups and downs of the journey. It will also give you the eyes of faith to expect and recognize His provision along the way.

> Taking the time to make a thoughtful decision about homeschooling through high school, coupled with prayer and wise counsel, will give you confidence in God's leading and provide staying power during the ups and downs of the journey.

2 THE ADVANTAGES OF DOING HIGH SCHOOL AT HOME

Let's take a closer look at the factors that tipped the scales for us in favor of long-term homeschooling.

HOME IS THE BEST PLACE FOR CULTIVATING SPIRITUAL GROWTH

Home is the most important place our children will see the power and mercy of the gospel on display and experience how it can affect their lives. Church is the second. If your faith and values matter to you—and these inform your daily attitudes, choices, and actions—then home is the best place for the spiritual development of your children. Sometimes this is a matter of faith for parents. All kids, prior to reaching adulthood, will evaluate and adopt or discard the values and beliefs held by their parents and other significant adults in their lives. Some kids will go through this process internally without much outward indication, while others will openly question and struggle. But no matter how your teen responds to the process, you can be confident this development is taking place and that he or she is moving toward a place of personally held beliefs and convictions.

Homeschooling allows for this fragile time to take place

in your home and amid your family. Research has repeatedly found that parents are the biggest influence in their children's moral development—*if* they do not abdicate that role. However, peers will become the chief socializing influence if the parents are not around. Quality time does not trump quantity of time; kids need both from us.

Homeschool is a natural setting for spiritual growth and the only one that truly can integrate a child's emotional, intellectual and moral development. And that's important if we want our kids to learn to live with integrity. Compartmentalizing our faith in life—being forced to leave it out of the equation at school or at work, especially during adolescence—is risky business. In public school, children learn to disconnect their academic achievement and their knowledge base from the moorings of God as Creator and center of all they know and do. It also fosters moral development for utilitarian purposes: *I will play by the rules because I want the reward that is offered for doing so.*

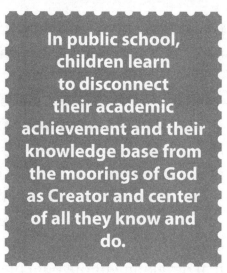

In public school, children learn to disconnect their academic achievement and their knowledge base from the moorings of God as Creator and center of all they know and do.

Today's culture is fragmented and idiosyncratic, and the same is true of public education. Kids have forty minutes for science, then—*buzz*—the bell rings, and they hurry off for forty minutes of English. All the components of the school day are divorced from one another. How does it all fit together? And for what purpose? *I was getting bored with science anyway. I've got more important things to think about. What am I going to do about my acne? And why did those girls laugh this morning when I walked by?*

I've found that much of the turmoil of adolescence is minimized in the context of homeschooling. Kids aren't asked to fight their internal battles while simultaneously coming to grips with living at odds with the culture. And at home you can seamlessly move back and forth in addressing your child's emotional upheavals, academic tasks, and spiritual questions. Homeschooling allows your teen to develop within a system that feeds his faith rather than eats away at it.

The psalmist understood that God was his source for peace and hope when his soul was wracked with disquiet and worry. He knew to look up, not within, for enduring solutions. But amid the noise of modern life, kids are not likely to figure out how to bring their faith to bear upon all of life on their own.

Prepared for Life

After spending eighteen years "at home," I have an incredible relationship with my family. I ultimately value my parents' and siblings' friendship more than any from outside of my family—their love is close, constant, and unconditional.

We took advantage of homeschooling by vacationing during the school year. By visiting Maine in September, when everybody else was in school, we experienced the best weather, the prettiest trees, and no bugs!

I also learned quite a few homemaking skills because I spent most of my time surrounded by five younger siblings and plenty of chores to be done. By the time I left for college, I knew my way around a kitchen, had been doing my own laundry for years, could keep my room clean and (relatively) organized, and knew how to care for other people when they were sick, bored, or just in need of a little "mothering." This proved to be very useful knowledge on a college campus.

Rebekah Wilhelm
Student at Hillsdale College

37

They need to see their parents daily demonstrate personal integrity by walking transparently with God. For Christians, this is a particularly important truth. If you want your children to believe there is a personal God who holds sway in our lives, then the surrounding culture must affirm that. Public school does not operate on this premise. In the face of all the changes going on in your adolescent's life, and the insecurity and awkwardness this breeds, it is a very tall order to ask your young teen to stand strong against the will of the crowd at school.

I am all for Christians entering and engaging the culture. That's the end goal. *But I'm convinced that adolescence is not the time to make this our priority*. It's like attempting to launch a rocket with a rubber band.

HOMESCHOOL OFFERS GREATER ACADEMIC OPPORTUNITY

Homeschooling has come of age. It's now an established alternative worldwide, and in the past twenty-five years, the homeschooling movement has matured and grown exponentially. Your access to this vibrant community and the opportunities it can provide is just a mouse-click away. The Internet will connect you to local and state homeschooling organizations, and it has already created a leveling playing field by making available quality online classes suitable for middle school through college.

Does your child need reinforcement and remediation in a specific subject? At home, you can plan for that without decelerating his progress in other subjects. Is she capable of working at a college level and accumulating college credit early? You can make that happen with online Advanced Placement (AP) classes or through your local community college system. Does your child have a specialized interest? An exotic language he wishes to study or a hobby to which he devotes extensive time? You can accommodate his interests without the burden of fulfilling someone else's diploma requirements.

Granted, the wide array of courses and expert teachers available in a large, affluent suburban school district or an urban magnet school are consolidated for your convenience. I admit upfront that I spent our high school years driving my kids to a lot of opportunities I didn't want them to miss. And you're the one who will have to master the logistics and scheduling in your quest to design the best program for your teenager at home, *but it can be done.* And if you're able to spring for the technology, many of the best opportunities are now or soon will be online at democratic prices.

The homeschool community, in particular, is the source of much innovation and self-sufficiency. When I first began this adventure back in 1988, our best bet was adapting curriculum designed for mass education. Today, the best products for home use are specifically designed for homeschooled students.

> **The homeschool community, in particular, is the source of much innovation and self-sufficiency.**

And if you are concerned that colleges and employers will look down their noses at a homeschooled applicant, rest assured, that's a myth. The trail has already been blazed in almost every career and academic arena by homeschool graduates who have gone on to great heights. I've been helping home-educated students get into the college of their choice the past fifteen years, and I can testify it is a non-issue. In many, many ways, homeschool applicants actually have an advantage—*if they've made the most of the opportunities homeschooling affords.* Colleges and universities are looking for diversity, and the student with the unusual background gets special consideration. Plus, many admissions officers have noted that homeschool kids come to college better equipped with independent learning and living skills than their public school counterparts. Their eventual graduation rate is higher, and they are more likely to assume leadership roles on campus. We continued to homeschool through high school in part because I was convinced it gave our kids a competitive edge, and this proved to be true. Recently my youngest daughter was embarrassed when one of her professors, upon learning that she had been homeschooled, announced to the entire class that homeschoolers have been the best students he has ever had. She felt pressured not to damage that opinion. (She didn't.)

HOMESCHOOL OFFERS GREATER FLEXIBILITY

The biggest advantage I found when I started to homeschool is one of the biggest reasons we chose to continue—I love the flexibility homeschooling allows. It's the only educational choice that wouldn't hold us captive to someone else's scope and sequence and schedule. Because homeschooling can be modified at a moment's notice to fit into the larger picture of family life, we were able to protect our priorities. If we wanted to focus on our spiritual life, we did. If we needed to increase the time devoted to math, we did. If we needed a vacation, we took it. If an educational opportunity we didn't anticipate appeared, we went for it. If we wanted or needed to change curriculum, we did. If we became interested in a new avenue of investigation, we pursued it. Our kids traveled abroad, took advanced courses, held jobs and internships, volunteered, and slept in when needed during their teen years because homeschooling allowed us that advantage.

This is a point I return to time and again in this book: If you choose to homeschool for the long haul, then make the most of the flexibility homeschooling affords you. Otherwise,

40

> **If you choose to homeschool for the long haul, then make the most of the flexibility homeschooling affords you.**

you'll miss much of what can be gained through your sacrifice. And to be sure, choosing to homeschool through high school does indeed come with a cost, as we will see in the next chapter.

3 COUNTING THE **COST**

THE CHALLENGES OF HIGH SCHOOL AT HOME

And now, the rest of the story. (I do try to be evenhanded and tell the truth as much as I know it.) If you are sailing toward the horizon into the great unknown of high school at home, then there is a cost you need to count.

HIGH SCHOOL AT HOME = TIME COMMITMENT

Homeschooling does require a greater time commitment as your kids get closer to graduation. Even if you've raised them to learn independently, which you absolutely must do—and I'll show you how to do this—your own time can quickly become absorbed by driving them to activities and planning ahead for the next season, especially if that season involves college.

If you've followed my homeschooling journey through my books and online articles, you know that I squeeze a lot into the margins of my life. I've been very active in the homeschool community, teaching at area co-ops, speaking nationally, and running a related business. I once thought that having four children all relatively close in age had many advantages; for example, I bundled a lot of subjects together for them in elementary. Well, most of these advantages evaporated when we found ourselves with four teenagers in the home! One kid going through the throes of adolescence is tumult enough, but four just about brought the house down.

I had to seriously scale back my life at this point. I backed out of commitments, turned down speaking engagements, and stuck very close to home. There was too much going on, and I didn't know when the next wave would crest. (My mother maintained justice was finally being served, considering what I put my parents through.) Maybe it will be different at your house, but my experience has been that teenagers need as much time as you are willing and able to give them. On the other hand, it's really worth it. I enjoyed the teen years, and the fruit my husband and I now experience surrounded by adult children who love the Lord and love hanging out with us means we have absolutely no regrets. But in the moment, homeschooling never felt so all-consuming.

> I enjoyed the teen years, and the fruit my husband and I now experience surrounded by adult children who love the Lord and love hanging out with us means we have absolutely no regrets.

Of course, my hope is that this manual serves you by eliminating much of the time I devoted to figuring out how to do the hard stuff, how to get my kids into the right college, and how to find money to afford it all. Right now, I don't have any grandchildren—*Lord, hear my prayer!*—and until I do, I'm going to write as much as I can to help other families continue homeschooling because I'm so grateful for the marvelous means of grace it was in our lives.

Okay, I'm supposed to be covering the disadvantages of long-term homeschooling. Back to the full disclosure.

KIDS NEED TO TEST THEIR METTLE

My experience with teens has been that most benefit from a widening circle of social and academic experiences during high school. Testing their mettle against other students is one way to raise the bar and inspire achievement. It is also the best way I know to gain an accurate picture of a particular student's strengths and weaknesses. If your child is planning on entering college or another competitive environment after high school, it's better to find out now how your child performs in a group context.

> Testing your child's mettle against other students is one way to raise the bar and inspire achievement. It is also the best way I know to gain an accurate picture of a particular student's strengths and weaknesses.

Our beloved pastor, Ken Mellinger, has noted that parents are inclined to overestimate their children's spiritual maturity and so encourages parents to set a purposeful transition period of testing the waters before sending them off into adulthood. I find parents can also overestimate their kids' academic abilities. Even knowing this to be true, Kermit and I still couldn't assess our children's strengths and weaknesses without seeing them in a variety of situations outside of our home.

44

My point is that traditional educational settings may facilitate testing their mettle most readily. Yet we had access to the same advantages through CHESS (Creative Home Educators Support Services), our homeschool co-op. My kids also took several classes online, and this served a similar function. As for their spiritual maturity, I've already mentioned some of the ways our kids got out and about in the world-at-large during high school. These opportunities to expand their horizons also revealed to us and to them areas of confidence in God's care in their lives, as well as areas where they were prone to doubt and wavering.

All four of our children benefited from taking high school courses in a group setting. (I'll go into greater detail about this in later chapters.) In particular, I found this to be important for our sons. Guys really need to get ready for the rough and tumble of the work world. Life demands a lot of resilience and perseverance from young men, and a mom who's acting as the primary teacher of adolescent boys faces some serious potential pitfalls. Although we decided not to enroll our sons in public high school, we felt they had made a valid point concerning "feminization." Therefore, we made an effort to bring other adult men into their lives in a mentoring way. They also both undertook apprenticeships that introduced them to the work world. And I learned how to back off from certain situations and not hover or micromanage the schoolwork. Again, it's easier to do this when teens are at school, out of sight and out of mind. Continuing on with homeschooling meant I had to learn how to let my kids, especially my sons, deal with situations and work through defeats or challenges without my interference.

WITH SIX, YOU GET VOLLEYBALL

Once upon a time, unless you had nine children and could start your own barnstorming baseball team, you were at a decided disadvantage trying to homeschool athletically inclined kids through high school. However, today many homeschool communities offer organized sports teams and other competitive extracurricular activities. There are leagues and tournaments, and sometimes college recruiters show up at games to scout for talent. Also, a number of states now permit homeschooled students to play on local public school teams. The

45

tide is definitely turning, and the opportunities are increasing.

Still, in general, your local school district offers far more opportunities for competitive levels of play that can lead to scholarship offers. Our sons were permitted to play for our school district, and they are very grateful for that experience. Because they played sports or trained year round, that meant I drove them to the school every day until they obtained their licenses. This really put a crimp in our schedule, and our daughters were often consternated by the limits this placed on our flexibility as a family. Once their brothers could finally drive, I was then free to take the girls on more field trips and allow them to pursue other opportunities offered by the homeschooling community.

In evaluating homeschooling as an option for high school, you will need to decide what priority you want to give to competitive sports in your children's lives.[1]

A MOM'S GOT TO KNOW HER LIMITATIONS

While every homeschooling mom has occasional doubts about her ability to teach high school-level coursework, I most often encounter this concern voiced by folks who do *not* advocate homeschooling. Fair enough, let me make a few comments.

I happen to be a credentialed teacher raised by credentialed teachers. Even my grandmother was a public school teacher. I grew up around public educators, and I think they're great people. I've always been particularly sensitive to rhetoric that categorically impugns the character and motivations of classroom teachers. In my experience, most professional teachers are really trying to make a difference in kids' lives, and they take their responsibilities seriously. My beef is with the public education system—its centralization, its mandates, its inflexibility, and the court-enforced secularization of its curriculum.

I also bristle at the notion that it takes degrees and certification and testing and a whole lot of money to figure out how to teach kids. Anything I learned in a college course I could have learned by checking a book out of the library or searching online. I learned more about teaching kids from experience and observation than from sitting in a college classroom. Good teachers are motivated teachers. Good teachers are self-educating. The homeschool parents I hang around with are both. It's also true that some are not, in the same way there are professional teachers who are not motivated or self-educating.

Any mother has a fair shot at becoming her child's best teacher. You just have to be able to identify and admit to your limitations and then do something about it. So how do you go about compensating for your limitations? First, your

> **I bristle at the notion that it takes degrees and certification and testing and a whole lot of money to figure out how to teach kids.**

goal should be to raise an independent learner. Second, you can pool your resources with other homeschooling parents—you teach a subject you already know or are willing to study, and the other parents each do the same.

On the other hand, if you aren't willing to take the time and trouble to offset your weaknesses, then your homeschooled student will be at a disadvantage at any grade level, but especially in high school when the curriculum does become daunting.

47

WHERE WILL THE MONEY COME FROM?

Homeschooling during high school costs more than it does during the elementary years. Textbooks cost more, and taking classes online or at a co-op often costs several hundred dollars. The cost of submitting college applications and visiting campuses adds up. Just raising teens costs more: They eat more, they drive cars and consume gas, they care more about their clothes, and they think they can't live without laptops and cell phones.

Many families feel pressed to find a secondary source of income during these years. Our kids started earning money, saving for college, and picking up some of the cost of living by the time they turned fourteen. Fortunately, we owned a family business and were legally free to put our kids to work for us. If you don't have that option, you may find that child labor laws hinder your teen's ability to help out. But you should know the added burden doesn't have to fall solely on your shoulders—in my circles, many teens are helping to cover their personal and educational expenses.

> If God calls you to homeschool through high school, He will supply the means.

As a family, we found other cost-saving avenues—eBay, used-curriculum sales, bartering for services, and splitting the cost of a video course with other families then alternating the years we used it. We had to believe in God's generosity and faithfulness and look for His blessings. I had many items on my homeschool wish list which I committed to prayer and then saw them surprisingly fall into our lap. If God calls you to homeschool through high school, He will supply the means. But in considering whether this route is for you, you must know your faith will need to be great in this regard. There are opportunities to be seized, but they come with a price tag attached.

BEWARE THE PITFALL OF SELF-RIGHTEOUSNESS!

On any path of life, even those we are called to by God, we will encounter temptation. In my own heart and in the hearts of some of my kids, we were tempted as homeschoolers to indulge in self-righteousness. How? Let me count the ways: We wanted folks to admire us; we wanted God to take note of our sacrifice; we often felt embattled and so elevated homeschooling to the level of suffering for Christ's sake; and we limited our interactions with those who needed Christ and so looked on from a distance with judgment instead of compassion.

These dangers await every homeschooling family. Here are faulty thought patterns to watch out for:

* Homeschooling is the choice made by the spiritually mature.
* Homeschooling protects our family from associating with sinners.
* Homeschooling increases my standing with God. He finds me more acceptable than other Christians who have their kids in a public or private school.
* Those who oppose homeschooling or promote other forms of education are our enemies; therefore, my judgment of them is justified.

I regularly had to check for these attitudes. It wasn't sufficient to recognize temptations to be smug about my schooling choice, demonize those who opposed me, or judge others based on their preferred method of education. And it wasn't homeschooling that caused these attitudes. The fault lay with my own idol-making heart. I am human, and I am tempted to think this way about all the choices I make—my strong preference for a college education, my standards for how my children relate to the opposite sex, my doctrinal convictions, etc.

I indulge in self-righteousness when I don't remind myself daily of the gospel: Christ's sacrifice, which should produce in me humility, not pride. I should renew every morning my gratitude for the Savior's unmerited favor upon my life. His amazing love should move me to compassion for those who have not

49

accepted His redemptive grace. His example should motivate me to do good works so that my Father in heaven, not I, might be glorified.

THE TENDENCY TOWARD ISOLATION

As Christians we are called to influence the culture around us and share the gospel of Christ with others. Homeschooling is a lifestyle choice that can, by its nature, cause us to become isolated and insulated from the lost of this world. We can live our lives so far removed from the society around us that we forget their peril and great need for salvation. Instead of responding with compassion to the needs of others, our lack of contact can harden into a lack of concern or, worse, a kind of judgmental arrogance.

I'm not sure to what extent our children should be expected to share their faith, but I know from experience that homeschooling puts a buffer between us and other adults. In this way homeschooling can hinder us from sharing our faith and responding to the visible needs around us, in which case our children may not learn to see these practices as a regular part of the Christian life. Mercy ministries—caring for the sick, feeding the poor, visiting prisoners, clothing those without—have always been a hallmark of orthodox Christianity and a mark of active faith in the believer's life.

Homeschooling through high school without any intentional effort toward reaching unbelievers will only widen the chasm between your family

> Homeschooling through high school without any intentional effort toward reaching unbelievers will only widen the chasm between your family and your neighbors and diminish your influence on their lives.

and your neighbors and diminish your influence on their lives. Academic concerns and training for adulthood can leave little time for reaching out beyond the community of faith. Sending kids to a traditional school, on the other hand, does force them to rub shoulders with those who do not know Christ.

Choosing to homeschool during high school means you must give prayerful consideration to the priority God assigns this privilege in your life, which may require you to modify your lifestyle to make time for acts of Christian charity and developing relationships that open doors to evangelism.

During our daughters' teen years, we elected to volunteer weekly with a ministry to inner-city kids. A good friend started an after-school tutoring program during the hours these kids would typically be home alone. This schedule prevented traditionally schooled students from volunteering, but our homeschooled teens had the flexibility to become a regular part of the outreach. This led to four of the girls—including my daughter-in-law and two daughters—becoming teachers in urban settings.

Some homeschooling families I know volunteered with the clean-up after Hurricane Katrina. Others started a ministry retrofitting homes for the handicapped. Some volunteered at crisis pregnancy centers, while others packaged medical supplies and Christmas boxes for ministries such as World Vision and Samaritan's Purse.

The flexibility homeschooling affords us is also our greatest opportunity for serving the needs of others.

51

WORKSHEET FOR OBJECTIVE DECISION-MAKING

This grid can help you decide which educational option is best for your family.

REALISTIC OPTIONS	SPIRITUAL CULTURE	ACADEMIC OPPORTU-NITIES	FLEXIBILITY	QUALIFIED TEACHERS	AFFORD-ABILITY
	Y/N		Y/N		
	Y/N		Y/N		
	Y/N		Y/N		
	Y/N		Y/N		
	Y/N		Y/N		

Assessing Your Child:

Spiritual maturity

Evidence of conversion

Evidence of cooperation with God's grace

Susceptibility to peer pressure

Academic needs

Interests

Talents

Needs

Probable course of study after high school

Possible career path following high school

Assessing Your Situation:

Practical considerations

Time commitment

Cost

Competing demands on your time and resources

PART 2

BEGINING WITH THE END IN MIND

4 PARENTING TEENS

A.K.A. RIDING THE MECHANICAL BULL

Homeschooling is not simply a style of education; it is a style of parenting. So while you probably picked up this book to figure out how to do the hard stuff, such as physics and calculus, the parenting issues that arise at this stage can often be the thousand-pound gorilla in the room no one wants to deal with.

The turmoil of the teen years catches many parents by surprise. It did me. Fortunately, there are some excellent resources I can recommend to help you shoot these rapids with skill and faith. Let me first give you a brief rundown on what is fueling the uproar—as if you don't remember.

Your teen is going through tremendous psychological and biological changes, and this is unnerving for both of you. These changes are often unpredictable and beyond the teen's control. My son Mike says he hated junior high because of his emotional swings. He never knew if he would wake up happy or angry. His emotions controlled him, and he had no idea how to explain this or manage them. Of course, he wasn't admitting this to us at the time because he wasn't mature enough to objectively analyze his situation. Instead we were on the receiving end of angry outbursts totally out of proportion to the situation or protracted seasons of silence emanating from behind a closed door. Our daughters, when they were teens, crumbled into tears at the drop of a hat. Now, with some distance, I wonder why I wasn't more sympathetic. The reason is that I was rooted in fear, so I acted out of fear instead of faith, thereby exacerbating the emotional upheaval.

A few general observations regarding this stage of life:

1. Significant physical changes take place as kids approach their adult height and sexual maturity.
2. Adolescents show increased interest in widening their social contact beyond the family.
3. Adolescents show increasing interest in the opposite sex.
4. Adolescents seek to establish their autonomy as individuals.

When you think about it, all of these are ultimately desirable outcomes. We do want our children to reach adulthood, to marry, to be responsible and independent of us, to establish meaningful social contacts in their church, their neighborhood, and the workplace. Right?

What I lost sight of was the physical process that God Himself designed for achieving these desired results. Our kids don't move from dependency to independence overnight. The transfer of authority over their lives from parent to child cannot be accomplished with the flip of a switch; it is a process that usually begins with them straining at the reins of parental authority.

I mean, I wasn't the first to say, "Hey, Mike and Gabe, why

> The transfer of authority over their lives from parent to child cannot be accomplished with the flip of a switch; it is a process that usually begins with them straining at the reins of parental authority.

57

don't you stay out later with your friends this weekend?" or "Why don't you take the car more often" or "Don't you think you should start including girls in your circle of friends?" No, they began thinking along these lines before questions of autonomy were even a blip on our radar screen. And as we weren't anticipating their interest in greater autonomy, we quickly took action to shut it down. Well, that was about as helpful as plugging a breaching dike with a finger: Temporary relief was more than offset by pressure building on the other side. Finally, with our youngest, we understood what was happening and didn't waste time trying to stop it. Rather, our best efforts as parents were directed toward channeling the waters that broke through the walls along an appropriate course.

> Our posture as parents should be to thank God for what He is doing in our children's lives, as difficult as that may be at times.

So the first thing to remember is that *this is a good thing*. Our posture as parents should be to thank God for what He is doing in our children's lives, as difficult as that may be at times. We can help them think about this season rightly, too, if they hear us expressing faith toward God for what He is doing in their lives.

The second thing to remember is that *most kids aren't going to make this transition smoothly*. They aren't really thinking about how they can make life easy for Mom and Dad. Psychologically, they've never been more self-conscious or more self-centered, and they will need your help to battle through this to a place of security and outward focus. You may find it helpful to just throw out any expectations of thoughtfulness or understanding on their end, and then be thankful and pleased when they do surprise you with consideration.

Of course, I'm not saying you should excuse your teen's

sin or sit back passively while she struggles to develop a more pleasant disposition. Not at all! Other than infancy, there is no time when hands-on parenting is more required. However, when we bring our baby home from the hospital, our primary responsibility is to provide care. When that child becomes an adolescent, our primary responsibility should be training. This may seem obvious, but it wasn't for me. My primary impulse was not to provide training but to establish *control.* I thought I needed to suppress my teens' impulses and restrain their attempts at freedom. I imagined that if I didn't do this, things would escalate to full-scale rebellion and dangerous behavior. I was responding to the natural course of events in fear and assuming my children's struggle for greater autonomy was fueled by sin. Instead, I needed to respond in faith and recognize that their resistance was in fact an imperfect response to the God-designed maturation process going on inside.

> When your child becomes an adolescent, your primary responsibility should be training, not to establish control.

When you first read the chapter title, did you picture yourself trying to ride the mechanical bull alone? Did you equate the bull with "parenting teens" in your mind? What happens if you picture you *and* your teen on that bucking bronco together, with you helping him to learn to remain astride the machine through the peaks and valleys of his undulating emotions and impulses?

Your teen is in a fight to gain control over his raging hormones. You need to get in his corner and coach him through this season. Someone needs to tell him how to *think* about everything that is happening. Someone needs to *point* him toward God and His available provision. Someone needs to *show* him how to traverse life's difficulties with faith and grace. Scripture makes it pretty clear that parents are God's means for doing this. And homeschooling your child will mean you're going to be on deck more than most, so be prepared.

OVERCOMING FAULTY ASSUMPTIONS

You need to identify any underlying assumptions about homeschooling your teen that may set you up for discouragement and unbelief. Here are a few I recognized in myself:

* If I homeschool my teens, they will love God.
* If I homeschool my teens, they will be happy.
* If I homeschool my teens, they will be grateful for my sacrifice.
* If I homeschool my teens, they will be like the population of Lake Wobegon: above-average and good-looking.
* If I homeschool my teens, they will receive a better education than they might get elsewhere.
* If I homeschool my teens, they will agree with and esteem my opinions.

You get the idea. Fill in the blanks with your own assumptions.

Am I saying you shouldn't have expectations? No. Scripture does promise a reward for our faithfulness and efforts. When you choose to homeschool through high school, you should definitely have faith in God for the outcome. But what I am cautioning against is going into it with an idealistic picture of what it's going to look like. Our kids are free moral agents, and the unexpected can and will happen. Your child may indeed skate through this season with amazing grace. Our daughter Kayte pretty much did. She's wired to please, not rock the boat.

But she's had to battle self-righteousness much of her life. Our other three came with more typical confrontations and challenges. God was at work transforming their weaknesses into strength of conviction and leadership, but the process for us as parents was not always pleasant.

> **Get ready for a marvelous opportunity to appreciate in a greater way how deep is your own need for a Savior and the empowering grace His sacrificial death has given you access to.**

Of course, my own flesh-based reactions contributed to these challenges in no insignificant way. This brings me to another assumption I made: *Homeschooling my teens will reveal what a mature Christian I am.* Not! Get ready for a marvelous opportunity to appreciate in a greater way how deep is your own need for a Savior and the empowering grace His sacrificial death has given you access to.

Recommended Resources

Gospel-Powered Parenting: How the Gospel Shapes and Transforms Parenting by William P. Farley

Growing Up Christian: Have You Taken Ownership of Your Relationship with God? by Karl Graustein and Mark Jacobsen

Age of Opportunity: A Biblical Guide to Parenting Teens by Paul Tripp

Do Hard Things: A Teenage Rebellion Against Low Expectations by Alex and Brett Harris

61

5 DISCOVERING YOUR TEEN'S GIFTS

Ideally, you are educating your teen with her future in mind. This includes not only the career path she may follow, but also the ministry efforts she undertakes and the particular strengths she brings to raising a family. If you have no idea what her future calling may be, then what you do in your homeschool is a shot in the dark. I don't believe that has to be our experience as parents. I believe we can trust God to provide us a direction for our kids.

* We need to ask Him for direction and trust Him to lead.
* We need to equip our kids to seek His direction and trust His leading.
* We need to learn to discern what that future call may be.
* We must pay attention to the changing needs of the global church and the job market.

Discerning God's will for our children must be a collaboration between parent and child. We need to strike an appropriate balance with our teens. We don't choose their future for them; we help them to learn to hear God's voice and understand His will for their lives. At the other end of the spectrum, we cannot dump the full burden of responsibility for making these huge decisions on our children's shoulders. Most teens I've worked with, including my own, find it overwhelming when faced with choosing the right college, the right major, the right career path. We must help them sort through the pile of options and together reach the best decision based upon what we can reasonably discern at the time a decision is required. Then we must model faith in God as our teens take those first tentative steps forward.

LOOKING FOR CLUES

So how can we know God's will for our children? In addition to devoting ourselves in prayer to seeking God's will, we must be on the lookout for clues He provides. Your primary clues are the gifts and interests of your child that emerge as he grows. Gifts, or areas of grace and natural strength, point towards God's future intentions.

The Bible tells us, "To each one of us grace has been given as Christ apportioned it" (Ephesians 4:7). Paul reminds us that these gifts have been given to us so the body of Christ can build itself up in love as "each part does its work" (Ephesians 4:16). We need to help our kids to see their gifts and talents as intended for God's purposes in maturing His body. This will include both their vocational and avocational pursuits.

How do we discern these gifts, talents, and motivational interests? By presenting opportunities where their innate graces can surface. I find this occurs through providing *many* experiences and *much* exposure

> How do we discern our children's gifts, talents, and motivational interests? By presenting opportunities where their innate graces can surface.

to different subject matter. Then we take note of what we observe, and prayerfully consider how to develop and direct the gifts that manifest themselves in the child.

Here is a partial list of the kinds of gifts we might be looking for:

Motivational Gifts	Talents & Interests	Grace
Leadership	The Arts	Obedience
Administration	Athletics	Love
Teaching	Speaking	Joy
Helping	Intelligence	Generosity
Caring	Intuition	Flexibility
Encouraging	Creativity	Humility
Pioneering	Sciences	Kindness
Gathering	Writing	Self-Control
Evangelism	Languages	Peacemaking
Organizing	Technology	Patience
	Learning	Faithfulness
		Diligence
		Passion
		Selflessness

In each case, you are looking for an innate strength that is more pronounced than others in your child. (I don't think comparing your child to other children is particularly helpful, as the strength you see may appear to be weak in comparison with another child who has a greater apportionment of grace in that area.)

We can all become better leaders or teachers with training, or more faithful in giving or being joyful by cooperating with God's transforming grace in our lives. What points to a future calling in our kids, though, are those areas of strength that emerge without much effort, as though God has woven them into the very fabric of their being.

For example, our son Gabe has loved being among people, lots of people, from his earliest days. When he was younger, this made him susceptible to peer pressure because he so wanted to be included in groups. This is a big reason we chose to homeschool him through high school. However, once he was regenerated by God's grace and submitted to God's sanctification process, this love for people motivated him both evangelistically and vocationally.

Gabe's capacity to be among people all day long and late into the evening amazes me. I find this level of social interaction exhausting, but Gabe is energized by being around people. Prior to entering law school, he worked in sales, meeting with people all day long, and he was also very involved in working with the young people at our church. Gathering is clearly an integral part of what Gabe will be doing the rest of his life. It only remains to be seen precisely in what context God intends for him to use this gifting.

On the other hand, his identical twin brother, Mike, has had a pronounced gift for organization and management since he was little. It's how he is wired. Mike was setting schedules for our homeschool at age five! Gabe has always been the one with a big idea for an event involving lots of people, while Mike is the one who brings some order to the event. Prior to grad school, Mike worked for the same company as his twin, but he quickly became a manager and also led a small group for adults at church. Mike is at his best when he's given responsibility.

Here are a few ideas for learning to recognize the indicators of God's future intentions for your own child.

Choices

What does your child choose to do when she is free to choose? Does she want to be with friends? Read a book? Study the

Word? Work on a project? Have a new experience? Start a project? Consider keeping a journal of your observations.

Kristen, my youngest, is a people person like Gabe. But while Gabe is wired to exhort and lead, Kristen is more apt to listen and empathize. She has always been caught up in the drama of her friends' lives and talks about people to the exclusion of things or projects. When she is free to choose, she frequently asks if she can organize a service project for others that she can do with her friends. Her mercy-oriented focus has led her to pursue a degree in elementary education, primarily so she can teach in an underserved area, such as an inner-city school.

Time

Does your child prefer to spend time with people or projects, or a mixture of both? A knowledge of your child's preference between personal interaction and projects will be valuable in helping them to evaluate potential choices for college and careers. Keep in mind that most kids are unfamiliar with the actual working conditions involving a particular career. Their notions often come from the romanticized depictions they see on television. The lives of doctors, lawyers, and law enforcement officers as shown in popular dramas often bear little resemblance to the actual working conditions and daily duties demanded of people in these professions. A good strategy involves arranging for your teen to talk with a professional working in an area of interest.

> A knowledge of your child's preference between personal interaction and projects will be valuable in helping them to evaluate potential choices for college and careers.

Debriefing

After your child has a new experience, be sure to debrief afterward. Listen carefully for which aspects he most enjoyed and areas he found most challenging about the experience. What part of the experience energized him? What did he find exhausting and depleting? Record this information for later use. Experience is a great teacher, so make the most of the opportunities that come along. If your teen learns he doesn't enjoy a certain type of work or activity, don't regret giving your child the experience. Find out what he learned and use it in making decisions down the road.

> After your child has a new experience, be sure to debrief afterward. Listen carefully for which aspects he most enjoyed and areas he found most challenging about the experience.

After Kayte returned from her first mission trip to Mexico at age fourteen, we noted the ease with which she had picked up conversational Spanish. She was already doing quite well with French. I also pointed out as we debriefed the apparent ease with which she moved among other cultures. She loved being in a foreign country and was invigorated by the new customs and foods. She had a cast-iron stomach and was undaunted by unfamiliar conditions. Later, many of her electives in high school and college were chosen to facilitate opportunities for travel. At twenty-four, she has already spent time in some of the most impoverished areas of the world and studied in the Middle East.

Another experience helped Kayte decide to steer clear of careers and activities requiring administration. I wanted to see how she handled a leadership position, so she shared the chairmanship of an end-of-year program for one of our co-op

67

classes. Well, it was a fiasco from beginning to end. She was just not innately gifted to manage people or large projects. She found the experience draining without any sense of satisfaction at the conclusion. During college, she grew quite a bit in her ability to administrate and manage when she needs to, but it still does not energize her. Realizing this early helped her quickly eliminate many such opportunities that have come her way. Her preference is to follow someone else's leadership or to work solo. This is great since we needed at least one person in the Bell household who didn't want to be in charge!

GIFTS ARE TO BE USED FOR GOD'S GLORY

Our kids did not deserve nor earn the strengths they innately have. If they are intelligent, it doesn't add to their value in God's eyes. If they are great athletes, it doesn't mean God loved them more than another person. However, our teens are not going to understand this without our help. Their tendency will be to determine their self-worth based on their gifts and talents and to use their abilities for their own glory and recognition, not to point others to God. The Bible does teach us to cultivate and multiply our talents, so athletic prowess or intellectual acumen shouldn't be buried in the ground. That's the easier route. The more difficult route is to earnestly develop the gifts we have, while asking God to make sure they are used for His purposes and recognition. Training our children in the purpose and use of their gifts is an important part of this process. If your heart is to see your teen ultimately find God's will for his life, then every gift he discovers needs to be sanctified for His use.

FACTOR IN SINFUL TENDENCIES AND IMMATURITY

I don't want to imply your teen should expect to build his life solely around what he enjoys or finds easy to do. A child who spends all his free time playing video games may be displaying an innate tendency toward laziness, not any kind of motivational gift pointing to a future calling. Or a child's dislike of new situations may be rooted in fear of man, not faith. Just because your teen doesn't enjoy an experience or activity the first time doesn't mean you should automatically cross it off the list of possibilities. Repeat exposure may increase your child's level of interest and success in an area. Remember, people are also wired to find satisfaction and motivation in working hard to accomplish a goal.

In the end, there are items on God's list of future responsibilities for each of us that we aren't necessarily going to want to do, such as the daily duties that go along with parenting, running a household,

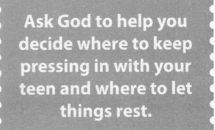

Ask God to help you decide where to keep pressing in with your teen and where to let things rest.

going to work faithfully, laying down our lives for others, etc. So ask God to help you decide where to keep pressing in with your teen and where to let things rest.

ASSESSMENT TOOLS MAY BE HELPFUL

Most teens enjoy taking personality and/or career guidance tests. However, you should not place too much stock in the results. Perhaps the main benefits of these tests are the thought-provoking questions that may help your teen become more self-aware about his preferences, passions, and inclinations. The aptitude test I took in tenth grade said I was most suited for a mechanical vocation. I think at the time I was an avid seamstress and considered all the questions in terms of my sewing projects. I haven't touched a sewing machine in years, and I ended up about as far removed from a mechanical-oriented career as one can get. With that caveat, here are two sources of assessment tools for teens from reputable Christian ministries. I'd recommend using these more toward the end of high school, after your teen has a broader base of experiences to draw upon:

The Call: Vocational and Life Purpose Guide, distributed by Focus on the Family, www.thecallonline.com

Career Direct Complete Guidance System, distributed by Crown Ministries, www.crown.org

6 ADAPTING TO THE DEMANDS OF THE CHANGING JOB MARKET

*"One of the only places operating largely as it did fifty years
ago is the local school."*
Renate Nummel and Geoffrey Caine
Making Connections

Uncovering your teen's innate gifts is only one part of the
equation. Figuring out how these might be used in choosing a
field of study, career track, or ministry is the other side. We are
in the midst of a cultural and global revolution at least as significant as the shift from an agrarian to industrialized society,
if not more so. Globalization and technology are transforming
every profession and corner of the world. New careers are ap-
pearing, while old standbys are slipping into the sea. Our kids
don't have time to figure out how this seismic shift should inform their decisions. Therefore, it falls to parents to get a bead
on how to factor the needs of a changing world into our teen's
high school choices.

The good news is that homeschooling puts our children at
an advantage. We can reinvent our course of study in a week
or two. Other schooling methods may take years to catch up
with current trends. We have more flexibility in our schedules

to investigate new occupations and become savvy in using new technology. We are able to quickly research, retool, and apply.

What follows is a series of recommendations for anticipating and navigating the shifting road ahead.

ENCOURAGE ENTREPRENEURIAL SKILLS

In *Being Digital*, Nicholas Negroponte writes, "By the year 2020 the largest employer in the developed world will be 'self.'" Long gone are the days of traditional company loyalties. Businesses

A Success Story

Homeschooling gave me the time for pursuing a hobby that I built into a business that has resulted in many opportunities, through media interviews and interactions with others, to encourage homeschooling and share my faith in Christ. At age twelve, while living in the city, I built a homemade incubator and hatched two roosters. We soon moved to the country, and I took my passion for animals and growing things and developed them into a business. I took a course in writing business plans at a local university and, ultimately, wrote a book on youth entrepreneurship, which I hope to publish soon.

I've learned to seek God's will and calling for my life, which means that just because I start a particular business and become well-known in it, I'm not necessarily locked into that. When I was eighteen, I started a real estate business and have found that it allows me the flexibility to pursue a passion for political and cultural involvement on the side. Like education, entrepreneurship is a lifestyle.

If I had been sitting in a classroom during my secondary education, I would more likely be dependent than independent, and I would not have had the opportunity or creative environment for any of this to happen.

Jason Heki
Real estate investor and a student at Patrick Henry College

are loyal to their shareholders, not their employees. Your teens need to be ready to work for themselves. Today, the average employee will change jobs seven times in his lifetime. Think about that. How many jobs did your father have? How many jobs has your husband had? That's why our kids need to be equipped to work for themselves, or at least think like an entrepreneur, even while employed. In fact, trends show a rapid increase in self-employment and nonstandard, decentralized work (i.e., distance work and outsourcing).

DEVELOP YOUR TEEN'S TECHNOLOGICAL SKILLS

This is *why* your kids will be able to consider starting a business or working for themselves. The playing field has been flattened by technology—that means little guys can go up against the big guns. Use the time your kids have at home to help them become computer savvy. In most cases, you just need to make sure they have the technology to mess around with. Forget about neat penmanship; it's becoming increasingly irrelevant. But they need to know how to use a keyboard with their eyes closed. Forget speeches with note cards; they need to know how to organize and deliver a PowerPoint presentation.

MAKE YOUR PROGRAM WRITING INTENSIVE

73

Business is all about communication, and no line of work is exempt from the need to write clearly and persuasively. E-mail, websites, faxes, PDF, text messaging—these are the communiqués of our daily lives. With all this information coming at us, content-rich delivery is the byword. The future is for the articulate. The power to write convincingly is the power to be heard.

TEACH YOUR TEEN HOW TO LEARN

There is no real way to determine exactly what knowledge kids should learn now to be ready for a rapidly changing job market and the cultural demands of the future. The only way to anticipate the curve is to learn how to learn. Focus on developing the skill of independent learning so your kids will know what to do when they discover their current skill set is insufficient or their knowledge base is outdated. Design your curriculum to emphasize research papers and projects, which will teach them to ferret out the information they need, synthesize it into cogent discourse, and use technology to present it.

> Focus on developing the skill of independent learning so your kids will know what to do when they discover their current skill set is insufficient or their knowledge base is outdated.

Lifelong learning is a current high-growth market, by the way, because ongoing training throughout our adult lives is necessary to keep up with the morphing marketplace.

As your teen's innate strengths and interests emerge, spend some time researching current career trends in fields relevant to those strengths. Make sure you are gleaning information from *credible* Internet sources (a research skill your kids need to learn). Here is a list of where the future jobs are for the U.S. population as compiled by the Department of Labor:

1. Professional and Business Services
2. Education and Health Services
3. Information Services
4. Leisure and Hospitality Services
5. Trade, Transportation, and Utilities
6. Financial Services

Growth is expected to be stagnate or decline in all areas of manufacturing or goods-producing industries.[1]

The biggest inference you should take from this list of growth industries is that jobs in these fields all require a college degree at the mid to upper levels of employment and at least some postsecondary form of training at the entry levels. A college degree today is almost equivalent to the high school diploma of yesteryear. More and more occupations, including teaching and management, require a Master's degree or its equivalent. Even a teen with self-employment interests will need an apprenticeship and ongoing training if he intends to remain competitive over his lifetime.

When you evaluate your postsecondary intentions for your son or daughter, do not be short-sighted in evaluating their future needs. You need to think about the cultural trends that are shaping our economy and consider the kind of skills they will require over the long haul. Certainly, lifelong learning skills should be on your short list—that way your teens can respond to the future no matter what shape it takes.

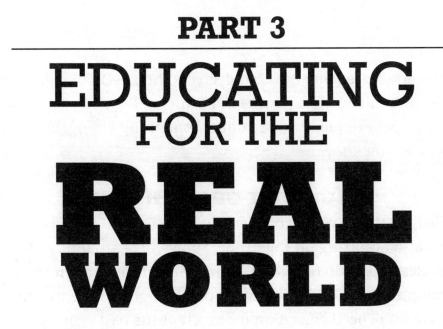

PART 3

EDUCATING FOR THE REAL WORLD

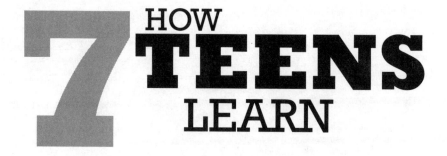

7 HOW TEENS LEARN

You don't need an advanced degree to homeschool your teen. However, there are a few helpful principles you need to keep in mind. Believe me, if you're doing something wrong, he or she will let you know.

COGNITIVE GROWTH SPURTS

First, all the physical changes you're seeing on the outside are also occurring on the inside. Somewhere around age ten or eleven, children begin to think and reason with greater complexity. Jean Piaget, a Swiss psychologist whose theories have influenced education for much of the past century, called this the "formal operational stage." Prior to this stage of development, children draw exclusively on prior experience and a trial-and-error approach to solving problems. But once learners reach this stage, they become capable of reasoning hypothetically, meaning they can apply reasoning to fanciful possibilities. For example, they can now imagine what might happen in a world without gravity. They can now handle abstractions, such as algebraic formulas. They can formulate hypotheses and systematically test them to arrive at a solution.

Here are a few indicators of formal operational thinking:

* Instead of relying on trial and error, your child can formulate a theory that predicts outcomes.
* The child quickly plans an organized approach to solving a problem.
* The child is able to think critically about a hypothetical possibility.

Recent researchers have determined that children can reach this stage of thinking earlier than Piaget originally supposed. They may also be able to handle abstract thinking in one domain—history, for example—before being able to do so in other domains such as mathematics.

In working with your teen, you may encourage this kind of problem-solving by steering away from curriculum resources heavy on rote learning and instead incorporate those that encourage open-ended activities, creative projects, and essay answers or research papers. You'll find many more suggestions for supporting your child's growth in higher levels of thinking in chapter eight.

THE IMPORTANCE OF PRIOR KNOWLEDGE

Educational psychologists recognize that learners must draw upon prior knowledge when mastering new skills and content. As your child enters high school and tackles more specific and compartmentalized subjects, consider the academic ground she has already covered. Does she have a firm foundation of experience upon which to build more abstract and theoretical knowledge?

My approach to teaching the elementary years was to cut a wide swath through the core curriculum. I was looking to provide my kids broad exposure to all the subject matter, and I seized upon new opportunities that came our way. I wanted to lay a strong foundation for future higher-level thinking and learning. This would require that they develop a lifetime

79

of experiential knowledge, so field trips became an essential component to our curriculum. I wanted to get my kids out in the broad world, seeing adults in a variety of professions, visiting museums and zoos, spending time with nature, studying the stars and tidal pools, and reading imaginative literature and eye-popping Eyewitness books by DK. I knew they would need this well of knowledge and life experience to draw upon when it was time to deal with the more abstract ideas presented by political science, physics, higher mathematics, and world history.

In areas such as arithmetic, grammar, language, and composition, I looked for opportunities for my elementary-age kids to use their newly developed skills in a variety of ways—playing games, budgeting their money, shopping for Christmas, writing thank-you notes, putting on short plays, and messing around with poetry. Students achieve greater speed and

> I wanted to get my kids out in the broad world, seeing adults in a variety of professions, visiting museums and zoos, spending time with nature, studying the stars and tidal pools, and reading imaginative literature.

sophistication in these areas by using these skills often and in a variety of contexts. This is one reason I didn't interrupt my kids for school when they decided to pull one of the games from the closet, where we had stocked the shelves with playing cards, chess, checkers, Muggins math games, Scrabble, Spell-It— anything that would encourage analytical thinking.

As you look ahead to the high school years, consider your present curriculum. First, are you giving your child a wide overview of each subject area? Has your child been exposed to the sweep of human history before entering high school, or have you focused exclusively on one time period or culture? In mathematics, has she been toying with elements of geometry, pre-algebra, and number theory? A focused, systematic approach to these subjects can, of course, wait until the student has reached her formal operational stage. What you want to do in advance is to provide her a glimpse of the bigger picture so she can build her knowledge base with the bigger picture in mind.

THE TEENAGER IS A NOCTURNAL CREATURE

The stereotype of the teenager who sleeps in till noon and stays up all night turns out to be rooted in biological fact. The physical and cognitive development going on in your teen will likely trigger changes in sleep patterns. Most teens need nine hours of sleep a night or more, and many are more alert in the evening than in the morning. You will have to decide if this is a hill worth fighting over. You aren't going to harm your child if you insist he keep hours aligned with your schedule, but you should know there is a legitimate biological component at work. I followed the lead of several of my friends and allowed my kids to start their school day around nine or ten o'clock. During high school, they were often doing school assignments after dinner, and typically they did not go to bed until after eleven at night. Fortunately, Kermit is a night owl and could handle evening supervision. I am a very early riser, and I'm usually off the clock (and out cold) by nine p.m.

81

THE ROLE OF EFFORT AND MOTIVATION

At the end of the day, neither you nor any professional teacher can truly teach a child anything, especially an adolescent. Children need to learn, and this can only be done by them. They must be active agents in the process. If they are not engaged, then all your efforts are for naught.

How does anyone learn?

Through effort. That's it.

The more time devoted to acquiring a skill or piece of knowledge, the more gains they will make. There is plenty of research to back up this assertion. Yes, innate ability plays a role, but you'd be surprised how small a percentage of importance that actually turns out to be. Malcolm Gladwell's book *Outliers* provides fascinating insight into the common denominators found among highly successful people. What is the recurring theme among experts in any field of study or talent? Time on task. They've been doing what they are doing *a lot*—and for *a long time*. Researchers have even been able to quantify the notion. It turns out that 10,000 hours is what it takes to become an expert, whether you're a basketball player, violinist, quantum physicist, or writer. That can be broken down into three hours of practice each day for ten years. And if you look into the background of any accomplished individual, chances are you will find that the person has done what he or she is good at consistently for long periods of time, usually starting in adolescence.

This is not to say that in homeschooling your teen you should burden yourself with the notion you are raising an "expert" in anything. Your job is to cultivate a work ethic that leads to later success. Your teen needs to be on task to learn. How do you make that happen? Enter motivation.

> Your job is to cultivate a work ethic that leads to later success. Your teen needs to be on task to learn.

Our job is to give our kids compelling reasons to engage. Motivation fuels persistence—it's why we don't quit when things get hard, whether it's homeschooling or doing calculus. Persistence is how we make gains. Learning doesn't happen while we are sleeping, and it doesn't happen just because we grow older. Learning occurs because we persist. And no one persists through difficulties unless they are motivated—something is giving them a reason to not quit.

So how do we provide those reasons? How do we keep that teenage tank fueled with motivation? We will discuss this in the next chapter.

8 THE STUDY-SMART STUDENT

The secret to making it through high school with your teens is to empower them to take ownership of their studies. Otherwise, you'll be spending late nights vainly attempting to figure out the trigonometry lesson, Latin conjugations, and chemical reactions before you teach the material the following morning. This way lies madness! As the teaching parent, your energies must be focused on equipping your teen to learn independently. So, if you're fortunate, your teen will be willing to read this chapter and apply its strategies. But if your kid is like most, then you'll need to digest this chapter and encourage ownership by setting up a program that takes the teen by the hand through these techniques:

What does an independent learner look like?

* An independent learner is *engaged*. He approaches each learning experience with questions in mind. He knows what he doesn't know, knows what he needs to know, and knows what he already understands.
* An independent learner *strategizes*. She plans, predicts, formulates hypotheses, and searches for evidence to support or nullify. In general, she directs her learning experience.

* An independent learner *initiates* learning. He decides what, where, when, and how to learn.

Most kids are not wired this way innately. Learning how to learn is usually an acquired skill, and parent-teachers must be committed to making this a goal of their home education program. A traditional school setting often detours a student's drive toward independence because classroom teachers retain control of the process and do not give students choices, flexibility, or autonomy—all essential ingredients for producing kids who can learn independently.

For their sakes and ours, we need to empower our teens to learn outside the traditional paradigm. Here's how.

GET THE BIG PICTURE FIRST

I conduct a seminar for teens called Study Smart Strategies. I open the session with jigsaw puzzles spread around the room for them to work on together. Once the session starts, I ask them what strategies they used to piece together these puzzles. Teens tell me they separated the border pieces or grouped the pieces by color. Then I ask if there is something I could have given them to make their task easier. I always get the answer I'm looking for—the picture on the front of the puzzle box. It's much harder to put together a puzzle when you don't know what the completed picture is supposed to look like. But that's what we often ask kids to do with school subjects—we insist they put together pieces of information without ever showing them the big picture they are constructing. We just give them bits of data and leave it up to them to make sense of it all.

When you start with the big picture in mind, you make it easier for your student to make connections. And connecting new knowledge with prior knowledge is how we build a network of skills and understanding in long-term memory where we can get at it whenever we need it.

So before you begin a unit on chemical bonding or sentence diagramming or dividing fractions, think about how the various pieces of discrete information fit into the whole of science or composition or mathematics and help kids make that connection. You may not intuitively understand the big picture—I know I didn't—but here are some strategies I learned to help me bring the big picture into focus over the years:

* Read a children's book on the topic. Whether it is the Civil War, geometry, or physics, children's books aim to hit the key facts and clarify overarching concepts.
* Watch a video on the subject produced for educational TV.
* Read the Cliffs Notes, now available free online, or similar type study helps. Titles from the Dummies series can also fill this need.
* Study the table of contents in the text you plan to use. Compare this with the contents of other texts on this subject. Key concepts and major divisions of information will soon emerge.

MAKE CONNECTIONS

Making connections is how kids remember and retrieve the knowledge they acquire, so invest in increasing their retention through "webbing." This imagery refers to the interconnections children make cognitively as they *use* newly acquired information in a variety of contexts. Does the text or study guide you're considering ask the student to work with the information in a variety of ways?

Think of your mind as a superhighway system with many different routes crisscrossing at key destinations. Every time you take a new route to the same destination, your understanding of the "lay of the land" increases. For instance, you probably know the way home from any starting point in your county. That should also be your goal for high school biology or calculus—no matter where your student starts, he should know how to arrive at his end destination because he's used the information in many different ways.

How do you facilitate this kind of flexibility and familiarity with the content? I have found it highly unusual for one textbook to use this multi-prong approach, so we used a variety of resources. For instance, we used Apologia science as our core text for the sciences, but we also watched science videos, participated in several science fairs, visited science centers, and checked many additional books out of the library on the various topics covered in the course. Juvenile titles, which were a quick read, were very helpful in grasping the nuances of cell division or genetics. Don't be afraid to use resources designed for younger students to help you build these connections.

> I have found it highly unusual for one textbook to use this multi-prong approach, so we used a variety of resources.

ORGANIZE YOUR STUDY AREA

In order to use the knowledge we have gained, we must know where we've filed it so that we can retrieve it at a moment's notice. Therefore, for our filing system to work efficiently, it has to be categorized in a predictable manner. Categorizing knowledge efficiently is another strategy employed by study-smart students. They know they can't retrieve endless reams of data, but they can find what they need in the annals of their mind if they've filed the information properly.

Learning how to categorize is an acquired skill. The first step

87

toward recognizing and labeling categories in your mind is to recognize and label categories in our physical world. This starts with organizing the place of study.

Determine with your teen what area of the house will be his domain for doing his schoolwork. Our teens preferred to work in their bedrooms, and we took steps to set these up for study. At minimum, kids need a desk, a storage area, and a bookshelf they can call their own. It's important that they keep the study area organized. This discipline will lead to organized thinking.

Next, set up a system for filing the knowledge they've gained. A fun field trip might be a visit to the office supply store just to see all the different organizational tools you might use for filing. We've used three-ring binders with dividers for some subjects and storage totes with hanging folders for ongoing ones, such as the sciences. I've also showed my kids how to set up filing systems on their computers, as that is where most of their work is done. But you cannot rely on computers alone—spatial organization of one's physical world gives teens the concrete and tactile experiences still important to their learning.

> **The best way for your teen to store information will emerge as he learns and looks for ways to connect information and make applications.**

Here is an important thing to remember about your filing system: *It needs to be organic.* It's not likely that any student will be able to predict accurately at the beginning of a course of study how to compartmentalize what he is about to learn. The best way to store information will emerge as he learns and intentionally looks for ways to connect information and make applications. New categories will emerge, and students will need to break down large groupings further into subsets. So start out with a labeling system that can quickly be redone. Store information in such a way that it can easily be reshuffled and re-filed. In fact, a good way to review material for testing and other evaluations is to practice recalling the information from a variety of different routes. There is any number of ways to organize information, so choose one way for filing during the course of your studies but be open to trying several different methods with the goal of increasing the interconnectivity of ideas.

Here are just a few examples of possible organizational schemes for your school subjects:

* Chronologically
* Geographically
* By historic era or cultural movement
* By important people in the field
* By ideological systems—i.e., economic, political, world-view, etc.

ORGANIZE INFORMATION VISUALLY AS YOU LEARN

We tend to think in pictures, not words. When I say the word "dog," you see an image, don't you? Not the letters *d-o-g* displayed across your mind. That's why the following tip works so well in mastering information.

Current research strongly suggests that students can improve their comprehension and retention of information if they construct *graphic organizers* or *concept maps* while studying material. Examples of these kinds of learning aids include Venn diagrams, time lines, flow charts, and matrices. Constructing these visual representations of knowledge requires students to decide how to organize and categorize; the visual format simply makes it easier to recall. You can download examples of

89

these organizers by searching the terms graphic organizers and concept maps online.

Simply look around you to see the increasing merger of image and text to communicate information. *USA Today* transformed the newspaper business with this concept. True, many such efforts represent attempts to accommodate falling literacy rates with claims that we are moving away from written language to pictorial communication. On the plus side, numerous studies have shown that most learners recall information represented visually more readily than with a text-only approach. This is important to keep in mind when reviewing potential curriculum and resource purchases. High school textbooks without charts, graphs, and pictures—especially for highly abstract subject matter such as science and math—just make the subject matter that much more difficult to learn.

DON'T BE A BENCHWARMER

As I've pointed out, motivation is a necessary ingredient in keeping teens focused and committed to a task. One reason kids stay committed to athletic endeavors is because there is a tangible goal at the end of all the drills and skill work—the opportunity to play in an actual competitive game where the outcome is decisive and success is empirically measured. No one wants to sit on the bench during the big game, watching others play. Applying this analogy to academics, at our house we found that our kids put their greatest effort into academic studies that clearly led to an important test or competition. Here are some suggestions for creating a sporting environment in your academic world:

* Arrange for your student take an AP test or SAT Subject Area Test at the conclusion of the course.
* Participate in an academic competition. See the appen-

dix for a list of competitions.

* Organize a project or science fair with your support group and arrange for judging and prizes.
* Schedule a recognition night at which students can display their best work.
* Undertake a project—such as building a shed, starting a home business, or traveling—that requires your student to master and use the information being studied.

End goals such as these give students a clear finish line to run toward and a reason *now* to achieve a high level of competency. Grades, especially over the course of time, lose their value as a source of motivation. They are artificial and typically not a source of recognition for the homeschooled student. Teens need a wider audience for their work, as well as recognition and meaningful rewards for their achievement. This is why teens devote the energy they do to athletics. If you want to see the same devotion applied to academics, then set up a similar rewards system.

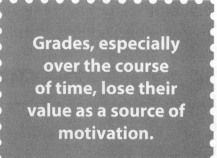

Grades, especially over the course of time, lose their value as a source of motivation.

Here's an example of how this concept works: I wanted my kids to learn a foreign language because most universities require at least two years of language study for entrance and the modern job market highly values applicants with second-language skills. But these long-distance goals were too remote to motivate my children. Then one summer, we were asked to host a French exchange student for three weeks. Kayte had been studying French at our co-op and begged us to agree. We did, with reluctance, and a whole new world of exchange programs opened up to us. We had a very good experience with our first French student, and our kids suddenly had a tangible reason for studying French. They wanted to talk to Clemence and the steady stream of other exchange students that followed. When I ended up a field director and roped my friends into hosting students, the French classes at our co-op became extremely popular as more and more kids hoped to converse with the group of foreign students that arrived each April. The Internet provided an ongoing way for kids on both sides of the Atlantic to practice their language skills as some of the students remained in contact for several years.

STUDY WITH A BUDDY

In preparation for "game day"—whatever your end goal may be—teens can benefit from studying challenging material with their peers, especially those also preparing for the same event. Buddy-study provides a supportive place for students to discuss material and reinforce their own understanding by verbalizing their thinking. It also helps ferret out areas where kids lack clarity. Students can share their graphic organizers with one another or explain how they solved a problem. As you may have seen in large families where older children work with the younger ones, the practice of explaining concepts and strategies to another person is an important learning tool.

> Buddy-study provides a supportive place for students to discuss material and reinforce their own understanding by verbalizing their thinking. It also helps ferret out areas where kids lack clarity.

We found the buddy-study method especially helpful in math and in preparation for the College Board entrance exams and Advance Placement testing.

I use these collaborative groups in my online AP classes, and they've become a main reason students say they enjoyed the course. The fact that they are all preparing for a difficult test at the end of the year helps students make the best use of these collaborations.

THINK LIKE A REFEREE

Students can really make gains with this strategy. Sticking with the sports metaphor, successful athletes and knowledgeable fans understand the rules governing the game. They know how to score points. They know what constitutes a foul, and so they feel justified in protesting a questionable call. In any game, there's a lot of action that the officials ignore, and then there is specific action they pay close attention to. Study-smart students likewise know what matters in a subject area and what doesn't. They take note of which skills will be measured when it counts and which are peripheral and can therefore receive less attention and preparation.

When my kids started working at the high school level, they tended to highlight way too much in the textbook. They understood the concept of taking notes, and they got the idea of highlighting important information. But highlighting *everything* nullified any benefit they might receive from this approach. They needed to learn to identify and categorize the information according to its importance. One strategy for figuring out what counts and what doesn't is to look through many different resources on the topic. Note what topics and skills appear over and over again. From this, generate a list of important concepts and focus on mastering them.

Another strategy for thinking like an official is to study scoring rubrics. A rubric is a scoring tool that lists the criteria for a piece of work or "what counts." In other words, a rubric helps the student figure out how their test or project will

93

be evaluated. I used the Great Source language arts program with my kids and co-op students in part because a rubric is provided for every writing assignment. I *always* provided this to students ahead of time—every player needs to know the rules governing the game. In my online AP Literature class, I provide the scoring rubric used by the College Board to score student essays. In addition, I've purchased the release exams of past AP Literature tests from the College Board and administer these to my students throughout the course. By the time they sit for the actual exam in May, they are rarely surprised by what appears on the test that year. They've learned to predict what skills and content will be measured.

You can help your teens think like an official by choosing resources with clear evaluation tools, such as scoring rubrics or standardized tests. Let students use these evaluation tools during the course to practice for the big game—the ultimate evaluation which determines their grade or score. You will find examples of various scoring rubrics in the appendix of this book.

> You can help your teens think like an official by choosing resources with clear evaluation tools, such as scoring rubrics or standardized tests.

94

THINK LIKE A COACH

Study-smart students need to think like coaches and not just like players. Coaches strategize by considering multiple scenarios for winning a game, and they can predict the competing coach's moves. The study-smart student needs to strategize how to "win" the game—whatever winning in a particular course of study constitutes—and anticipate what the teacher or test maker or judges will select to measure their success.

Allow me to use another example from my AP Literature course: I've coached students to recognize *why* they are being asked to write about a particular excerpt from literature. They need to understand from the course description provided by the College Board which skills they need to master. They then must apply that list of skills in analyzing a particular piece of literature. For one thing, they know the AP test makers choose literature passages that are accessible on some level to all students—those with the most basic level of skill in analyzing literature—but also sophisticated or subtle enough for the very best students to demonstrate higher levels of critical reading and grasp of artistry. For example, most high school students know a simile when they see one, so you might want to skip writing about similes and instead choose to analyze the irony of the situation set up by the author, as that is a more difficult element to recognize. I also coach students to pre-read questions on the reading comprehension section before reading the passage. Students are then primed to read the passage strategically.

The best material I know for teaching kids how to think like a coach in preparation for high-stakes tests are produced by Princeton Review. These are not the only test prep materials I recommend, but they are the ones that focus on strategies for thinking like a test maker, not the test taker.

95

PRACTICE, PRACTICE, PRACTICE

You can help your students prepare for the big game by simulating "game" conditions during practice or coursework. The College Board periodically releases exams used for their Advanced Placement tests, so I administer several of the exams to my AP students under modified test conditions: The first one they may take un-timed, at their own pace. The second they may take in two sittings but within the prescribed time constraints. The final they must complete according to official test conditions—three hours in one sitting. By the time they sit for the actual test, they have rehearsed test conditions several times and are better equipped to control their nervousness and give a true picture of what they have achieved during the course.

IDENTIFY YOUR LEARNING STYLE

"Know thy self," Socrates urged his students. As surely as your child has a unique personality, he or she has a unique learning style. In *The Ultimate Guide to Homeschooling* I spend an entire chapter discussing learning styles where I present a model based upon David Keirsey's theory of personalities. I like this model because a student's learning preferences can be determined through simple observation: Does your son come alive when he is in a group? Does your daughter enjoy spending the afternoon reading in her room? Does your teen busy himself with construction projects whenever he has any free time? All of the things your child chooses to do when she is free to choose are clues to how she learns best. A wise parent not only uses these observations to better mold a program to each child's preference, but a wise parent also encourages her teens to figure out what learning strategies work best for them.

Here's a quick summation of the four types of learners:

> All of the things your child chooses to do when she is free to choose are clues to how she learns best. A wise parent not only uses these observations to better mold a program to each child's preference, but a wise parent also encourages her teens to figure out what learning strategies work best for them.

Type A Learner

The Type A learner prefers group work, activity, and construction and learns best with these types of methods and strategies:

* Co-operative learning
* Short units of study spanning two to four weeks
* Creative projects or performances as a method of evaluation
* Audio or video presentation of information
* Interactive software
* Academic competitions

Type B Learner

The Type B learner prefers traditional teaching methods and materials and learns best with these types of strategies:

* A consistent schedule for studies
* Short lessons with immediate evaluation, such as quizzes and objective tests
* Opportunities to teach younger children as a method of reinforcing her understanding
* Written reports as a method of evaluation
* Reading to learn
* Well-organized resources with logical progression of information and a simple layout

Type C Learner

The Type C learner prefers focused independent study and learns best with these types of strategies:

* A mentoring relationship with an expert in his field of interest
* Lots of reference materials
* Access to his own computer
* Equipment specific to his areas of interest
* Freedom to manage his time

Type D Learner

The Type D learner prefers a wide scope of studies and co-operative learning and does best with these types of strategies:

* Co-operative classes
* Creative projects
* Unit studies
* Opportunity to present her work to an audience or perform in front of groups
* Biographies
* Flexibility to change routines

Resources

Study Guides and Strategies (www.studygs.net). This learner-centric website is neatly organized.

What Smart Students Know by Adam Robinson. Even though the 1993 copyright appears dated, any book by Adam Robinson, the founder of the Princeton Review, is worth your while.

9 CRITICAL AND CREATIVE THINKING SKILLS

I want to spend a few pages talking about the importance of equipping our kids to think critically about academic subjects and life in general. By *critical*, I don't mean teaching our kids to *criticize* everything—most do this without our help, and we'd like them to do it much less. No, what I mean is fostering their ability to think deeply about what they are studying—to dig beneath the surface and grapple with it on a profound level. There are some compelling reasons for pursuing this level of thinking, but first let's define our terms.

Just what are critical thinking skills, and why all the fuss? I find two models particularly helpful in identifying higher-level thinking. The first is the classic model developed by Dr. Benjamin Bloom and his colleagues in 1956.

Bloom's Taxonomy of Thinking and Learning

Knowledge or Memorization: The ability to remember facts without effort.	Demonstrated by the ability to define, describe, identify, label, list, match, name, state, outline, reproduce, tabulate, select, and/or underline.
Understanding or Comprehension: The ability to grasp the meaning of the material.	Demonstrated by the ability to convert, defend, distinguish, estimate, paraphrase, predict, rewrite, and summarize.
Use or Application: The ability to use or apply what one has learned (i.e., rules, methods, concepts, principles, laws, and theories) in a situation other than the one in which the student has learned them.	Demonstrated by the ability to use the knowledge understood to solve different types of problems; to apply, demonstrate, calculate, complete, illustrate, show, solve, examine, modify, relate, change, classify, experiment, or discover
Analysis: The ability to break down the material into its component parts so that the underlying organizational structure can be understood. It requires the ability to see similarities between things that are different and differences between things that are similar.	Demonstrated by the ability to diagram, distinguish, illustrate, outline, infer, subdivide, connect, select, and separate into categories.
Synthesis: The ability to rearrange the basic parts of something and put them together to create a new product.	Demonstrated by the ability to create, design, formulate, modify, substitute, plan, and revise.
Evaluation or Judgment: The ability to choose, on the basis of supporting evidence, among more than one possible points of view. The difference between a reasoned judgment and a simple guess is the amount of evidence offered in support of the choice made.	Demonstrated by the ability to compare, contrast, conclude, rank, evaluate, criticize, choose, recommend, justify, and support.

This model represents a progression from lower-level to higher-level thinking, with *analysis*, *synthesis*, and *evaluation* representing the more complex and desired outcomes.

When we analyze a thing, we break the whole into its discrete parts and we recognize the relationship between those parts. Remember writing out chemical formulas in high school? Or diagramming sentences? Putting together a jigsaw puzzle by studying the box cover? These are all examples of analysis.

Synthesis is the creative process—we take what we know and understand and put it together in a whole new way. This can mean writing a short story, designing a house, inventing a hybrid car, or proposing a new program or solution to a political problem.

Evaluation involves critical judgment, being able to decide the best solution to a problem or determine the weaknesses in an argument. Analysis is recognizing all the moves one can legally make at a given point in a chess match; evaluation is recognizing the *best* move to make for strategic purposes.

Another model for thinking skills was developed by Vincent Ryan Ruggiero. The following definition of terms is excerpted from his book *Saving Your Child's Mind:*

Creative Thinking (The Production of Ideas)
* Skill in defining problems and issues
* Skill in identifying and pursuing the most promising areas for investigation
* The ability to postpone judgment
* The ability to produce many ideas with ease
* Skill in divergent thinking (achieving a broad, rather than a narrow assortment of ideas)
* The ability to shift perspectives while producing ideas
* Imaginativeness

Critical Thinking (The Evaluation of Ideas)
* Fair-mindedness in analyzing issues
* Skill in asking relevant questions
* The ability to select appropriate criteria for judgment
* Skill in interpreting factual data
* Skill in evaluating the reliability of sources
* The ability to make important distinctions and recognize unstated assumptions
* The ability to detect errors in one's own and other people's thinking (for example, illogical or hasty conclusions, overgeneralization, and oversimplification)
* Skill in evaluating arguments
* The ability to draw sound conclusions from evidence
* The ability to recognize when evidence is insufficient
* Vigilance concerning one's own tendencies to irrationality

As you can see, although Ruggiero organizes his taxonomy according to creative thinking and critical thinking, he too emphasizes analysis, synthesis, and evaluation as the more desirable thinking skills.

WHY DEVELOP HIGHER-LEVEL THINKING SKILLS?

A higher-order level of thinking will benefit your students in two very important ways: retention and usefulness. Let's look at each of these more closely.

Retention

Many programs teach children to memorize and comprehend material, but they remember as little as two percent of what they "learn" through this method. However, a child may retain up to ninety-eight percent of material they learn through analysis. Let me illustrate this for you. Take a moment to memorize the following list of ten numbers:

13, 6, 3, 42, 87, 11, 31, 17, 62, 24

Now put down the book and complete another task—make up a bed, practice a song on an instrument, or just mentally walk through the steps required to perform a similar task. After doing this, grab a sheet of paper and jot down the list of numbers you memorized. How many can you recall?

Okay, now that you know the drill, let's try this again. Here's another list of numbers to memorize:

7, 14, 21, 28, 35, 42, 49, 56, 63, 70

You're chuckling, aren't you?

How many numbers do you think you will remember this time? All ten, right? Why? It's because these numbers are all multiples of seven. And that's analysis. You figured out the relationship between the parts. Therefore, you are able to quickly move all this data from short-term memory to long-term memory where you will be able to recall it at will.

Two hours from now, how many numbers on the first list will you be able to retrieve? Very few, if any. But if I meet you at a conference sometime in the future and ask you to retrieve the second set of numbers I asked you to memorize here, will you be able to do that? You bet.

If your students learn material through analysis, synthesis, and evaluation, you won't have to teach it over and over again. Try this experiment: Lay math textbooks from two or three different grade levels side by side and compare the table of contents. Notice a lot of redundancy? That means the material is being taught at a lower level and, because kids are forgetting it all over the summer, a great deal of review is necessary. Teaching at a higher-level saves a lot of time, the time you need to s-l-o-w down the process so kids can grapple with the material at a more profound level. Once they do, they will be able to recall the information whenever it's needed in the future.

Usefulness

We use higher-order thinking skills to problem-solve, invent, and make decisions. Are these skills you want your children to develop? Consider the complexity of the adult life waiting for them. The answers to life's dilemmas are rarely easy or obvious. Your kids need to be equipped to navigate these difficulties successfully. Think about the job market. Will they need to make decisions, invent, and solve problems in order to compete in the global job market? Absolutely. Our teens are entering a very sophisticated and competitive marketplace; they need to be far more skilled and analytical then we were required to be at their age.

> Our teens are entering a very sophisticated and competitive marketplace; they need to be far more skilled and analytical then we were required to be at their age.

I trust you are a better decision-maker today then you were twenty years ago. One reason is because you've had many chances to make decisions and to reap the consequences of those decisions. When we consider the potential moral and ethical dilemmas our kids may have to face in the future, we shouldn't leave these kinds of skills to chance. They need to practice now under our tutelage. And they need to practice in daily situations where the stakes are not as high as they will be in the future.

Kids become better decision-makers by making decisions.

They become better problem-solvers by solving problems, and they become better inventors by inventing. But many teaching strategies do not keep these long-term goals in mind, nor do they allow kids time to hypothesize, experiment, fail, try again, and consider multiple outcomes—they only ask kids to read, fill in the blanks, regurgitate the information on a test, and relentlessly keep moving.

Sure, it takes more time to set up a program that values higher levels of thinking, but you have that time in the home-schooling environment. And if you begin to revamp your approach and curriculum now, you will gain a lot of traction as your child progresses and becomes an increasingly motivated and independent learner over time.

STRATEGIES FOR DEVELOPING THINKING SKILLS

Helping kids to build creative and critical thinking skills is much easier than you may imagine. Here are several simple strategies for encouraging analysis, synthesis and evaluation.

Teach Your Teen to Ask Questions

Kids who think critically demonstrate the characteristics of the study-smart student. They are engaged in the learning process, they initiate and strategize, and they do not hesitate to ask questions while learning.

The Greek philosopher Socrates was immortalized by Plato in his *Dialogues* as the consummate teacher who trained his students to think by posing a question to them, which the students then answered, followed by another question from the master. Socrates never told his students what to think or what the correct answers to these questions were. Rather, he led the students to logical conclusions and revelation through the art of questioning. The Socratic method has been used for centuries, most notably at the universities of Oxford and Cambridge. However, in this form of exchange, it is the teacher who asks the questions, not the student. Posing the right question is actually the more difficult part, so to develop critical thinking skills, the student should be the one figuring out the questions he needs to answer.

Your teen should begin asking questions while reading the assigned text. This internal dialogue will lead him to a more profound and analytical level of understanding. In his book *What Smart Students Know*, Adam Robinson provides a list of helpful questions for students to ask while learning. Here are some of them:

> Your teen should begin asking questions while reading the assigned text. This internal dialogue will lead him to a more profound and analytical level of understanding.

What is my purpose in reading this?
What do I already know about this topic?
What is the big picture here?
What is the author going to say next?
What questions does this information raise for me?
What information is important here?
How can I paraphrase or summarize this information?
How can I organize this information?
How can I picture this information?
How does this information fit in with what I already know?

I would add to this list the simple practice of asking who, what, when, where, how and why as means of jump-starting this inner dialogue.

Secondly, encourage your teen to ask questions of others,

especially interesting folks who have a wellspring of knowledge—museum curators, field guides, professionals on the job, missionaries on furlough, and anyone with an unusual background or experience. View your extended network of relationships and contacts as a library of valuable resources.

Finally, model the characteristics of an independent learner for your teen yourself. Cultivate your own curiosity about life by asking questions of others and expressing curiosity in the course of daily life.

Analyze Your Resources

Review the materials you are already using with your kids. To what degree do they encourage analysis, synthesis, and evaluation? A quick way to assess this is to examine the review questions posed to the student at the end of chapters. Do all these questions have short, simple answers? Or do some of them pose open-ended questions that can be answered in multiple ways? Is your student being asked to apply what he has learned or to explore further lines of inquiry? Is she being challenged to think more deeply about the implications of what she has learned?

> To what degree do your materials encourage analysis, synthesis, and evaluation?

If you find your current resources lacking, you can still use the material. But you may want to check out other books from the library to augment your teen's reading list. Also, consider creating secondary assignments to reinforce the material, such as having your student generate his own questions then search out the answers.

Dialogue with Your Teen

Talking reveals thinking. Engage your child throughout the day in conversation about what she is reading or studying. Following an activity, field trip, or educational video, ask your child to explain his thoughts about what he's learned. Ask her how she is connecting what she's just heard to what she already knows, or ask what he is curious to learn more about.

At first your child may have difficulty voicing questions, answers, or curiosity. That's okay. Don't give up. Keep engaging your children, and they will begin thinking more actively about what is going on to prepare themselves for the inevitable discussions. I found this to be true over and over again in my homeschool co-op classes. If kids are used to a more passive approach to learning, they won't have any comments or questions at first. But once they realize I'm going to run a discussion-based class, they gradually open up and begin to participate.

> One strategy I've found that works particularly well is to furnish questions ahead of time for the students to think about.

One strategy I've found that works particularly well is to furnish questions ahead of time for the students to think about. Then the kids look for answers to these questions during the learning process. Sometimes I separate the kids into groups of three or four to discuss these prompts together for twenty minutes or so. When I bring them back together to discuss the questions as a group, I get a lot more participation from the quieter students. Many kids are not experienced at thinking on their feet—they need time to ponder and consider, or they want to "test out" their thoughts on a few others before submitting their ideas for a teacher's evaluation.

Another thing to keep in mind is that it's very important not to constantly correct your child's erroneous thinking, especially in the areas of judgment or evaluation. If they have their facts wrong, then okay, maybe correction is appropriate. But when the flaws in their reasoning are primarily the result of inexperience or immaturity, let time work its course. You want to encourage active learning and build your child's confidence in his ability to figure things out. Instead of correcting or stating what you believe to be the right conclusion, ask another thought-provoking question for her to consider. Get comfortable with letting opinions and assumptions evolve. My kids are adults now and, in many areas, have come around to sharing our values that they once questioned. In other areas, they have not. And in some cases, I've had to reevaluate my own conclusions for possible faulty thinking.

As a family, we have found the dinner table to be a great place for the type of dialoguing that supports and encourages thinking deeply about the issues of life. The day's headlines, the sermon at church, the books we're reading, or an interesting guest all stimulate discussions that can last long into the evening. This practice began when our children were very young as we encouraged them to listen thoughtfully and gave them opportunity to throw their own ideas on the table. The old adage that says children should be seen and not heard is not a good principle for promoting learning.

CHOOSE PURPOSEFUL ACTIVITIES

The problem with much of what we ask students to do in a traditional educational setting is that there is a big disconnect from any meaningful goal. More often it's just another day of putting the jigsaw puzzle together without the box cover. You may understand the future need for today's grammar drills or math problems, but do your kids? It's hard for anyone to stay motivated and engaged when the purpose escapes them.

Here are two ways to add purpose to your curriculum:

1. Allow your teen to choose an activity, and he will have a built-in sense of purpose. Of course, getting your teen to choose to complete studies in the right areas is the trick. But even though you will need to provide parameters, you can be flexible within them. Let your teen choose which books to read, projects to complete, papers to write, resources to use. Your kids should be going to the curriculum fair with you at an early age and participating in choosing the program. Choice creates a sense of ownership, and ownership produces motivation. You can also give your teen more control over the school day—the order of his studies and the time he allots to each subject. Of course, this may be scary if you already have a child who tends to waste time and is not motivated to learn. My principle is this: Limit the parameters to those that are necessary. If your child is disinclined to read, then you will have to say that he must be reading a book, but still let him choose which book. If he is only willing to read books by one author or in one genre, then require him to choose to read a book from another specific genre. But still allow him to choose which book within the category. Make the corral as big as possible, and give him free rein within it.

> **Choice creates a sense of ownership, and ownership produces motivation.**

2. You can make the purpose clearer for your kids by tying activities and assignments to the context in which they will use the content or skills in real life. When you separate grammar drills from authentic writing experiences, you sap the work of meaning. Instead, show your teen how to use a grammar handbook to look up the punctu-

ation or capitalization rules she needs to use as situations occur in her writing. Creating such situations across the curriculum may simply take too much time, but with a bit of effort, you should be able to locate resources that show teens how certain math concepts or science can be applied in real life. Examples of application help students to connect the dots and understand the big picture.

Decrease Direct Instruction and Lecturing

In a traditional setting, the teacher tends to stand at the front of the room lecturing to silent children. As you probably know from experience, this method, over time, produces a loss of interest and a lack of motivation in students. As a high school English teacher many years ago, I inherited a classroom full of teens who no longer cared to initiate learning on their own or who stared stonily at the clock regardless of what I tried to do to rekindle their interest.

We can produce the same results at home if we expect our kids to sit quietly plowing through textbooks and workbooks for hours on end. This passive approach to learning is counter-productive. A teen needs to be more of an active participant in the process. Study groups, collaborative learning, discussion, projects, papers, performances, field work—these are methods that allow kids to use the lessons they've learned to analyze, synthesize, and evaluate.

111

Encourage Risk-Taking

Risk is an essential component for making forward progress and the development of any skill or talent to its fullest potential. If kids never try to accomplish something that they might very well fail at, they will always underachieve. For the Christian, this means a life lived without faith or trust in God and a squandering of the talents He has given our kids to use for His glory.

Today in public education, high-stakes testing has virtually eliminated risk from the classroom. There is no time for experimentation, trying new things, or reconsidering goals and priorities. The rat race has gone global, and our schools have had to quicken an already hectic pace. Often, homeschoolers take their cues from what the schools are doing. Our goal is to keep up, to show we are just as good. We think our teens will lose a shot at college if we don't follow a conventional approach or use traditional materials. Instead of capitalizing upon the freedom homeschooling affords us to individualize our programs or live at a more adventurous level, we take a conservative approach more concerned with not failing than with maximizing the opportunity.

> **Taking risks means failure is a possibility we can tolerate, even learn from.**

Taking risks means failure is a possibility we can tolerate, even learn from. Winston Churchill once said, "Success is proceeding from failure to failure without the loss of enthusiasm." Henry Ford said, "Failure is the opportunity to begin again, only this time more wisely."

How do you see your own mistakes? Do you stagnate with regret and discouragement? Or do you thank God for the lessons learned and trust His redemptive power to transform the experience into part of His sovereign plan for your good? How do you see your children's mistakes? Are you overly critical of what they produce, pointing out more of what is wrong than encouraging them where you see potential?

If you see your teaching role as primarily to correct what is wrong, kids will choose to do only what they know they can already do. The stories they write will be filled with only words they can spell. The books they read will be those they already understand. They won't sign up for a new sport or try a new experience. They'll be conditioned to think the cost of failure is too high to take any chances.

Give Your Teens Time

In this culture, we live at a hectic, harried pace that has a corrosive effect upon our health and creativity. Leisure is an important aspect of invention. So is daydreaming and play. Read the biographies of Einstein, Edison, or the Wright brothers and you'll see that their daily schedules made generous allowances for time to think. How regimented is your family's life? How many activities are your kids enrolled in? How much time is spent over-stimulated by a computer, television, or iPod? Electronics do not provide time for thinking deeply—they are mind-numbing.

Kids need time to think, raise questions, hypothesize, test theories, fail, try again, experiment, explore, and ponder. This is what I mean about s-l-o-w-i-n-g down your curriculum. You need to build time into the schedule for messing around with stuff like math manipulatives, science apparatus, creative writing, art supplies, machines, and musical instruments. Even though David Elkind is primarily writing about preschool children, his research in *The Power of Play* (2007) supports the importance of play as a precursor for formal learning in any subject area at any age. First we mess around with the stuff, and then we begin to uncover the underlying concepts and structures, be it music or math or language or cooking.

> Kids need time to think, raise questions, hypothesize, test theories, fail, try again, experiment, explore, and ponder. This is what I mean about s-l-o-w-i-n-g down your curriculum.

Value Creativity

Take an active interest in your teen's creative efforts. Allow time for these ventures and provide an appreciative audience. Praise originality. Make your program project-oriented so they have an opportunity to create. When possible, arrange for art or music lessons. Study the creative process and the great minds and artists of history.

Study Concepts, Themes, and Ideas in Addition to Facts

Vincent Ruggiero calls this mind-building vs. mind-stuffing. Certainly factual knowledge is to be valued, but you encourage critical and creative thinking by studying the prevailing forces that pushed human endeavor toward a discovery or caused a historical event. It's especially important that you set scientific, mathematical, and technical knowledge in context. What was going on historically? Culturally? How did the discovery or event in question affect daily life? What is the contemporary application of this information?

> Factual knowledge is to be valued, but you encourage critical and creative thinking by studying the prevailing forces that pushed human endeavor toward discovery or caused historical events.

Many good resources are available in all disciplines that approach learning from this perspective. And I'll point out some of my favorites later in the book. While this approach may not appear to be the simplest to use, remember, we want our kids to be able to retain what they learn and make use of it, and so we must be willing to take a bit more time setting up a program that will encourage higher-level thinking.

Use the 3 P's as a Means of Evaluation

Instead of using tests to measure a student's comprehension, I prefer assigning one of the three P's—projects, papers, and performances. For high school students, I require at least three reference sources to be used in completing an assignment; these can include (but are not limited to) reference books, websites, educational videos, field trips, articles, and interviews with experts or eyewitnesses.

In my English courses I use a mix of creative projects, objective tests, and analytical papers to evaluate students' grasp of the material. This combination, I find, gives each student at least one method of evaluation that best suits his or her learning style and also requires kids to use different types of critical thinking skills.

ACTIVITIES THAT FOSTER HIGHER-LEVEL THINKING

* Play strategy games such as chess, checkers, or Othello.
* Problem-of-the-day: Take an issue from the headlines, history, or your family setting and discuss ways to solve it.
* Brainstorm: List possibilities before making a decision.
* Use puzzles, brain teasers, mindbenders, and word games for leisure.
* Investigate the creator behind a work. Study the lives of inventors, writers, artists, composers, and directors. Look for information about their unique process for discovery and creation.
* Encourage your teens to look for patterns in math, in nature, in music, in language, in art, in history, etc. Look for repetition, order, design, and predictability.
* Predict outcomes in science experiments or before finishing a story or movie.

115

* Ask your teens what they think a character in a dramatic dilemma should do? This is a good way to rehearse moral choices before finding oneself in a real-life dilemma.
* Examine news stories for biases, opinions, and facts.
* Review articles you find about inventors and creators or new inventions.
* Visit an artist's studio, bookbinder, or other production facility.
* When you and your spouse are problem-solving, do so in front of your kids. If you're deciding where to move, what job to take, what church to join, or how to allocate your funds, let your teen see the process acted out.
* Have your teen keep a blog of ideas and issues.
* Encourage your teen to hypothetically redesign his or her room, a house, a street system, or a process.
* Select employment for your teen based upon the opportunity to invent, problem-solve, and make decisions.
* Analyze and apply timely quotes and scriptures. For example, the writer G. K. Chesterton said, "The Christian ideal has not been tried and found wanting. It has been found difficult and left untried." What did he mean? How can this thought be applied in your teen's life?
* Encourage imitation. This is the best way to discover the process required for invention.

* Let your teen try out an idea you already think does not have merit.
* Let your children make decisions daily.

Recommended Resources

Saving Your Child's Mind by Vincent Ryan
 Ruggiero

The Art of Thinking: A Guide to Critical and Creative Thought by Vincent Ruggiero

The Critical Thinking Company (www.criticalthinking.com) publishes classroom materials that foster creative and critical thinking, particularly deductive reasoning and logic.

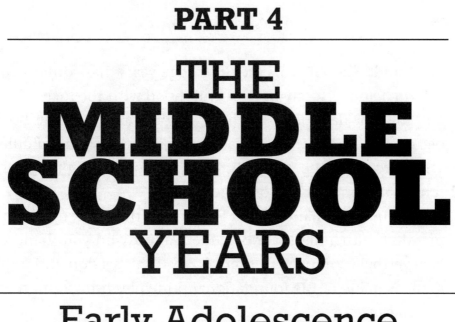

PART 4

THE MIDDLE SCHOOL YEARS

Early Adolescence

10 LAYING A FOUNDATION IN JUNIOR HIGH

The middle school years are the bridge years that connect the informal and leisurely days of childhood with the focused and strategic days of high school. If you are reading this book because you're planning ahead, congratulations! The middle school years are the perfect time to begin preparing for high school at home and beyond.

On the other hand, if you are picking this book up for the first time with a high school student already on your hands, it is nevertheless important that you read this section and implement as many of the foundational principles into your program as you can.

In my experience, the first set of priorities teens need to focus on during the middle school years includes:

* Time management
* Study skills
* Reading comprehension
* Preparation for advanced studies

For high school to really be doable at home, teens need to be willing to learn independently and shoulder the bulk of the responsibility. We equip them to do just that by breaking down the process into bite-size morsels. Remember: Assume the posture of a coach, not a teacher. You are training and equipping; the students must do the work. They break a sweat.

Let's look at each of these six priorities individually.

TIME MANAGEMENT

You need to think through with your spouse the amount of time you envision your teen eventually capable of managing. We were open to the possibility of our high school graduates going directly to a four-year university and living away from home. That meant they had to be ready by age eighteen to essentially run their daily lives independent of us. Working backwards from this end goal meant transferring responsibility and control to our teens in incremental steps. As they demonstrated maturity and faithfulness in little, we allowed them to become progressively responsible for much. And we communicated clearly that this is what we were doing. Make sure your kids know the training program you are following, as well as your expectations of them.

I believe that responsibility, not age, is the primary tool God uses to develop maturity in His children. Wise counselors recommended to us this guiding principle of parenting, and I'm glad they did. We didn't allow our kids to drive at age sixteen just because the law allowed it, nor did we send them away to college simply because they had turned eighteen. We allowed them to exercise these privileges when they were *responsible* enough. But we had to help them get there.

What areas of responsibility do your children currently

> I believe that responsibility, not age, is the primary tool God uses to develop maturity in His children.

121

manage? Their personal hygiene? Laundry? Cleaning their bedroom, bath, and other areas? Cooking? Caring for younger siblings? Lawn care? Determining their own bedtime? Working for others? Service at church or other organization?

If you are micromanaging your young teen's life, you need to see the importance of relinquishing control in a systematic fashion. If there is no priority placed on time management in your home, then perhaps your entire household needs an over-haul. Diving into the high school years without some distribu-tion of responsibility in your household, especially a laissez-faire lifestyle across the board, is going to culminate in a very stressful and discouraging homeschool experience. There is just too much to do, and typically, what doesn't get done defaults to mom. This is a survival strategy I'm preaching here!

Evaluate the strengths and weaknesses of your time-man-agement system, then script out a timeline for transferring responsibility to your kids. Your timeline should probably span several years; I'm not advocat-ing radical overnight change. At the same time, consider eliminating or decreasing ac-tivities that merely waste time. Leisure is important, but what does your child do to relax? Watch television? Play computer games? Cultivate a sedentary lifestyle? Your ability to influence their lifestyle choices is wan-ing as your children age. You have a better shot at breaking bad habits during the middle school years than you will during high school. And whenever possible, you want to be ahead of the curve, not caught behind it.

> Your ability to influence their lifestyle choices is waning as your children age. You have a better shot at breaking bad habits during the middle school years than you will during high school.

One area in particular you might want to think through with your spouse is the computer: computer games, text messaging, Facebook, Twitter, etc. These are activities that can consume lots of free time while flying under parents' radar. My sons were very surprised when they arrived at college to find how addicted their peers were to online gaming. Even though they were living in honors housing with the university's brightest students, many of the young men whiled away the hours transfixed by computer games, and several eventually flunked out.

Our daughter Kristen accepted Christ at a summer youth camp during junior high—that detail is important to note—because this gave her access to the power she needed to make some significant changes in her life. She was subsequently convicted by the Spirit of wasting time with entertainment—specifically, watching television and instant messaging with her friends. Because of God's grace in her life, she radically changed her TV viewing habits and completely stopped chatting online with friends for about four years, until it became necessary for a class she was taking at our co-op. But at that point, she found she had developed the maturity she needed to keep her messaging under control. During another season in college, she realized Facebook was consuming large portions of her time, so she deleted her Facebook page and stopped visiting the site. For your child, managing time in this area may not require such extreme action. But are there other ways your young teen is prone to mismanage time? Is there a gentle way to begin reining that in? Delaying action will only allow the practice to become more entrenched in your child's life.

Here are a few suggestions that may help:

* *Set deadlines* for schoolwork and chores and stick to them. It's very easy and tempting to move deadlines

while homeschooling. And flexibility can indeed be a real blessing at times, as we are free to rearrange schedules when the unexpected arises. However, it's equally tempting to just drift into a lackadaisical approach toward scheduling that doesn't really prepare our teenagers for adult life. I tried not to set unnecessary deadlines, but I did establish enough deadlines that we could practice timely completion of duties. Help your child map out his daily, weekly, and monthly schedule. Find an organizer she likes and help her learn to use it. Set your schedule together at a specified time each week.

* *Establish routines* wherever possible. In school and personal areas of responsibility, routines will first free you from repeatedly assigning chores and schoolwork. Set up a repeating schedule at the beginning of the year with reasonable levels of accountability. You will periodically have to come along and encourage faithfulness, but you won't have to keep starting from scratch over and over. Secondly, routines will foster habitual behavior in your preteen and this is the secret to good time management and actually achieving the goals we set.

* Show your preteen how to break down assignments and responsibilities into *measurable steps*. Kids and adults alike often procrastinate because the goal is as intimidating as a mountain rising before them. Scripting out a plan will help your teenager learn to gauge his progress and avoid cramming at the end to get something important done.

* Help your preteen learn how to *prioritize* and *set goals*. Invariably, he will not complete all he sets out to achieve—but folks who set priorities and goals accomplish more over the course of a lifetime than people who never bother to plan ahead.

* Help your child develop *responsibility* through babysitting, lawn care, service at church, small jobs for neighbors, etc. This is also an effective way to help your young teen walk out of the inherent self-centeredness that infects this season of life.

* *Consider organized sports.* This can help you to promote a healthy lifestyle and motivate your child to get things done on time. For my family, scheduled afternoon practices helped to quicken our study pace earlier in the morning.

Recommended Resource

The 7 Habits of Highly Effective Teens, Sean Covey

STUDY SKILLS

Study skills help your teen to learn and retain knowledge *efficiently*. Many of these were covered in the chapter on the study-smart students. Here is a brief overview of the most basic study skills kids should start developing before they enter the high school years.

Taking Notes

Junior high is the time to start expecting your child to take notes on the material she is studying. The study-smart student has her own personalized method that develops over time. You can help your child start down this path by sitting down together and discussing how to take notes. Most conscientious kids will first try to take notes on everything, which is counterproductive, while other students won't take enough. They need your help in figuring out how to recognize what information is important. They will need to learn both how to take notes from

125

> Students should learn that note taking helps us to organize the information in our mind. This is an important step towards storing the material in our memory so we can retrieve it for later use.

a text and how to take notes from a lecture.

Students should learn that note taking helps us to organize the information in our mind. This is an important step towards storing the material in our memory so we can retrieve it for later use. Current research suggests concept mapping may be a more effective method of note-taking, especially when the student wants to broadly outline subject matter, not just a chapter in a textbook. (This approach is briefly discussed in chapter eight.) Graphic organizers are powerful tools for keeping important information we need to recall, especially when we want to condense large amounts of knowledge. Outlining is a simpler way to take notes on a chapter or lecture.

Kids also must decide where to *keep* their notes. Most of my kids took notes in a notebook with subject dividers. Some kids will prefer to take notes on a laptop, PDA, or even on index cards. Whatever their preferred method, help them decide where to store their study notes so they don't become lost. If you have several kids, you might want to standardize the color of notebooks each one uses so that they recognize their own notebook on sight.

Highlighting

Many students will also find it helpful to mark up a textbook for later review. They should be free to highlight and add notes in the margins that help them make connections. I realize this compromises the resell value of the text or means a younger sibling may not be able to use it. You have to balance this against allowing your child to develop study habits that support his learning. Allowing your children to personalize their resources in ways that support their learning preferences will give them an advantage in mastering the material.

Test Taking

While I do not advocate tests as a frequent assessment tool, they will nevertheless be a big part of the college-bound student's life. Junior high is the place to start getting accustomed to the test maker's game. Our kids began receiving grades for the first time in seventh grade. Because they weren't burned out from an intensive elementary experience and constant testing and grading, they found this new approach exciting. Objective tests—some of which I made, while others were obtained from test banks—became a part of their experience. Our co-op classes and activities at home remained heavy on research papers and creative projects as evaluation tools, but the kids became experienced test takers before the high-stakes testing game began in earnest in tenth grade.

Doing a Google search on "test taking skills" will bring up some helpful websites to review, including www.testtakingtips. com. As mentioned earlier, test prep books by The Princeton Review are also very helpful in developing test-taking strategies.

Recommended Resources

What Smart Students Know by Adam Robinson. Robinson is the founder of The Princeton Review.

What Smart Students Know: Maximum Grades, Optimum Learning, Minimum Time by Adam Robinson

The 7 Habits of Highly Effective Teens by Sean Covey. I recommend Covey's book with this caveat: It is heavy on self-esteem teaching as motivation for teen's to manage their lives well. While I do believe that responsibility and achievement, not positive thinking, are how a child improves his or her self-image, I want my teens to be essentially motivated by God's grace. And they should be striving for His glory, not their own recognition. That said, this practical approach to life management is worth your student's time.

How to Become a Superstar Student by Dr. Tim McGee. An excellent DVD series from the Teaching Company.

COMPUTER SKILLS

Today the personal computer is an indispensable tool, and reliance on this tool at home and in the workplace is only going to increase. However, your child will need your help to safely and confidently navigate these waters. If you, as the parent, have not yet developed basic computer literacy, then you might want to take an inexpensive course at the local community college or purchase a resource that helps you make sense of it all.

Currently, most colleges and employers are looking for proficiency with Microsoft Office software. This suite of programs includes Word, Excel, Access, PowerPoint, and Outlook. (Open Office is the free, open-source alternative.) I suggest you develop a plan for incorporating these programs into your student's scope and sequence over the next few years so that he or she achieves competency prior to graduation. Working through a self-study book about Office can be a good use of time, and you should consider requiring the use of these programs regularly in completing assignments.

Internet Skills

In your case, as it was in mine, it may be that your children will teach *you* how to do things efficiently with technology. However, one area where you need to take the lead is making sure your kids know how to safely search for information online.

The first step in guaranteeing that kids are safely searching the Internet is to choose a search engine that allows parents to set family-friendly filters. All the major search engines include this feature, typically located under "search settings" or "search preferences." Firefox, by the open-source company Mozilla, may be your best bet in this area.

> **The first step in guaranteeing that kids are safely searching the Internet is to choose a search engine that allows parents to set family-friendly filters.**

We also dealt with the temptation of the Internet during the high school years by keeping the computer face-out in the family room. This way, I could easily see what my kids were doing online. If you have purchased a laptop for your child, you may want to set restrictions on where and when it can be used. We established with our children at the outset of adolescence that mom and dad should be able to look over their shoulders at what they were doing online at anytime. In fact, we had access to our children's e-mail accounts until college. If our kids requested privacy with explanation, we certainly respected that. However, the argument that teens should have relationships and activities that are kept completely closed from parental oversight is dangerous territory to wander into. Yes, you need to give your teens room to grow and make mistakes; but once you concede an area of authority, it becomes a battle to regain your role in this area of their lives.

129

Recommended Resource

Cyber-Safe Kids, Cyber-Savvy Teens: Helping Young People Learn to Use the Internet Safely and Responsibly by Nancy E. Willard

Recommended Reference Materials

The middle school years are the right time to set up a reference library for your teens, either on a bookshelf or online. Independent research should become the hallmark of their studies in every subject area, and keeping references tools handy will be critical to their future success. Some of the kinds of tools kids need to know how to use include a student or college dictionary, atlases and maps, a thesaurus, almanacs, and style guides that set standards for academic writing. Examples of quality style guides include *The Chicago Manual of Style*, *The MLA Handbook for Writers of Research Papers* and *The Associated Press Stylebook*.

Recommended Online Reference Materials

Dictionary: www.dictionary.com
Thesaurus: www.thesaurus.com
Maps: www.mapquest.com
        maps.google.com
Google Earth (earth.google.com)
Online databases:
    www.infoplease.com
    www.ipl.org (Internet Public Library)
    www.ask.com
    www.about.com
Virtual Reference Shelf from the Library of Congress:
    www.loc.gov/rr/askalib/virtualref.html
Encyclopedia: www.wikipedia.com. A quick note regarding

Wikipedia: It's true that virtually anyone in the world can edit an entry in Wikipedia and, therefore, the information contained therein may not always be entirely accurate. However, continuous activity by experts on the site now reduces greatly how long inaccurate information may appear. I have found it a great starting point for information on any topic imaginable, though I would never suggest citing Wikipedia as a source in a scholarly paper. Keep in mind that any information gleaned here needs to be verified elsewhere.

READING COMPREHENSION

During the junior high school years, reading comprehension becomes an essential skill. Today there is simply too much information to process to rely on hands-on activities or multimedia presentations, though these are certainly strategies you should use to augment a student's studies whenever possible.

Vocabulary

The foundation of understanding what we read is word comprehension. This is why building vocabulary should be an emphasis during middle school. If your child has poor reading comprehension scores, studying vocabulary is the single most effective strategy you can implement to dramatically increase his achievement in this area. However, completion of a basic vocabulary program alone will not do the trick. The following is some of what we know to be important in increasing vocabulary comprehension.

Remember what I said about *webbing* in chapter eight? I've found this approach to be helpful in increasing a child's vocabulary. New words must be *defined* with language and examples from the student's experience. Context is nice when encountering a word for the first time, but context only helps if the

131

surrounding text is discussing a situation the young reader has some familiarity with. He will assimilate the word into his own vocabulary bank only after he uses it in a variety of contexts, thus increasing his webbing, or network, surrounding that word. You can see why figuring out what a word means from the context of a chemistry lesson may be difficult if the student is studying chemistry for the first time. You need to provide additional connections between the word and the student's prior knowledge.

For example, let's take the word *bellicose*. Here it is used in a sentence: *Phillip II was reputedly bellicose and intractable.* In this example, you can see the issues. Young students not versed in European history are unlikely to know anything about Phillip II (a Spanish king during the Inquisition) from which to deduce the meaning of *bellicose*. And if they don't know the meaning of *bellicose*, they are unlikely to know the meaning of *intractable*. This sentence might be easier to work with: *Attila the Hun's bellicose and unyielding nature earned him the nickname "The Scourge of God" from those he conquered.* Students are far more likely to deduce that bellicose means "war-like" in this context. If you then accuse your teen of being bellicose in the midst of breaking up a fistfight with his brother, you've wisely made the most of the "teachable moment" to reinforce the webbing support for his new vocabulary word.

Keep in mind that a good vocabulary program defines words with examples and illustrations and shows students how they might be used in a variety of contexts. On the high school level, it's very important for students to also study the connotations associated with words. This is essential to a

132

> Your teen will assimilate the word into his own vocabulary only after he uses it in a variety of contexts.

student's understanding of the implied meaning, or subtext, of what they read. For example, a news report might call the same group *insurgents* or *freedom fighters*. While the literal meaning of both labels is the same, the connotation is very different. *Insurgents* implies a group of armed rebels attacking a legitimate government, while *freedom fighters* implies that they are fighting against an oppressive regime.

Also remember that retention is greatest when a student learns a few words deeply. Less retention is likely when learning a long list of words, as when memorizing definitions in preparation for a weekly test.

My recommendation is that you take vocabulary studies into consideration when selecting subject area resources for the middle school years. Consider texts for science, history, and literature that provide the student with a short list of vocabulary words taken from the reading assignments. Find ways to talk about and use these words in your everyday conversation. When working online, keep www.dictionary.com open to look up unfamiliar words. This only takes a moment, but it gives students immediate support and deepens their comprehension.

Recommended Resource
Vocabulary for Achievement, courses 1–5, by Margaret Ann Richek

133

Strategic Reading
Readers with high comprehension skills read strategically and efficiently, and they adjust their reading approach to match the text. For example, reading a textbook is different than reading a novel, though middle school students are unlikely to know this. We can help them by bringing the different approaches to their attention.

SQ3R is a popular and proven strategy for effectively reading textbooks. Here are the steps this odd acronym represents:

Survey. Before you read, scan the titles, headings, pictures, and chapter summaries. Check out the questions at the end of the chapter you may have to answer. Surveying the material is necessary to get a bird's-eye view or big picture of what's being taught.

Question. Actively ask yourself questions as you read. For example, what are the key topics in this chapter? Turn section headings into questions you can answer: *George Washington's Farewell Address* becomes "What did George Washington say in his farewell address to Congress?"

Read. Read for comprehension, locate concepts and facts, and record and reduce the information in the margins. Read like a hunter looking for his quarry: You're after big game, not small rodents. Figure out why the author has included a particular piece of information in a particular place—what is this section's relationship to the larger topic of the chapter?

Review. Practice and rehearse the main concepts, reflect on key points, and anticipate potential exam questions.

Recite. Transfer information to your long-term memory. If you can't state the main ideas verbally, you do not understand them, you have not connected the information to prior knowledge, and you will not be able to recall it later.

134

Instruction in "How to Read"

Finally, a student's comprehension of material is increased when he or she is instructed how to read the text. There are many lively, well-illustrated textbooks and resources now available for use, but studies have found that simply handing these colorful books to students does not result in higher comprehension. Rather, kids are more often confused and overloaded by information that is cluttered with graphics. First, choose a resource that is logically organized—that is, the pattern is evident to you. Then take time to go through the book with your teen. Show her how to use the table of contents to anticipate the big ideas and classification of information. Review the index as a source of discrete information the student may have to look up in the future. Preview chapters together. Point out the level of importance indicated by chapter titles, chapter divisions, and subheadings as well as how to read charts and graphs and captioned illustrations. If there are vocabulary words or terms highlighted, go over a strategy for mastering these.

Recommended Resource
Deeper Reading: Comprehending Challenging Texts, 4–12 by Kelly Gallagher

Time to Read

Finally, make sure your teen has plenty of time to read. Home-schoolers can easily be as busy as their traditionally educated counterparts. For years, our family maintained SSR (silent, sustained reading) after lunch. At first, some of the kids balked at this mandate, but once they knew I wasn't going to budge, they quickly became engrossed in a book of their choosing. You will probably have to remove distractions, such as competing media, to help direct attention to the goal at hand.

And it isn't too late to enjoy audio books together as a family or entice your teens into a book by reading aloud to them. My daughter-in-law teaches in an urban setting where many of her students are easily distracted and some have attention-deficit disorders, but they love when she reads a compelling story aloud to them.

135

PREPARATION FOR ADVANCED STUDIES

This is the time to anticipate the future. Determining what foundational knowledge you need to focus on in middle school won't necessarily be the same for every family or even every child. You want to work backwards from your end goals. For instance, if you want to get through calculus by the end of high school, then you will need to teach algebra in the seventh or eighth grade. If you want to take Advanced Placement U.S. History in tenth grade, you will need to cover high-school-level history in junior high.

> You may be able to see only one foot in front of you, but the expectation that God will lead the way is a critical one.

This is the season to begin praying about just what these goals might be. You can have faith that God will give you direction in these matters as you commit your plans to Him. Yes, you may be able to see only one foot in front of you, but the expectation that God will lead the way is a critical one. Then you will be more positioned to read the signs He has set before you.

Focus on Areas of Interest

As you consider what to study during the middle school years, it is time to start building a program around your child's interests and strengths. You'll want to develop and direct those gifts that have surfaced in his life. If you still feel stumped about what these are, then you need to increase your child's exposure to a broader swatch of subject matter and look for new experiences to try to joggle those clues free. In the meantime, keep your curriculum structured around what you *do* know she needs no matter what: research skills, writing skills, reading comprehension, and learning how to learn.

136

Work Backwards

Here are a few additional questions to help you figure out just what God's future plans for your child may be:

1. Should your teen prepare to go to a four-year institution? Or do you believe living at home and attending a community or junior college is a more desirable option? Or is he or she more likely to go to a trade school or straight into a career?

2. Do you anticipate your teen's being more interested in a field of study in the hard sciences or humanities? Business or education? The coursework he or she should complete in high school, especially in mathematics and foreign languages will depend upon that answer.

3. What is your child's potential for doing advanced studies in high school? Are college-level classes a realistic possibility? If she is reading well above grade level now, or accelerated in mathematics, then college-level work during the latter part of high school is something to consider.

4. What are your child's greatest areas of strength? Don't try to figure this out by comparing your child to other kids. Rather, evaluate his strengths in comparison with areas not of interest or gifting in his life. If you don't immediately recognize his areas of strength, then begin by crossing off what you know is not of interest to him. Also, consider his temperament if an academic domain is not yet obvious. Think about the careers best suited for your child's personality.

The reasons you need to know the answers to these questions is so that you can work backwards to determine how your

137

child will go about preparing to meet the most demanding entrance or life requirements. If you would like your child to attend an elite four-year school with a demanding major such as engineering or nursing and receive scholarship, then the high-school-level studies he completes will need to be very demanding. On the other hand, if you plan to use the community or junior-college system available to you, then that takes some of the pressure off. Your child can use coursework there to qualify for his or her next career step. If you aren't in a hurry—if you are open to your child taking a gap year before going to college, or if college isn't an end goal at all—your teen can pursue more leisurely and unconventional coursework during the teen years.

> The student shooting for the most demanding colleges will need to pursue the most advanced high school work in these areas.

The subject area guidelines provided in the following chapters are not exhaustive but are intended to provide you with an overview of core content and key skills kids need in place to prepare for high-school-level studies. The student shooting for the most demanding colleges will need to pursue the most advanced high school work in these areas. In fact, you may want to go ahead use the ninth- and tenth-grade material suggested in later chapters with the truly gifted seventh- or eighth-grade student.

CREDITS TOWARD GRADUATION?

One caveat about doing high-school-level coursework in middle school: Many colleges and states do not count junior high coursework as credit toward high school graduation. So if you do algebra 1 in junior high, as I'm about to suggest you do, you will still need to complete three to four credits of math in high school. If you complete American history in junior high, and your state requires American history as part of the high-school-level requirements, you still need to show this as being met *during* high school. Whether or not this needs to be a full yearlong course, or just a topic covered in the context of another course such as American government, will vary from state to state. Ask for clarification from your state organization or any institution you plan to apply to that has specified certain subjects be covered in high school.

11 WHAT YOUR MIDDLE SCHOOL STUDENT NEEDS TO KNOW

Everything kids need to learn in school can be divided into a skill area or a content area. In general, skill areas are the more important as they build in complexity to become the tools students will use to complete important tasks and objectives. Examples of skill areas include writing, math, computer, and research.

The content we study, I believe, is up for debate. We live in the Information Age, with more knowledge than ever available readily and cheaply to everyone; we will never learn everything there is to know in a lifetime. So how do you determine what is important to know? That depends on your end goals.

At our house, Scripture is irrefutably essential—the more scriptural understanding we gain, the wiser we will be in negotiating life's minefields and choices. After that, what's considered important among academic subjects is determined by each child's needs. There are plenty of good reasons for studying the roots of Western Civilization, as emphasized by the classical Christian movement, especially if your child's eventual goal is a liberal arts college and his career ambitions lean toward the humanities. But a compelling case can also be made for a more culturally relevant, globally-focused agenda, especially if the student is interested in cross-cultural work or heading into any field connected with business or technology.

In this chapter, I'm going to emphasize the *skills* your child should master by the end of eighth grade, while only mentioning options to consider in terms of content.

ENGLISH

You will need to consider both literature and language arts skills when determining your child's course of study.

Literature

During the middle school years, your reading program should begin to focus on quality literature. By this, I mean books that are more theme-driven than plot-driven. For instance, Katherine Paterson's *Jacob Have I Loved* won the Newbery Award for children's literature in 1981. This story of twin girls growing up on a Chesapeake Bay island during the 1940s vividly captures the lifestyle of those who earned their living by crabbing. The sibling rivalry between the two girls is the conflict that drives the story forward. However, Paterson uses this setting and story primarily to explore the themes of familial love, the function of community in forming our adult selves, and our own responsibility in determining our happiness. The biblical allusion of the title is the first clue that this story is to be read on a deeper level. Well-chosen literature of this caliber is especially helpful with teens because you can use the adolescent situations as a springboard for discussion.

> During the middle school years, your reading program should begin to focus on quality literature. By this, I mean books that are more theme-driven than plot-driven.

141

If your teen is reading above her grade level, then she may be ready to read and understand more adult literature. In evaluating choices to study, I recommend you choose works that are appropriate to your teen's experience level. For example, even though *The Adventures of Huckleberry Finn* and *To Kill a Mockingbird* were intended for an adult audience, their adolescent narrators and Southern settings provide an excellent starting point for discussing with teens the themes of prejudice and justice at work in both novels. However, the themes of revenge, deception, and the moral order of the universe, combined with a setting in medieval Denmark, make it a stretch for young teens to understand the complexity of Shakespeare's *Hamlet*.

Literature textbooks may be appealing because they condense your reading program into a single volume while providing study questions. However, most of the literature in English textbooks is abridged or excerpted, and this is problematic, as students never get to experience some works in their entirety. Also, be sure to check the study questions for their ability to develop higher-level critical thinking. Literature is one of your primary tools for cultivating this skill, and you don't want to the waste the opportunity by teaching literature at a rudimentary level.

142

Recommended Resources

eNotes.com is an online source I've used for quite a few years. This website has the best online material for studying literature. As of this writing, the site offers study guides to more than 3,500 texts, including nearly 1,000 appropriate for adolescents. All content can be downloaded for later use, so I suggest subscribing for one year and downloading everything you might want for your homeschool.

Bookrags.com is a similar online source for literature guides, though their content and analysis are not as comprehensive or penetrating as those on eNotes.com. The difference is that Bookrags currently offers almost 200 of its 4,000 guides free of charge.

Sparknotes.com provides most of their online study guides for free, so I allow my AP students to use Sparknotes for quick overviews of literature. However, I would not use Sparknotes as a source for an analytical paper.

Progeny Press Study Guides are easy-to-use study guides that examine literature from a biblical perspective. I'm enthusiastic about them because they teach a reasonable amount of vocabulary, ask analytical questions, provide writing prompts, and teach the elements of literature in context. Study guides are available for elementary through high school at www.progenypress.com.

There are several other online sources for literary guides I do *not* recommend—PinkMonkey.com, Barron's, JiffyNotes.com, and ClassicNotes among them. I often find their critiques deficient and their content questionable.

Language Arts

Writing skills make up the primary target when it comes to language arts, so whichever resource you choose to use to teach grammar and mechanics should have real writing as its end result. Kids who write well, write frequently. Kids who fill out worksheets related to language arts, but never complete actual writing assignments with a purpose, do not write well.

The current trend is to teach the six traits of effective writing. You may see this mentioned frequently in your curriculum research, so let me define them for you here:

143

* *Ideas.* Good writing presents clear ideas with a purpose.

* *Organization.* Any written piece should have a beginning, middle, and an ending and be well organized and easy to follow.

* *Voice.* Your writing should connect with your audience, fit your purpose for writing, and reveal the author's voice. (In the same way a friend recognizes your spoken voice without seeing your face, a knowledgeable reader should be able to recognize the author's written voice through his preferences in word choice, subject matter, organization, and syntax, even if the author's name is not included on the work.)

* *Word choice.* Good writing uses specific nouns and verbs and strong words that deliver the writer's message.

* *Sentence fluency.* Sentences should vary in length, with a variety of sentence beginnings. The writing should flow smoothly from sentence to sentence.

* *Conventions.* Strong writing should be edited for grammar, punctuation, capitalization, and spelling so the writer's ideas can be easily understood.

You will find many good Internet sites built by teachers using the six traits approach to teaching writing. You can also find more information at www.thetraits.org, a site hosted by the Northwest Regional Educational Laboratory, creators of the six traits approach.

Recommended Resources

Great Source Writing (www.greatsource.com). While I would strongly recommend the Great Source program, it can prove problematic for homeschoolers. Designed for classroom use, the complete program is expensive and overloaded with information. Still, it is the best available for creating a writing-intensive program and is the only one I'm aware of that emphasizes content over mechanics, form, and style. This program teaches kids how to think and how to compose thoughtful, original work. Every other program I've considered overlooks the fact that writing is fundamentally about having something worthwhile to say and that saying it well is a secondary goal. Here is how to make Great Source work for you: First, buy the Write Source student book for the appropriate grade level (e.g., *Write Source Grade 7*) and work through it chronologically. Do not buy the teacher's guide—it is very expensive and doesn't provide the daily lesson plans you are looking for. If you read through the student book, you should be able to grasp the scope of the program and how to make assignments from it for your kids. Instead, you may wish to purchase the grade-level SkillsBook and the SkillsBook Teacher's Edition to practice mechanics, usage and grammar.

Great Source iWrite (www.greatsource.com/iwrite). This site, which supports the Great Source program, is full of helpful and highly interactive information for students and parents. The grammar guide, for example, explains key grammar rules with voice and animated illustrations.

WriteatHome.com offers online writing classes designed by a homeschooling father, and these are a must at some point in your teen's curriculum. The courses are reasonably priced and can last nine weeks, a semester, or the entire school year. A writing coach guides the student through the writing process, providing constructive feedback and a score for finished assignments.

Write from the Heart (www.denisebotsford.com). Denise

145

Botsford's online writing classes for junior high and senior high students are very popular, and she is now adding writing coaches to help her with the demand. I know Denise personally, and her students and parents are very satisfied with her teaching.

Our Mother Tongue: A Guide to English Grammar by Nancy Wilson. This inexpensive one-year course is written in a lively style with a lot of good background information about the history of the English language. I like this element because it helps students understand the reasons why grammar functions the way it does. This allows them to make analytical connections that allow them to store and recall the rules governing usage.

Standards for the English Language Arts, published by International Reading Association (IRA) and National Council of Teachers of English (NCTE). You can download this document at www.ncte.org/standards.

Recommended Books

In the Middle: New Understandings About Writing, Reading, and Learning by Nancie Atwell
Teaching Adolescent Writers by Kelly Gallagher

Acceleration in English

If you want to prepare your junior high student for college-level achievement by the end of high school, then the literature and composition work he or she is completing in eighth grade must be equivalent to the skill level of a rising eleventh grader.

One way to do this is to begin using the Tapestry of Grace curriculum (www.tapestryofgrace.com) in seventh grade, with a view toward completing the four-year program in tenth grade. The program is multi-level, so you will need to follow the reading assignments for high school (the rhetoric stage). Then transition to college-level coursework through a community college or AP coursework in the humanities beginning in eleventh grade.

Tapestry of Grace is a classical Christian curriculum I can recommend with enthusiasm if you want to emphasize the humanities in your program. However, if your junior high student is not reading above grade level, do not attempt to plow through all the reading and writing required at the rhetoric stage. If you follow this plan, the composition work integrated into Tapestry of Grace is sufficient and you will not need to add Great Source or another writing program to it.

For additional ideas for acceleration in this subject area, consider implementing some of the suggestions provided in chapter thirteen for high school English.

Mathematics

I have some very fresh experiences to draw upon in writing this section. In order to qualify for my doctoral program, I had to retake my GREs (Graduate Record Exam). My scores from thirty years ago were a bit outdated, and my math knowledge was too. Fortunately, the GREs test competency in mathematics typically covered in junior high—i.e., arithmetic, simple algebra, and geometry. So I scripted out a six-week study program and dug in. I wanted to master the material for future use, as my program requires a lot of statistical analysis and analytical research. Though at first daunting, my studies gained traction as the test date neared. Because of my interest in how students learn, I took note of not just *what* I was learning but *how* I was learning as well, keeping a mental list of what worked, what didn't, and why. In the end, I went from below-average scores on the pre-test to achieving a personal best on test day with scores well above average. Here are just a few strategies I believe contributed to my success:

147

* I used several different resources to study—two online tutorials, two test prep books, and a software program that gave me three practice tests with a diagnostic report.

* I dedicated at least a hundred hours of focused study on the subject matter. I always had my math problems with me: I solved math problems while waiting in the car, at the doctor's office, before going to sleep at night, during the day, and first thing every morning. Research shows students make significant gains with this approach to remediation. Conversely, students do not make gains if remediation is gradual and integrated with the rest of the curriculum. In other words, if your student lacks remedial skills in an area of math or reading, that's all you should cover in that subject area for at least 100 hours.

* The Princeton Review test preparation program was the most helpful because it gave me mnemonics and graphic organizers to help me remember math concepts and problem-solving steps. Where abstract thinking is required, visual representation of information or concrete experience is necessary for mastery.

There are three things you should know about teaching mathematics:

1. There is more than one way to solve any math problem, and students should be encouraged to development a variety of approaches to mathematical reasoning.
2. Students should begin by discovering the purposes of math in the context of real-world problem solving. The SATs, for instance, measure mathematical reasoning, not computation skills. You need to design a junior high program that fosters mathematical thinking.

3. Math is a language—the language of science—so learning it well is critical to understanding other important subjects. Teach math as you would any other living language. Immersion and using math in context are the best approaches for developing mastery.

Arithmetic

The first objective in mathematics during the junior high years is to make sure your teen has a solid foundation in arithmetic, or solving for known quantities. Far too many high school students have not yet mastered the basic operations of adding, subtracting, dividing, and multiplying known numbers, making algebra next to impossible for them. So start by assessing your teen's proficiency in calculating solutions not just for problems using whole numbers, but also for those requiring the use of decimals, percentages, and fractions. There are plenty of resources that can help your child complete a focused study in basic arithmetic.

Recommended Resources

The Keys To . . . series includes *Keys to Fractions*, *Keys to Decimals*, *Keys to Percents*, etc. These can be used for reinforcement and review during the summer months or as a six-week study to begin your school year. Available from www.keypress.com, these workbooks are supplemental and not sufficient to be used as your math program for college-bound students.

Math.com provides instruction and practice in all the major areas of junior high and high school math. I used it daily in preparation for my GREs.

Mathdrills.com. This site contains 6,000+ free worksheets with drills in basic math facts and operations.

Calculadder, levels 4–6, drills kids in intermediate arithmetic in less than ten minutes a day and include easy-to-use keys for checking work. The goal is for students to complete the drill every day until they hit their target time. That simple challenge was incentive enough for our kids to complete their Calculadder tests without reminder.

Saxon Math. Despite the fact that my kids did not learn to love math using Saxon, research continues to show a strong correlation between high mathematical achievement and Saxon's middle school math program. (The results were mixed for Saxon's newer elementary level program.)

Word Problems

Students need to learn to use math in the context of real-world problems. Indeed, the major tests college-bound students will face in high school are loaded with word problems. The challenge in solving word problems is typically not the mathematics involved but, rather, figuring out which mathematical process is required to solve the problem.

> The challenge in solving word problems is typically not the mathematics involved but, rather, figuring out which mathematical process is required to solve the problem.

There are two things you can do in this area that I believe will contribute significantly to your kids' success in mathematics. The first involves the use of Figure It Out, a very inexpensive program from Curriculum Associates intended for the elementary grades. These simple workbooks teach important problem-solving skills. The word problems are not overly easy, and because learning the strategies is what's important, books

4–6 provide quality word-problem work for a middle school student.

Step-by-Step Math: Understanding and Solving Word Problems is a follow-up program from Curriculum Associates with inexpensive workbooks developed specifically for middle school students. Spanish versions are also available.

This brings me to my second strategy for middle school mathematics: math competitions. Jane Rimmer, a homeschool mom in our area, started a math club and invited us to join when my sons were in third grade. We met monthly at her home and occasionally for all-day math games. She then started coaching homeschool kids for math competitions. (Jane did not have a degree in math; she learned alongside her students.) Even though Jane's daughters are now grown, she is still coaching Math Olympiad and Math Counts teams and teaching math strategies at our local co-op.

Math Olympiad (www.moems.org) is a math competition open to fourth- through eighth-graders. Problems are sent to the math coach and must be administered on a predetermined date set by the organization. Students have thirty minutes to solve five non-routine word problems using mathematical thinking and strategies learned through resources recommended by Math Olympiad. All problems can be solved without using algebra.

Math Counts (www.mathcounts.org) is a competition for sixth through eighth grades and is not associated with Math Olympiad but dovetails nicely with it. Some of their word problems require the use of algebra and geometry. Homeschoolers are welcome to participate but must form teams. The prep material for coaching "mathletes" is free, though there is a cost to enter a team into competition. The actual competition begins in February with a written exam administered by the coach. Teams with qualifying scores then move on to regional, state, and national competitions.

My daughter Kayte, who is now a math teacher, was a member of a successful Math Counts team, finishing fifth in their region. Not only did they draw attention for being a home-schooled team, but more so for being an all-girls team. Kayte credits her involvement in these competitions for her high math scores on the SATs. She feels that the problem-solving strategies taught in preparation for these competitions reflect the type of thinking required on college-entrance exams.

> If your teen has any interest in focusing on math and science in the future, you should consider making competitions such as these a priority in middle school.

If your teen has any interest in focusing on math and science in the future, you should consider making competitions such as these a priority in middle school. The activity may seem supplemental, but that the mathematical reasoning taught here and the energy generated by team competition is excellent preparation for your teen's future. If you can't pull off a team or math club, at least send away for the materials created by these organizations and consider devoting one day out of five to this type of problem solving.

152

Algebra

Working backwards, if your teen plans to complete college-level math work before the end of high school, she will need to complete algebra 1 before starting high school. This will enable her to finish calculus 1 by the end of her senior year, which is now the expectation for anyone heading to college to study mathematics, engineering, or the sciences. (My kids did not get through calculus in high school but still earned degrees in finance and math. However, their college years would have been easier had we known we needed to go this route.)

Completing algebra 1 by the end of eighth grade is also helpful for the newly recommended regimen in science. Perhaps you have heard that there is a concerted push to strengthen U.S. students' achievements in math and science, as we have been getting left in the dust by the rest of the world. This has created a space-race-like urgency to revamp curriculum in the U.S. This makes things difficult for homeschooling families trying to stick to a mom-teaches-the-lesson model. Fortunately, innovators in the homeschool market are providing a way. Online classes and new-and-improved product lines are making advanced math classes at home very doable, even desirable.

The resource you choose to use for algebra, I believe, may be the most important curriculum decision you make in homeschooling. Algebra is the language of mathematics, and it lays a foundation for all of high school math to follow. Not all programs are equal, so spend some time researching and reviewing products. Talk to knowledgeable friends. Interview students who have succeeded at higher-level math and get their opinions.

We used Chalk Dust videos (now on DVD) for higher-level math. Many families in our homeschool community have been enthusiastic about Math-U-See. Both programs feature great instructors explaining material to the kids. My daughter Kayte gives two enthusiastic thumbs up to Shawn and Greg Sabouri, founders of Teaching Textbooks. She has found their materials the best to use for her summer tutoring sessions. These Harvard graduates have created engaging, technologically savvy math courses designed for independent learning. Featuring *lots* of practice and review problems, their programs include a CD-ROM with up to 160 hours of teacher instruction accompanying the text. The real power of the program is the integration of mathematics with real-life application and a well-designed

153

presentation of finance, economics, and mathematical history woven into the lessons. Currently, they have published textbooks for Grade 4 through Pre-Calculus.

 **Recommended Resource**

The National Council of Teachers of Mathematics website (http://standards.nctm.org) offers many helpful resources, including online lesson plans and interactive models for many mathematical concepts. You will also find national standards adopted for each school stage, including grades 6–8. Use this list to evaluate any math program you are considering.

Parting Comments

Before we move on to other subject areas, let me close with this: Language arts and mathematics are where you should devote your energies during the middle school years. These are the skill areas that, once mastered, will set your child up for success in every other endeavor lies ahead. We all have good days and bad days in homeschooling, and we all have uneven spots in our programs. But as you prioritize your time, allocate plenty of time each day to the 3 R's. What curricula you settle on in both these subject areas is an important decision, *but* not as important as just being consistent in practicing these skills. No matter which program you choose to go with, your teen will benefit by completing work in these two areas daily.

SCIENCE

The standard course sequence in science includes teaching life science in sixth grade, general science in seventh, and physical science in eighth. Be aware that many institutions no longer give high school credit for physical science. Where your child is in math should drive the science choices you make. Algebra 1 is typically taught concurrently with biology, but the student who completes algebra 1 at the same time as physical science and prior to biology has a definite advantage.

My good friend Vicki Dincher has taught high school science at our co-op for more than ten years, and she believes that middle school science programs need to be hands-on and experiential. Vicki's concern is that a textbook-only approach to science is very boring for kids at this age, causing them to lose interest and motivation. This is unfortunate for several reasons. First of all, the wonders of God's creation are fascinating, so any study of these wonders should also be fascinating. Second, our nation and our faith need more kids prepared to enter science-related fields. Third, if your children are bored and unmotivated in junior high, high school science is going to be unbearable.

> **The wonders of God's creation are fascinating, so any study of these wonders should also be fascinating.**

Vicki suggests that parents get kids outside exploring nature, collecting specimens, and classifying the flora and fauna. She also advocates emphasizing the scientific method. Our family and co-op are bullish on Apologia Science, which is specifically developed for homeschooling and promotes a creationist worldview. The experiments are interesting and easy to follow. Integrate science videos, field trips, collections, and visits to museums, and you're all set.

155

Apologia's general science course focuses specifically on teaching the scientific method. You may be familiar with this as a multi-step process used to produce the typical science fair project:

1. Ask a question about something you observe.
2. Formulate a hypothesis about why this happens.
3. Design an experiment to test the hypothesis.
4. Analyze results.
5. Draw conclusions based on the data gathered.

> A thorough understanding of scientific method should inform your child's science studies, and this should be one of the criteria you use for evaluating new ideas and opinions.

In reality the scientific method is much more complex than just a few basic steps. It is, in fact, a systematic approach to the study of the natural world. A thorough understanding of scientific method should inform your child's science studies, and this should be one of the criteria you use for evaluating new ideas and opinions.

The American Association for the Advancement of Science is an influential organization in the development of science standards and curriculum. The organization's website includes an insightful article by Stephen Budiansky entitled "The Trouble with Textbooks." In it, Budiansky writes:

One of the key findings of Michigan State University researchers who developed an experimental middle-school science curriculum was the importance of leading students through a logical chain of evidence, of showing them a variety of phenomena that can be explained by the same basic principle, and of providing students with a chance to put to use the ideas they have learned. This is crucial in breaking down students' preexisting misconceptions—which are often deeply held and based on intuitive but naive beliefs about the world. It is also essential to making the insights stick. And it is also how science actually works: Science is not just facts to be memorized or terms to learn, but a process for building up a picture and explanation of the world from evidence.

Most children, for example, find it hard to accept the notion that air is matter; common sense says it is not, for it cannot be felt. Most children also believe that solids weigh more than liquids; again, in everyday experience they usually do. In the test curriculum that the Michigan State researchers developed on matters and molecules, the unit begins with a series of experiments and demonstrations to convince students that one substance—water—can be a solid, liquid, or gas and that gases, even though they are often invisible, have weight and really are matter. In one experiment, students weigh an ice cube in a Ziploc bag, then let it melt and weigh it again. In another the teacher boils water in a flask, the top of which is connected to a glass tube that leads to another flask; the students can see the water disappear from the first flask and reappear in the second, even though no visible substance is passing through the tube. These hands-on exercises are simple, but vivid and to the point.

157

Science is a great area to emphasize the critical thinking skills discussed in chapter eight. We also found science to be a good subject to build a co-op around. When Mike and Gabe were in sixth grade, we worked for a year with another family for the explicit purpose of strengthening our science program.

We found that meeting one day a week for three hours was more effective than trying to do science daily. For curriculum, we used Janice VanCleave's science titles, including *Janice VanCleave's A+ Science Fair Projects* and *Janice VanCleave's Biology for Every Kid.* You need to choose titles appropriate for middle school, but VanCleave explains scientific concepts clearly and with numerous illustrations. And all her science experiments are designed to be completed with household items, making her activity books easy to use for the non-scientific mom. My friend Cindy and I took turns preparing and leading the lessons, which meant twice-a-month duties for each of us. I found this approach to be much more manageable for me than trying to oversee daily science lessons at home.

We extended VanCleave's experiments by having our middle-school-aged kids compile follow-up reports on the topics she suggested for deeper study. They then reported back to the group for the benefit of all, including their younger siblings who only did the experiments. This year of dedication to strengthening our science background served us well in preparation for the rigors of a later, more formalized study of science.

The other source we found helpful for science classes at this level was TOPS Learning Systems (www.topscience.org). The TOPS founder, a former Peace Corps volunteer, is committed to making do with limited resources—a perfect match for homeschool families teaching on a shoestring budget. Some of our co-op's more enterprising moms spent a summer collecting and collating TOPS science labs for the group, which then made using the TOPS materials a breeze to use.

Science Fairs and Competitions

Science fairs and science competitions can provide motivation for most kids. If your child is interested in pursuing science studies in college, science competitions in middle school can help him to build toward excellence in high school and provide him something substantial to put on his résumé.

Recommended Science Competitions

National Science Bowl. The U.S. Department of Energy sponsors this annual competition for both high school and middle school students. Learn more at www.scied.science.doe.gov/nsb.

Science Buddies (www.sciencebuddies.org) provides a list of science competitions and tips and advice for students aspiring to compete at the highest levels.

Greater Philadelphia Homeschool Science Fair. This home-school organization has developed an impressive science fair competition worth emulating. Visit www.fair.science-resources.org.

HISTORY

Our family found history to be one of the easiest subject areas to complete at home, as well as one of the most flexible. It's your choice as to which specific areas (i.e., local, state, national, or world history) you focus on in middle school, but again, you should be anticipating what kind of work you want your child to be doing in high school and beyond. For example, determine which Advanced Placement courses are potentially of interest up ahead and design a middle school history or government course that is equivalent to what would be covered in a high-school-level course on that subject.

I learned this the hard way with my sons. They took several AP courses in high school without a solid foundation in place, and they struggled with making the leap from essentially a junior high level to a college level. We did much better anticipating Kayte's college-level work in high school. During middle

159

school, Kayte completed a thorough course in world history using the *Western Tradition* video series available through Learner.org (now available *free* through their site) and Beautiful Feet's History Through Literature courses (www.bfbooks.com). This prepared her well for AP courses in U.S. history in tenth grade and European history in eleventh. The University of Pittsburgh eventually awarded her six college credits for each of these courses.

We also extensively used the History of Us series by Joy Hakim. This ten-volume set covers U.S. history in a compelling style and is targeted toward fifth through eighth grades. My goal was for each of my kids to complete these books by the end of eighth grade. Sometimes we used these as a core resource—several volumes are integrated into the Beautiful Feet curriculum—and sometimes as supplemental reading. Study guides are now available for the series, one set for elementary students and one for upper-level grades. Christian families will not agree with Hakim's interpretation of American history at every juncture, but you will not find a better-written text on the market. I liked this resource most because I never had to tell my kids to do their history reading—they read these texts for fun.

If you are drawn to the classical Christian movement's emphasis on history and literature, then the middle school grades may be the most advantageous time to complete materials developed by Tapestry of Grace, Peace Hill Press (*The Well-Trained Mind*), or Veritas Press.

As mentioned earlier, skills are more important than knowledge in my book, and

160

> Skills are more important than knowledge in my book, and what your teen needs in the area of history and social sciences are research skills.

what your teen needs in the area of history and social sciences are research skills. These are best accomplished through short-term assignments (two to six weeks) that require research, reading, analysis, and synthesizing information and data. These can either culminate in a research paper or project. For the students I've taught at our co-op, I've required that at least three sources be used in every research assignment. Relying heavily on a single source will not require students to compare and contrast the information they've gathered.

An exciting way for students to develop strong research skills is through the National History Day competition for grades 6–12. Students work in teams or as individuals on year-long projects that are then presented at the state level and may qualify for the national competition. Check it out at www.nhd.org.

FOREIGN LANGUAGES

Foreign language study was a subject area I always felt stumped by as a parent. I believed it to be important but kept striking out with every approach I tried. Only Kayte learned to speak a second language—French—before leaving home, though our sons were able to use what little we accomplished in this area as a springboard for language studies in college. Here are a few things I learned about teaching foreign languages.

First, the earlier you start, the better. I'll spare you the details of lengthy neurological studies, but they clearly show that young children can acquire a second language with greater ease than teens. So it makes no sense at all that our schools in the U.S. do not start foreign language studies until high school. Kayte's strength in French is actually her accent. She could pass for a native speaker if it weren't for syntax errors. The fact that she began studying and speaking French prior to the end of puberty is likely the reason for this. She started speaking Arabic in college but laments that there are sounds she will never be able to pronounce accurately in Arabic because she's beyond the developmental stage that allows for this. An interesting vignette: Henry Kissinger emigrated from Germany to the U.S. at age 15. Despite decades of speaking flawless English, he has never lost his Bavarian accent. His younger brother, Walter, who was 14 at the time of the move, speaks unaccented English. This difference is due to the fact that the younger Walter was quicker to adapt to the new culture, in part because of Henry's childhood shyness, which made him hesitant to speak.

> We need to make an effort to learn the native language of other peoples instead of expecting them to first learn ours in order to hear the truths of God's Word.

If your kids dream of an adventurous life or are committed to seeing the gospel shared with every tribe and every nation, your kids need to become adept at learning other languages. After all, it demonstrates our love for other people groups if we make an effort to learn their native language instead of expecting them to first learn ours in order to hear the truths of God's Word.

Just as with mastering musical instruments, the first foreign language they learn will be the most difficult. It gets easier from there on. My sons found, after learning the basics in French and Spanish, they quickly became conversant wherever they went, including Bangladesh and Thailand.

The first thing you need to determine is whether your students' goal is to become conversant so they can travel or speak with internationals, or if their goal is simply to fulfill academic requirements. The approach is different for each. College requirements are commonly fulfilled through proficiency testing in reading, writing, listening and speaking. This requires the same teaching approach we take with English classes during the elementary grades—a lot of language arts work. If the goal is to become conversant, then you can forego much of the literacy work.

Learner.org is the website for Annenberg Media, a leader in educational video courses. Many of their courses are now available free online. Among these are *French in Action*, *Destinos: An Introduction to Spanish*, and *Fokus Deutsch* (German). Completing any of these programs is equivalent to four years of high school language studies, or two levels of college coursework (now a requirement for many humanities-centered majors). I like the Spanish course best because it is a good blend of Spanish with English explanations, whereas the French course is completely in French. You will need to buy all the ancillary products—textbook, workbook, and audios—to make a complete course. We found all these products used at Amazon.com.

Rosetta Stone (www.rosettastone.com) has been gaining popularity in the homeschool market. I think it's a great product and is *almost* sufficient for your foreign language needs. The program is very effective for learning to speak another language, but it is not sufficient for the written requirements expected by most schools. Your child is unlikely to test out of levels 1 and 2 in college just by using Rosetta Stone. Most placement tests measure written work and grammar, and that isn't Rosetta's Stone's purpose. It's a product designed to get you ready to visit a country and converse with the locals. While you can *hear* native speakers pronounce the words, you cannot see them, which is a definite aid for most types of learners. My recommendation is to include Rosetta Stone in your repertoire of resources but choose a program such as those at Learner.org for your core curriculum.

Our sons definitely found it challenging to learn a language during high school. They used classes at the co-op to meet their high school requirements, but it wasn't until they studied abroad that they really accomplished something in this area. For them, learning a language through immersion is the only way to go.

TALENT IDENTIFICATION PROGRAMS

One last item you may want to consider before completing the middle school years with your teen is some of the nationally known talent searches. The better ones are run by top-flight universities and seek to identify and challenged academically gifted students with out-of-level coursework. Seventh- and eighth-grade students qualify for recognition and classes by taking the SAT or ACT college admissions exams. Each university sets its own qualifying scores for ongoing programs.

If your child routinely scores at the ninety-fifth percentile or above on standardized tests, you may wish to consider the benefits of out-of-level testing and participating in a talent identification program. However, be aware that the cost of the ongoing programs may be cost-prohibitive for most families, unless you qualify for financial aid.

Recommended Resources
Duke Tip (www.tip.duke.edu)
Johns Hopkins Center for Talented Youth
   (www.cty.jhu.edu)
Stanford Education Program for Gifted Youth
(epgy.stanford.edu)
University of Denver Rocky Mountain Academic Talent
   Search (www.du.edu/city)
Northwestern Center for Talent Development
   (www.ctd.northwestern.edu)

PART 5

THE HIGH SCHOOL YEARS

12 THE FOUR-YEAR PLAN

Before we delve into specific subject areas in high school, I want to provide you with a simple tool that will preserve your sanity as you set sail for the great unknown. Think of this as your set of navigation instruments. Columbus would never have made it across the ocean and back without them, just as I can't find my way home without a GPS. Think of your Four-Year Plan (FYP) as your GPS for the future. (Wise parents also bring their teenagers into this process so they can then make their own FYP when they get to college. Otherwise, their FYP may become an SYP—a six- or seven-year plan.)

In my day, the FYP was designed with a pencil, paper, and a huge eraser because every FYP goes through many revisions. In your case, you just need to open a Word document and create a template like the one seen here:

	9th	10th	11th	12th
Math				
English				
Social Studies				
Science				
Language				
Electives/ Other				
Tests				
Summer				

169

You can find a full FYP template with drag-and-drop subject tiles at www.debrabell.com. The subject tiles I've created include many numerous high school course options as well as a list of potential tests to be taken. By shuffling these tiles around the template, you can complete a sound, achievable plan without overwhelming yourself, your student, or the schedule at any point. This will help you to avoid a logjam come senior year, which is going to be stressful enough with college decisions and applications—it's not the time to try and double up on credits still needed for graduation.

Here's a sample four-year plan (plus one) I've created for an ambitious college-bound student:

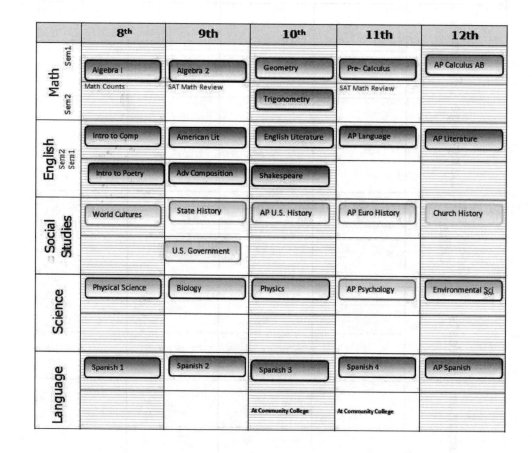

		8th	9th	10th	11th	12th
Math	Sem1	Algebra I	Algebra 2	Geometry	Pre- Calculus	AP Calculus AB
	Sem2	Math Counts	SAT Math Review	Trigonometry	SAT Math Review	
English	Sem1	Intro to Comp	American Lit	English Literature	AP Language	AP Literature
	Sem2	Intro to Poetry	Adv Composition	Shakespeare		
Social Studies		World Cultures	State History	AP U.S. History	AP Euro History	Church History
			U.S. Government			
Science		Physical Science	Biology	Physics	AP Psychology	Environmental Sci
Language		Spanish 1	Spanish 2	Spanish 3	Spanish 4	AP Spanish
				At Community College	At Community College	

	8th	9th	10th	11th	12th
Electives/Other	Music	Music	Music Theory	Music/Recital	Music
			Internship	College Visits	College Apps
Tests			AP	PSAT	SAT I
				SAT I	
			AP History	AP Psych, AP Euro, AP Language	AP Spanish, AP Lit, AP Calculus
Summer			Missions Trip	Missions Trip	

Before you start building your FYP, begin by profiling your teen—I mean the one you really have, not the ideal teen who understands the stakes and can be expected to cooperate fully with the plan. Here are a few questions for you to answer and keep in mind as you begin laying out a potential scheme for your teen's high school work:

* What his preferred learning style?

* In what areas does he show the greatest effort and interest?

* In what areas are his strengths?

* In what areas does he need your greatest involvement?

* In what subject areas does he already have a good foundation?

* In what subject areas does he still need to do fundamental work?

Keep this profile in mind as you begin formulating a four-year plan. In those areas where your teen has already shown herself to be a self-starter with a high degree of interest, you do not need to invest your greatest personal energy. For example,

171

if your daughter loves math, then a lot of different math programs will do—choose the most convenient program and the easiest setting to facilitate this. Where there is a lack of drive, however, spend more time thinking about the kind of resources your teen will find most motivating and how you can best support her learning.

Working backwards from your child's educational goals, begin building your FYP by starting with the coursework required for high school graduation or admissions to a target college. You will need to check with your state homeschool organization to learn what requirements exist for homeschool graduation in your state. The following are typical course requirements expected by most colleges:

* 4 credits in language arts (literature, composition, grammar, vocabulary)
* 3 credits in social studies (geography, U.S. and world history, government)
* 3 credits in mathematics (from algebra, geometry, algebra 2, trigonometry, pre-calculus, calculus)
* 3 credits in science (from physical science, earth science, biology, chemistry, physics)
* 2 credits in a *living* foreign language (not Latin or sign language)
* 2 to 6 credits of electives

If you are shooting for an elite school or merit scholarship consideration, then here is the kind of coursework that represents a rigorous schedule:

* 4 credits in language arts (including AP English)
* 4 credits in social studies
* 4 credits in mathematics

* 4 credits in science (biology, chemistry, physics, and advanced topic—all with labs)
* 4 credits in a living foreign language
* 4 to 6 credits of electives

Tips for Writing Your Four-Year Plan

There are several things to keep in mind as you start thinking through the FYP and considering potential high school courses.

Get your teens involved. Your teens need to be involved in making coursework decisions, especially during the later years of high school. If they don't take ownership of their school and activities, you're likely to experience a lot of unnecessary tension in the

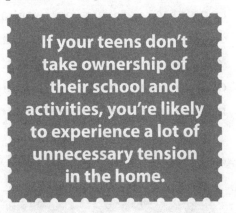

If your teens don't take ownership of their school and activities, you're likely to experience a lot of unnecessary tension in the home.

home. It's fine for a teen not to take every course that might be advantageous. It's fine for him to take a "gap" year prior to going to college. It's fine to use the community college system as a bridge to university. It's not fine to "drag" your teen through this process. Preserve your relationship with your children and get them involved. And be willing to extend the timetable if one of your teens is just not emotionally or intellectually ready to run this race—it's okay to walk the course. Invest your energy into keeping everything on track, but let your teen set the pace.

Use the FYP as a tool, not a bible. Having a plan will help you and your teens remain strategic and intentional and, in the end, accomplish more. But it is likely that some of the goals you choose to include in your plan will never be completed. Life happens, and as homeschooling parents, we tend to be more ambitious in our planning than our execution.

173

Your FYP will have strengths and weaknesses. In the end, the four-year plan will become a transcript and, like most transcripts, will have both strengths and weaknesses. In order for your teens to develop mastery in the skills and knowledge necessary for your chosen college or for entrance into today's specialized job market, you may need to settle for a minimalist approach in some other areas. In theory, we want our kids to have a well-rounded education, but not at the expense of being competent yet unexceptional across the board.

The most important years are the tenth and eleventh grades. You may be relieved to know that many universities largely disregard a student's ninth grade work, placing an emphasis instead on achievement in grades 10–12, especially if the student's ninth grade grades are spotty. So if you need the freshman year to reinforce remedial skills in areas such as math and reading, don't be afraid to do so. Tenth and eleventh grades are where the meat and potatoes of coursework belong. If your student plans to attend college, the best demonstrations of her academic potential— SAT scores, AP test results, internships, academic camps, travel etc.—must be completed before twelfth grade in order to impact her college applications.

> Tenth and eleventh grades are where the meat and potatoes of coursework belong.

For twelfth grade, you may need to factor in time for college visits, so leave yourself and your child some breathing room on the schedule. Save a few courses you know will be less demanding for the end. However, your student will still need to show a reasonable amount of rigor in senior year, even if the credits required for graduation have already been completed. Colleges see sloughing off as a sign of underachievement. However, there are acceptable ways for showing rigor while still accomplishing other important goals, such as earning money. Hold tight and we'll get to the nuts and bolts of getting it all done.

Know what colleges are looking for. E-mail the admission offices of target colleges and ask what type of high school coursework they prefer for admissions and scholarship consideration, especially from a homeschooler. If your teen already has a college major in mind, mention this, because some departments will have definite preferences. For example, an incoming engineering major will need to have completed specific science and math coursework. Even if your teen does not apply to these schools in the end, the advice you receive will be helpful when applying to schools of similar size and focus.

Extracurricular activities are important components, not just "extras." Academic coursework is not all that matters. In fact, the experiences your teen accumulates outside the "classroom" may better prepare her for the future. These additional activities will also differentiate her from others on her college and job applications, so you need to be strategic in working these into the schedule. These activities may include:

> The experiences your teen accumulates outside the "classroom" may better prepare her for the future.

Sports
Financial training
First-aid training
Mission trips
Worldview camp
Driver's education
Community service
Study abroad
Child-care training

175

Travel
Music, drama, or art
Entrepreneurial endeavors
Internships
Leadership development
Cooking and life skills
Apprenticeship
Political action
Competitions
Debate
Computer skills

The list is endless, and yours may differ from mine. That's a good thing. Our teens will enter a marketplace in which highly specialized skills are sought after by admissions offices and future employers. However, it's probably in your teen's best interest to think in terms of focus or areas of spe-

> **Forget about compiling a scattershot résumé. Clusters of interest should emerge when an outsider reviews your child's high school transcript.**

cialization. Forget about compiling a scattershot résumé. Clusters of interest should emerge when an outsider reviews your child's high school transcript.

Our sons' transcripts showed appropriate rigor for incoming business majors. Their outside activities—which included working for a variety of businesses, some entrepreneurial endeavors, and a competitive streak reflected in their athletic accomplishments—convinced a scholarship committee that they were a good investment. Schools are looking to give money to kids who will not drop out, and departments are looking to subsidize kids who will not change their major.

13 HIGH SCHOOL ENGLISH

As in the middle school years, English and math are the primary skills to focus in on in high school. Your kids will have the rest of their lives to master content in areas of interest, but in order to get off to a good start in college or in the workplace, they need to be able to write, read, and compute at a competent level. Setting themselves apart from their peers in these areas can lead to scholarship offers and position them to do well grade-wise once at school.

Because of what's at stake here, English is a great subject to farm out to an online class, co-op, or tutor at some point. If you are not confident of your own abilities in this area, then look around for someone who is qualified to work with your teen. Also, you want to make sure you have an accurate assessment of your teen's strengths and weaknesses in this area, and outside evaluator can help you with this.

English as a content area presents great flexibility. You and your student can choose from a wide array of subject matter, so let the interests and the needs of your teen drive your decisions. In other subject areas, the curriculum will be more prescribed. It's even okay to do double duty here—the writing projects for other subject areas can provide partial credit for English or literature. For example, a research paper for a science class can double as an assignment for a composition course. Reading *Uncle Tom's Cabin*, *Up from Slavery*, or *Invisible Man* can also be considered coursework in U.S. history and American literature. See the appendix for a list of books of literary merit that can also be used for credit in other subject areas as well.

The Critical Skills to Master

Ability to read on a college level

Ability to write analytically using college-level vocabulary and grammatical standards of the English language

Understanding the interconnectedness of the arts, history, and culture

Recognition of the basic artistic components of literature and poetry—i.e., symbolism, plot, characterization, point of view, figurative language, theme, tone, etc.

READING COMPREHENSION

Reading comprehension is an absolute must, as most subject matter during high school will require extensive reading. My family did a lot of hands-on activities and took a lot of field trips up until ninth grade, and that was critical to developing the background knowledge and conceptual understanding as a springboard for high-school-level work. But once we turned the corner into ninth grade, there was a lot of ground that needed to be covered by staying home and reading heavily within each discipline.

As a rule of thumb, I like to see a verbal score of 600 or above on the SAT or 26 on the ACT as one indication of college-level comprehension. Here's what you might consider doing in order to improve your teen's reading comprehension skills.

Build Background Knowledge

Learners are always building upon what they already know, as new material is integrated with prior experiences and understanding. Previously acquired information in a subject area helps students comprehend more of what they are reading. My daughter Kristen struggled with reading early on. Fortunately, I recognized this as an isolated problem that did not mean she wasn't ready to think more deeply or grapple with difficult material—it just needed to be presented through different media. I made sure she kept acquiring through other means—field trips, audios, videos, and software—the background knowledge her peers were gaining from reading. Then when her reading finally took off, she had a similar knowledge base to that of her peers.

Learners are always building upon what they already know, as new material is integrated with prior experiences and understanding.

While we are still a print-dependent world, new technology is definitely making it possible for non-readers to acquire knowledge once only found in books. Here are suggestions for helping teens to build their background knowledge in preparation for higher-level reading:

* Preview subject matter with juvenile titles such as Eyewitness books and DK Visual Dictionaries.

* Build up background knowledge with educational videos such as those available from the Discovery Channel and PBS. Discovery Education Streaming is a subscription service that gives you online access to their incredible library of high-quality media. You can find your best deal for this option at www.homeschoolbuyersco-op.org.

179

* Teaching Company audio courses (www.teach12.com) are an alternative for covering certain subject matter.

* YouTube is a good source of short videos that illustrate difficult concepts and capture content vividly. However, I don't advise allowing your teen to log in to this site without monitoring or filters. One solution may be TeacherTube.com, where you will find great content efficiently organized for use in the classroom. Also, you can find official content from partner colleges and universities at www/youtube.com/edu.

Develop Subject-Specific Vocabulary

Vocabulary is the key to reading comprehension, and *Vocabulary for Achievement* by Margaret Ann Richek remains my favorite vocabulary program for several reasons:

* Words are pulled from authentic texts.

* Words on the weekly lists have a logical connection to one another—e.g., words derived from Spanish or words describing boldness.

* The history of language is discussed throughout, so students understand the source of language development.

* Reading comprehension is the goal, and exercises are designed around this skill, not memorization of word meaning.

* One year of the program is dedicated to reading comprehension only.

If your teen is not reading at grade level as he enters high school, consider making your ninth-grade English course a reading comprehension course. Kristen experienced a breakthrough in reading once she started taking classes at our home school co-op in junior high. At home, I had been inclined to select resources in keeping with her reading level, but no such accommodation was made at the co-op. Because Kristen wanted to do well, she devoted hours that first year reading and re-reading material. It may be that I had been holding her back by not challenging her.

Consider ways to motivate a reluctant reader—rewards of value come to mind—and then use the reading required in other subjects—science, history, art, etc.—to fulfill your student's English requirement for the year.

> **Kids need to build upon background knowledge, recognize vocabulary in context, draw inferences from what is stated and implied, make connections between cause and effect, and sum up the parts into big ideas and themes.**

Direct teaching of reading comprehension skills will help. Kids need to build upon background knowledge, recognize vocabulary in context, draw inferences from what is stated and implied, make connections between cause and effect, and sum up the parts into big ideas and themes. You can facilitate the development of these skills by discussing challenging texts with your teen and by demonstrating for him the kind of thinking you do while reading—asking questions, figuring out challenging words, predicting what will come next, and summarizing in your mind what you have just read. This kind of cognitive engagement comes naturally to some learners, but needs to be taught to those who are struggling.

There is a massive amount of information on the Internet about adolescent literacy. You can find a number of free, diagnostic tools at the Merit Software site. Their software is also relatively inexpensive and considered pedagogically sound as a

181

tool for building vocabulary, reading comprehension, and writing skills. Check it out at www.readingcomprehensionconnection.com.

Eliminate Deterrents to Reading

How much time daily does your child spend reading? What is she doing otherwise? Physical activity increases thinking ability, while time in front of the television or video games does not. Gaming and TV viewing not only takes time away from activities that support reading, but these have also been shown to stunt cognitive development. A growing body of research reveals a direct link between time spent gaming and poor school performance, violent behavior, and obesity. In some cases, video gaming can become a full-blown addiction. Consider eliminating gaming from your home. I know it's tough, and the move may be met with a lot of moaning and groaning, but stick to your guns and don't back down. Your teen will eventually find other things to do.

For more research-based information on the effects of video games and television on adolescents, visit the National Institute on Media and the Family at www.mediawise.org.

LITERATURE

There is far too much noteworthy historical and cultural literature to attempt read it all in four years, so you have a range of options here. Your goal is to cultivate in your teen an appreciation for the artistic pleasures of prose and poetry and help them to develop a lifelong love for reading.

First of all, students need to leave high school with some sense of the "grand conversation," as it is sometimes called, the continuous discussion writers and thinkers have with one another across the span of time as they respond to the thoughts and ideas of prior generations. Given that the "dead white

> **Your goal is to cultivate in your teen an appreciation for the artistic pleasures of prose and poetry and help them to develop a lifelong love for reading.**

guys" have become less revered and emphasized in our public high schools, your student will be at an advantage in college if she can draw correlations between the ancient texts of Homer and Plato and the literary voices of the past few hundred years. This is where I find the greatest benefit in a classical Christian approach to content, such as you will find in material developed by Veritas Press, Peace Hill Press, and especially Tapestry of Grace. These curriculum suppliers make the connections vividly for us as they trace the streams of Western Civilization and the continuing rise and fall of culture.

If you find classical Christian materials attractive, then consider shaping your coursework around this content. You can include it on the transcript as Humanities 9, 10, 11, or 12 and award credits for literature, history, art, and music, if applicable, while including an annotated list of the reading material used. Or you can break your program down into individual course titles for greater clarity—e.g., Ancient Literature for English or Ancient History for social studies.

Here is the essential literature for college-bound teens to cover. We're talking exposure, not mastery—you are not going to be able to do all these writers justice in high school. Rather, design your program so your teen develops an appetite for quality literature.

Ancient Literature—Homer, Sophocles, Plato, Virgil
English Literature—the Bible, Geoffrey Chaucer, John Milton, William Shakespeare, Charles Dickens, Jane Austen, Alexander Pope, and Jonathan Swift. Anyone buried at

183

Westminster Abbey is a good bet here.

American Literature—from the Puritans to modern day. If you cannot cover all that ground, then focus on the nineteenth-century Romantics and their detractors: Thoreau, Emerson, Whitman, Poe, Hawthorne, Melville, Emily Dickinson, and Mark Twain. From the twentieth century, focus on Hemingway, F. Scott Fitzgerald, E. E. Cummings, Faulkner, Steinbeck, and Robert Frost.

World Literature—Dante, Dostoevsky, Hugo, Tolstoy

Modern Literature—post-colonial and ethnic writers are currently ascending in importance, making the grand conversation all the more interesting. A few I can recommend: Chinua Achebe, Maxine Hong Kingston, Sandra Cisneros, Chaim Potok, Amy Tan, Gabriel García Márquez, and Jhumpa Lahiri. These folks are being taught more and more in college-level literature courses.

Possible Courses Titles

English is a subject area with a lot of latitude. Take advantage of that. Colleges appreciate course titles on transcripts that make sense to them. Here are some suggestions:

English 9, 10, 11, 12—This is perfectly acceptable but not very descriptive. This kind of course heading gives you plenty of flexibility to pick and choose whatever literature you wish to cover. You need to also incorporate language arts and writing into each course. If you choose to go this route, attach an annotation to the student transcript that includes the texts used.

World Literature—This heading presumes you are excluding British and American authors and focusing on selected works of significance from several different cultures and historical eras.

English Literature—This excludes American literature but can include post-colonial literature published in English from former British colonies, such as India and Africa.

American Literature—This includes colonial writings through modern day.

Modern Literature—This heading includes twentieth- and twenty-first-century works from around the world.

The Novel—This heading implies you will cover the evolution of the novel as a major literary genre and then study the most important novels from several historical eras.

Drama—This heading assumes you will cover the evolution of drama from the Greek tragedies to modern day, selecting representative pieces from each era. Ideally, the student will attend several dramatic performances during the course. If your teen is involved in a dramatic production, you may count the hours devoted to that activity as partial fulfillment of an English credit.

Poetry—This is a study of the oldest literary form in the world. Anthropologists have yet to find a culture that does not have a poetic tradition, so you can approach this subject from several different angles since it will be impossible to do a survey course with any integrity. The most common approach is to focus on poetry of the Western tradition. Or you can organize material around a specific time period and do a comparative approach across cultures. However, only a few students will be able to sustain a yearlong interest in poetry exclusively, so it might be best to integrate poetry into a broader literature course.

Nobel Prize Authors—This might be an interesting way to cover world or modern literature.

Christian Literature—See the appendix for list of suggested works in this area.

185

College-Level Courses

For the advanced student, AP English Literature and Composition is a survey of important imaginative literature—i.e., poetry, the novel, short stories, and drama. Students learn to recognize how literary devices—figurative language, characterization, setting, choice of detail, diction, etc.—are used by authors to create meaning through theme and tone. The course commonly replaces an introductory literature requirement at most colleges and can often be used as an exemption from introductory composition because of the amount of writing required. A course description can be downloaded at the AP Central section of the College Board website.

AP English Language and Composition is a course focused on the rhetorical strategies used by writers to express a point of view (sometimes called *argument*). The works studied in this course are predominantly non-fiction, though fiction may be used if it focuses on the author's rhetoric. The primary purpose of the class is to teach students how to effectively respond in writing to the arguments posed by others in print and to logically construct one's own argument. A major component is learning how

> A major component is learning how to properly synthesize and attribute quotes from other writers into one's own research.

to properly synthesize and attribute quotes from other writers into one's own research. MLA (Modern Language Association) formatting should be emphasized. (See www.mla.org/style.) This course typically replaces a freshman composition requirement and is intended to teach students how to write across the curriculum. A research paper should be a major assignment. A course description can be downloaded at the AP Central section of the College Board website.

If you take a college-level English course at a community college or online for the purpose of knocking off some college credits in advance, make sure it fulfills a requirement toward the intended degree and not just an elective. You will find a lot of unique classes offered by the English department at most colleges, but typically these do not count as fulfillment of a general education, or "gen-ed," credit most freshman and sophomores must complete. You will find more about the ins and outs of earning college credits in high school in a later chapter.

Suggested Approach

In thinking through what literary material you want to cover in high school, consider organizing the texts your student reads according to their historical time period. Keep in mind that more difficult texts such as Homer, Virgil, and Shakespeare will require greater reading comprehension skills than those by Hemingway, Fitzgerald, and Frost.

If your teen is not ready for this approach because of maturity level or reading skills—and many will not be—then make a concerted effort to set the literature they do read into its historical and cultural context. Have your teens keep an ongoing timeline or notebook of the authors and works they study so that, by the end of high school, they have a good feel for how these works relate to one another. Mortimer Adler's *How to Read a Book* is a good source for figuring this out.

187

Recommended Books

Invitation to the Classics by Louise Cowan and Os Guinness is the best survey from a Christian perspective I can recommend. This is a very readable reference book that most teens should be able to use independently.

How to Read a Book: The Classic Guide to Intelligent Read-

ing by Mortimer J. Adler and Charles Van Doren. Adler single-handedly created the notion of the grand conversation with his formulation of the first Great Books program and subsequent Great Ideas program. You can find out more at www.thegreatideas.org or pick up this book, which will give you a list of Adler's picks as well as a layman's guide to reading analytically and syntopically (comparing works and thinkers to each others).

How to Read Literature Like a Professor: A Lively and Entertaining Guide to Reading Between the Lines by Thomas Foster. This easy read will give you a quick and engaging overview of how authors transform a storyline into a work of literary merit. What is the significance of rain? Why do allusions to mythology and the Old Testament matter? How does the choice of setting give us a clue to theme? The only caution about this text is the graphic discussion of sexual themes in chapters 16 and 17.

Perrine's Literature: Structure, Sound and Sense. Any edition of this standard college anthology is an invaluable source of appropriate literature for a college-bound high school student. The introductory material explaining how to analyze and write about literature is the strength of this volume.

Perrine's Sound and Sense: An Introduction to Poetry. This thin volume includes just the poetry section from the above anthology and is the best resource for studying this particular art form.

Recommended Websites

Annenberg Media's exceptional video courses have now been made available free of charge online at www.learner.org. Of particular interest to high school students will be *Voices and Vision*, an introduction to thirteen American poets; *American Passages: A Literary Survey; Literary Visions; In Search of the Novel*; and *Conversations in Literature*.

Outline of American Literature is a historical overview of significant writers from the U.S. Government's Office of Information. Visit www.america.gov/publications/books/outline-of-american-literature.html.

Project Gutenberg (www.gutenberg.org) is one of the oldest and largest sites for e-books. Most works from the literary canon in the public domain are now available. To my own surprise, I've found reading books online to be much more convenient than I had imagined, and it is now a frequent habit of mine.

Web English Teacher (www.webenglishteacher.com) is a well-organized site where you will find endless resources applicable to a homeschool setting.

World Literature Online is Bedford/St. Martin's site to accompany their college-level anthology. However, the free content available here is phenomenal! Among other things, you will find an interactive timeline, a guide to reading in the literary canon, and a link through to The Bedford Research Room, where there are many writing aids. Visit http://bcs.bedfordstmartins.com/worldlit.

189

Recommended Online Study Guides

E-notes (www.enotes.com) is a subscription site with high-quality study guides to more than 4,000 literary works. This is the best source of reliable, scholarly content to support the study of literature.

Free Book Notes Online (www.freebooknotes.com) is a collection of online sources of free study guides and notes for literary works. Just remember, "free" may mean the information is not reliable or authoritative.

Other Recommended Resources

I'm really fussy in this area, so there isn't a course of study I'm particularly enthusiastic about recommending. I've tended to use a mix of resources and pick and choose from each what I like best. Here's the best stuff I've found for homeschool use:

Bob Jones University Press (www.bjupress.com) publishes literature anthologies for tenth (*The Elements of Literature*), eleventh (*American Literature*), and twelfth (*British Literature*) grades. I find these anthologies acceptable, especially the American and British literature texts, as these are survey courses that expose students to the sweep of literary history. The teacher's guides are particularly well done. I have used the *American Literature* text for many years in my co-op course, though BJU has a tendency to squash enthusiasm one might have for a particular work by a gifted author by pointing out the author's decadent lifestyle or less-than-biblical worldview. I'm much more interested in directing students to the aesthetic pleasures of great literature and encouraging their own participation in the arts with a goal toward establishing a standard of excellence. Used BJU materials are widely available.

For Such a Time as This (www.forsuchatimeasthis.com). Dr. James Stobaugh has produced several literature courses for college-bound students, with an emphasis on development of a Christian worldview, and his materials may be the easiest to use for completing an English literature course at home. You will, however, need to purchase or borrow the texts covered in these courses, and the reading load for each course is substantial. However, reading the full work is, in the end, much better than only reading an excerpt.

Canon Press, a publisher of classical Christian materials, is the best source of study aids extolling the study and creation of literature and the arts as a distinctly Christian endeavor. Anything by Peter Leithart, especially *Brightest Heaven of Invention: A Christian Guide to Six Shakespeare Plays*, is invaluable. I also love *The Roar on the Other Side: A Guide for Student Poets* by Suzanne Rhodes. Materials from Canon Press should be included in any homeschool program where thinking Christianly is the goal. Visit www.canonpress.org.

COMPOSITION

Running a writing-intensive program is the best thing you can do for your teen. There has never been a time in history when the ability to communicate effectively in writing has mattered more. The competition just to be heard is intense, so in order for opinions to rise above the roar, they must be compelling, original, and clearly presented. And that, in a nutshell, is what you should look for and cultivate in your teen's writing.

> There has never been a time in history when the ability to communicate effectively in writing has mattered more.

191

If you feel inadequate to teach this subject, then you may want to work to increase your own confidence and competence in written expression. I know that homeschooling my kids definitely increased my own skills as I spent years reading books on writing, teaching writing courses, and writing alongside them.

I completely understand that parents must pick and choose carefully where to invest their time, but let me encourage you to spend at least a bit of time learning about the writing process and how to best implement the information in your program.

The best resource for helping to understand writing this is Great Source Books at www.greatsource.com, where you can purchase a *Write Source* handbook for the appropriate grade level. The latest editions incorporate the six traits of writing (as outlined chapter 11) into their already well-established program for teaching kids to write. If you don't want to spend money on brand-new material, then earlier editions of the best-selling high school handbook *Writers Inc: A Student Handbook for Writing* and Learning are easy to come. The middle school handbook, *Write Source 2000: A Guide to Writing, Thinking and Learning*, will also do the trick of bringing you up to speed. Spend a few hours reading through the handbook. Every grade level in the series takes the same approach to writing—the steps and writing models simply increase in sophistication and complexity. So once you figure out how to implement the material into your curriculum (use the Forms of Writing section for your assignments), you are set for the each subsequent year.

I love Great Source's approach to writing above all others because it focuses on developing a teen's unique writing voice—a personal style and originality that makes what she has to say interesting. This is the kind of writing your kids need to produce to set themselves apart on a college application essay or résumé cover letter, sell a short story to a magazine, or persuade someone to reconsider their position on an issue of importance. Most kids who dislike writing feel do because they are told what to write. This is equivalent to telling kids what to say, and no one derives any satisfaction from this approach. Writing is an expression of your child's personality. Develop an approach to writing that helps your kids express themselves convincingly and with clarity and originality.

Here are a few things to keep in mind when developing a writing-intensive high school program.

Writing reveals thinking. If a child cannot write clearly, he is likely not thinking clearly. The development of logic and reason is an important skill to work on. Experience is also necessary to stimulate thinking. If your teen can't think of anything to write about, then have him read a provocative book or take a field trip somewhere new or unusual. This will help generate ideas, especially if the student is interested and engaged during the experience.

> **Experience is also necessary to stimulate thinking. If your teen can't think of anything to write about, then have him read a provocative book or take a field trip somewhere new or unusual.**

Writers write all the time. Writing projects should be underway as often as possible during high school. In my Monday morning tutorials with my own kids, where we met to discuss their week's work, I always asked what writing projects they were working on and what they planned to complete for me to review by Friday. The one caveat to this approach is an understanding that projects will not always be brought to the same level of completion or refinement. Real writers always have many projects underway, and years can lapse before they finally finish a project or abandon it altogether. It is not helpful to require teens to finish every writing assignment they start. My kids probably averaged eight to ten polished assignments a year, including a ten- to twenty-page research paper.

Writers write across the curriculum. Writing is a method of learning, so use it liberally in all subject areas. Study journals

193

for history or science are an excellent way for kids to increase their fluency in writing while helping them process what they are learning. Use research and report writing as a method for learning how to analyze and synthesize information, as well as an assessment tool to demonstrate knowledge and comprehension. See Sharon Sorenson's book under "Recommended Resources" for more information on writing across the curriculum.

Writers need an audience and purpose. Authentic writing is created with an intended audience in mind. Adults don't spend time on mere composition assignments, and neither should kids. Your kids will work more diligently on their writing if they know they will be sharing that writing with an audience. So have them create picture books to share with the preschool class at church or write a research paper to submit to a contest. Ask them to compose a poem to share with the family or write an editorial for the local newspaper. Participate in writing contests or start a writers group for homeschooling families where students can share their work with one another. You don't have to make this overly complicated—kids are motivated by the opportunity to share.

> Your kids will work more diligently on their writing if they know they will be sharing that writing with an audience.

By now, you're probably wondering where all the information is about teaching (and grading compositions for) grammar, mechanics, usage, and punctuation. This is often viewed as the heart and soul of any English course. Yes, kids need to master the conventions of the English language. However, it's often a fruitless effort to try to teach this year in and year out by having your kids complete grammar exercises. *Research does not support this approach.* Kids who achieve mastery in this area have two things in common: They *read* good books a lot, and they *write* a lot. This is why I emphasize reading, literature, and composition over language arts. The best way to learn the rules that govern usage is by *using* language to accomplish legitimate goals—hence, a writing-intense program built around assignments for authentic audiences will motivate students to master the rules. Forcing kids to memorize rules without ever producing real writing projects is a quick route to raising kids who detest English. The most effective strategy is to teach grammar on a "need to know, need to use" basis. Simply keep a couple of good English handbooks at the ready as you help your child achieve the greater goal of effective written communication.

Recommended Resources

Warriner's English Grammar and Composition: Complete Course. Do you know when I actually learned English grammar? The weekend before I started teaching a nine-week course on the subject at my first teaching job. Grammar wasn't emphasized in my college training. Fortunately, I grabbed a copy of Warriner's from the stockroom and spent the weekend reading it cover to cover. English grammar actually makes sense in large doses like that. I took this same approach with my kids: I ordered a used copy of Warriner's and kept it close at hand. It's well organized, with lots of examples. This meaty tome is really all you need.

Eats, Shoots & Leaves: The Zero Tolerance Approach to Punctuation by Lynne Truss. You need to read this book with your teens, if only to demonstrate that a revolution can be started about anything in the hands of a knowledgeable, passionate, and witty writer. Truss has now taught the common man on both sides of the Atlantic to

195

properly punctuate with conviction because of her best-selling manifesto.

Daily Grams and Great Source SkillsBooks provide practice in mechanics, proofreading, and editing. You will not need to use both every year. Please note that these resources do not make use of sentence diagramming, which is a helpful skill to expose your teen to at some point. *The Complete Book of Diagrams* by Mary Daly is the best resource available in print. I suggest teaching diagramming in ninth grade or earlier.

Our Mother Tongue: A Guide to English Grammar by Nancy Wilson. If you haven't used this resource for middle school English, be sure to squeeze it into your curriculum at the beginning of high school.

Webster's New World Student Writing Handbook by Sharon Sorenson. This is a must-have reference. Sorenson has created a comprehensive guide to the most common writing assignments across the curriculum for high school and college students, including science lab reports, history research papers, book reports, creative writing, journal entries, newspaper stories, movie reviews, summaries, and short essays. This well-organized book features step-by-step instructions and excellent student models to follow.

The Purdue Online Writing Lab (OWL) is generally regarded as the best of the college OWLs you will find online. I use it extensively in my online AP courses. Visit http://owl.english.purdue.edu.

HOW TO EVALUATE YOUR STUDENT'S WRITING

Most homeschool parents are at a loss when it comes to evaluating their children's compositions. Our default position is to merely circle spelling and grammatical errors, but this can do more harm than good. Content is the most important element. If the student's writing lacks thought but is perfectly punctuated, nothing has been accomplished.

Below is a quick overview of the kinds of things you should be looking for in a writing assignment. Try using a writing rubric (available online) to score or evaluate writing—kids need to know what they are shooting for. Remember to give the scoring rubric to students prior to beginning the assignment.

> **If the student's writing lacks thought but is perfectly punctuated, nothing has been accomplished.**

Precise Vocabulary

English is arguably the greatest language ever constructed for written work. Whereas French claims 100,000 words, English is now rocketing past 500,000. This is because English is the language of assimilation and amalgamation. As the English were conquered or conquered, they absorbed the languages around them and made the vocabulary distinctly their own. For this reason, we can say something in English with great precision of thought. How expansive is your teen's vocabulary? Compare her word choices with the language found in any section of a compelling novel. Can you spot the differences together and use this to make improvements? Additionally, the vocabulary you are studying in other subject areas should be showing up in her writing.

Syntax

Syntax includes word order and sentence structure. How does your teen order the words in a sentence? Does he understand that arrangement can affect the meaning, emphasis, and impact of what he's written? This is where the importance of punctuation comes into play. The comma, dash, semi-colon, and colon are used to organize more complex thought into well-defined sentences. As your student is reading quality literature, have him note the author's use of punctuation and attempt to copy their sentence structure. This will help your teen to order his thoughts more compactly and clearly. Reward his attempts to include varied sentence structure and experimentation in his own writing.

Focus

What is the work's main idea, theme, or thesis? What is the work about? After reading the assignment, you should be able to state the main idea in a single sentence. If not, help your teen figure out what is making the focus unclear. Is there too much information covering too many topics? Is the central idea and purpose of the work not fully developed? Think of a photograph that is unfocused or lacking a central subject, and make an analogy to the writing your teen produces.

Logic and Organization

Does the composition build a persuasive argument in a logical manner? If the student is writing fiction, then the logical arrangement of the story may be driven by the need to create suspense. Ask your teen to explain why she has organized the material in the order she has. Then make necessary suggestions for improving the logic accordingly.

Detail

How well is the focus developed? Does the work paint a picture in bold, vivid colors, or is it rendered in black and white? Does the writer enrich the information with concrete details that are easy to visualize? Is the main point supported with good examples, illustrations, or anecdotes? Here is where "voice" is partially achieved—the details the writer chooses to include is one way she conveys her unique personality as an author. Does she select vigorous verbs to convey momentum or action? Is the descriptive imagery sharp and visceral? Does it put you at the center of the action where little imagination is required? Are the illustrations fresh and unusual, or have you heard all these arguments and stories before? Commend your young writer for every aspect of the composition that is memorable in its details.

Voice

The whole is greater than the sum of its parts, and that is voice. The way the five preceding elements work together is how the voice of the writer is heard and recognized. Good writers make habitual choices in each of these areas, and that creates their recognizable, individual voices. Young writers must be free to experiment in this area—they need to try different personas on for size and see if they like the fit. Too many teens spend a lot of time trying to write what they believe someone else wants them to say. Just as a student must, through experience and maturity, learn to be comfortable with his own personality, he also needs to, through practice and opportunity, arrive at his own unique writer's voice.

Recommended Online Writing Classes

Since I'm highly recommending you consider outside help in this area at some point during high school, allow me to pass on some of the best online options:

Write At Home—www.writeathome.com
Write from the Heart—http://denisebotsford.com/
Brave Writer—www.bravewriter.com
Write Guide—www.writeguide.com
The Potters School—www.pottersschool.com

COLLEGE-LEVEL ENGLISH

The university-bound student capable of accelerated work is advised to pursue college credits in English during high school. Whether headed into the sciences and the humanities, students are well served by completing certain English requirements prior to entering college. For science majors, this will save them from a taxing workload in composition or literature during their freshman and sophomore years when they will need to devote as much time possible to math-intensive courses. And the humanities student can qualify to bypass introductory coursework and begin taking upper-level classes sooner in order to devote more time to diversified studies.

The accelerated high school student has two options in this area: She can take an Advance Placement test or a CLEP test and, depending upon her score, receive college credit or exemption from certain college requirements; or she can take college-level English at a local community college or university that accepts high school students. We will discuss the implications of doing college-level work in the chapter on AP, CLEP, and Equivalency Testing. For now, let's examine what kind of student is ready for college-level English.

There are three college courses most students must take in this department, regardless of their major: Speech, Introduction to Literature, and Introduction to Composition.

Speech is not available as an Advance Placement or CLEP test, so your only option here is a course held at a local college. Speech can be a very easy course for many high school students. In most cases, its unassuming goal is to get kids comfortable presenting information orally. In some cases, the course may delve into rhetoric, logic, and debate and therefore be a bit more challenging.

Introduction to Composition is intended to get incoming college freshmen ready to write across the curriculum. Many colleges are running writing-intensive programs these days; my daughter Kayte, a math major, was required to take four writing-intensive classes in four different disciplines. Introduction to Composition is generally doable for a student capable of writing a five-paragraph essay with few grammatical errors. Most colleges these days require a placement test in writing, so you may have to submit to this before your teen can enroll. If he scores high enough to be admitted, he has nothing to lose and everything to gain by knocking this course off his workload early (especially if the colleges he's looking at are giving high school students or homeschoolers a price break for doing so).

> **AP English Language and Composition is is a good place to start if you think your student is capable of college-level work.**

AP English Language and Composition is the test that can exempt students from the Introduction to Composition requirement. This is a good place to start if you think your student is capable of college-level work. And while taking an AP course as a precursor to taking the exam in May is not required, kids who take a course in preparation perform significantly better than those who try to study on their own and then sit for the test. Before taking the test, students should be ready to read fifty or more pages a week from a college-level text, usually an anthology of essays. They should also be comfortable writing essays, as creative writing alone will not prepare a student for college-level writing.

AP English Literature and Composition often qualifies students for exemption from both Introduction to Composition and Introduction to Literature on the college level. AP Literature, though, should not be attempted until students have a solid foundation in English literature. I recommend taking an

201

American or British literature course first and only in eleventh or twelfth grades, as kids need to be ready to discuss mature themes. Younger teens just don't have the life experience to begin to think deeply about the revenge ethic of *Hamlet* or the ambiguity of Hawthorne's treatment of Hester Prynne in The *Scarlet Letter*. Students need to realize that much of literature explores the gray areas of life and that a range of responses is possible, even for the Christian student. Because of the reading and writing load in any AP Literature class, and the difficulty of the test, I recommend that this be one of the last AP courses you consider.

There are several CLEP exams in composition and literature. Review the exam contents for each of these at the College Board's website, www.collegeboard.com. We will discuss this option further in chapter 26.

14 HIGH SCHOOL MATH

Homeschoolers need to be careful about being shortsighted in the area of mathematics. Technical and computer skills in almost all fields of employment are rapidly increasing in complexity. Students intending to move directly into the job market will likely find mathematical skills or mathematical reasoning essential as they learn to grapple on the job with changing software and technology. Therefore, I think it wise to cover a minimal level of higher math with all students, thus keeping open the possibility of completing college-level coursework at a later date.

Students preparing for trade or technical school or direct entrance into the job market should complete a minimum of algebra 1 and 2 and geometry. Some states still require only two years of math for a high school diploma, but as graduation requirements are being revised across the nation, three years of algebra-level work and higher is becoming the minimum. Consumer math is no longer awarded high school credit in many places.

Students preparing to earn a four-year college degree in the humanities should complete at least algebra 1 and 2 and geometry in high school. To be competitive for scholarship consideration, they should take four years of high school math, including trigonometry or pre-calculus. If your college-bound teen is capable of handling calculus, then she should do so if the schedule permits. Students who demonstrate high attainment in math will find favor in many quarters, as math aptitude is considered a strong predictor of future success on campus and in life. However, if math is an area of challenge for your college-bound teen, then your priority must be building a solid foundation in algebra so he can build upon it somewhere down the road.

> Students who demonstrate high attainment in math will find favor in many quarters, as math aptitude is considered a strong predictor of future success on campus and in life.

Students preparing to earn a four-year degree in the sciences, math, or engineering should *minimally* complete algebra 1 and 2, geometry, and pre-calculus. But they will be better served by completing a robust calculus course, too. Many colleges require calculus as a prerequisite before entering a science-oriented major. For example, Kayte had to complete three semesters of calculus before she even began the forty-credit course of study required for a B.S. in mathematics.

It's not uncommon for kids who have completed calculus 1 in high school not to score "calc-ready" on their college placement exam, meaning they must retake calculus in college. However, this doesn't mean calculus in high school is not advised. Top colleges understand the importance of a solid foundation in calculus for science and engineering majors and set the bar for the placement test relatively high, reasoning that a review of basic calculus is a better place to start than to send students on their way to struggle repeatedly with the math end of their coursework.

Indeed, the rigorous course of study in engineering and the sciences often necessitates a five-year program, so getting through as much math as your science-oriented teen is capable of in high school will help him control to some extent the length of study later required in college. So the more you can get done in advance, the better. Your teens may not thank you now, but they will realize in hindsight that establishing a solid foundation in mathematics during high school was in their best interest.

Course titles for high school math

Algebra 1, algebra 2, geometry, trigonometry, pre-calculus, discrete math, probability and statistics, calculus. Additionally, college-level work completed at home can also be used to fulfill high school math requirements.

PLANNING AHEAD FOR COLLEGE BOARDS

College-bound students need to complete algebra 1 and 2 and geometry before taking the SAT or ACT College Entrance Exams, which are sometimes referred to as "boards." The new SAT now includes more advanced math topics, and the ACT includes a few questions from trigonometry. This is not a subject area to be using a text with a dated copyright. Use this list provided by the College Board to evaluate your textbook options:

205

Number and Operations

Arithmetic word problems (including percent, ratio, and proportion)
Properties of integers (even, odd, prime numbers, divisibility, etc.)
Rational numbers
Logical reasoning
Sets (union, intersection, elements)

Counting techniques

Sequences and series (including exponential growth)

Elementary number theory

Algebra and Functions

Substitution and simplifying algebraic expressions

Properties of exponents

Algebraic word problems

Solutions of linear equations and inequalities

Systems of equations and inequalities

Quadratic equations

Rational and radical equations

Equations of lines

Absolute value

Direct and inverse variation

Concepts of algebraic functions

Newly defined symbols based on commonly used operations

Geometry and Measurement

Area and perimeter of a polygon

Area and circumference of a circle

Volume of a box, cube, and cylinder

Pythagorean theorem and special properties of isosceles, equilateral, and right triangles

Properties of parallel and perpendicular lines

Coordinate geometry

Geometric visualization

Slope

Similarity

Transformations

Data Analysis, Statistics, and Probability
Data interpretation
Statistics (mean, median, and mode)
Probability

Students applying to top-tier schools or engineering and science programs may also be required to take the SAT subject test Mathematics, Level 2. There is trigonometry and pre-calculus on this test. Students must take this test by the fall of their senior year, so they will need to complete a pre-calculus course by the end of eleventh grade. Remember, keep working backwards. Check the website for potential colleges and see what they expect of their incoming freshman in a particular major or department.

STRATEGIES FOR DOING MATH AT HOME

Of all the subjects, math is the most far removed from your own high school experience. Technology has revolutionized the minimal standards for math literacy. So throw out everything about how you learned math and the limits of your study. Your teen needs to go well beyond that, and the approach should be much different as well. That doesn't mean there's any reason for you to start hyperventilating or throw in the towel on homeschooling. You will find plenty of help online, and great curriculum choices abound. Homeschooling, more than any other option, can provide the motivated student a tremendous advantage in math studies.

> Homeschooling, more than any other option, can provide the motivated student a tremendous advantage in math studies.

I decided pretty quickly to go the tutor route to teach my kids math. Learning math is in many ways like learning a foreign language—there are limits to how far one can go without a native speaker to guide the way. If you feel uncomfortable teaching math and a tutor or math class through a co-op or community college is not possible, then consider purchasing a resource that includes a "teacher in the box" (such as Video-Text) or a highly interactive curriculum such as Teaching Textbooks.

> If you feel uncomfortable teaching math and a tutor or math class through a co-op or community college is not possible, then consider purchasing a resource that includes a "teacher in the box."

Algebra is the language used for all other math coursework that follows, so this is the subject requiring the greatest amount of thought. What is your best option here? Make sure the year you start algebra that other subjects do not overly compete for study time. Most teens realistically need ninety minutes a day for math. (And math is a subject that should be done daily. Others, such as, history, may reasonably be completed in one block of time weekly.)

We also found that math is best grasped in context, and the Apologia science courses we did concurrently with our math studies provided this context. The Apologia physics course is particularly effective for reinforcing algebra, geometry, and trigonometry—a strong reason for making physics one of your high school sciences.

The use of a calculator for high school math is now expected, so make sure the math program you choose works the use of a scientific and graphing calculator into the course. Teaching Textbooks, for example, has thoroughly integrated learning how to use a graphing calculator into its pre-calculus program. There are many websites showing the keystrokes and functions for Texas Instruments' TI-83 and 84 graphing calculators, the standard for high school math. All my kids, except math major Kayte, found the TI-83 sufficient for their college coursework, too. Science and engineering majors will need a more sophisticated (read: expensive) calculator.

Yes, your kids will need to know how to perform computations without a calculator, and they need to be able to graph simple curves from algebraic equations. However, many of the math problems on the SATs and in real life are too complex to solve without a calculator. Students need to use their time efficiently, so after they learn how to solve math problems longhand, permit them to use a scientific calculator. When it comes to trigonometry, pre-calculus, and calculus, they will need a graphing calculator by their side from the beginning.

My son Gabe, the finance major, has asked that I suggest students also learn how to use Microsoft Excel for math computations. He argues that Excel converts mathematical problems to graphs and charts, which has the added benefit of allowing you to show your work to others—something that cannot easily be done with a graphing calculator.

Recommended Resource

Georgetown Independent School District Student Online Resources (www.georgetownisd.org/libraries). Select "mathematics" for a list of the best Internet sites that support a high school student's math needs, including links for SAT preparation and using graphing calculators. This is a very extensive, well-organized list.

CHOOSING A MATH CURRICULUM

Because topics can be placed differently within the scope and sequence of different programs, it's wise to pick one program's math curriculum for high school *and stick with it*. I am not going to recommend the old standby, Saxon Math, here because of their approach to geometry—it is integrated into their algebra 1 and 2 courses. This does not provide students with an adequate introduction to geometry, and it takes time away from important algebra topics that must be covered in those two courses. Saxon is also thin on application problems, and visual presentation is non-existent. I do know families who swear by Saxon for high school math, but their teens tended to have a strong math aptitude to begin with, and bright kids can often make any resource work well.

> Because topics can be placed differently within the scope and sequence of different programs, it's wise to pick one program's math curriculum for high school and stick with it.

There are three programs I recommend reviewing first: Teaching Textbooks, Chalk Dust video courses, and VideoText interactive courses. The one component all three have in common is the use of visual representations of math models. While each does this differently, what is important is that each program understands that abstract concepts must be converted to concrete application and graphically rendered if students are to comprehend and remember what any array of numbers represent.

I love the relative newcomer of the group, Teaching Textbooks. Harvard-educated brothers Shawn and Greg Sabouri have designed their math courses for homeschooled students to use independently, and it works. The companion CDs include audio explanations of all lessons with animated graphics, as well as solutions worked step-by-step on the CD. Your only job as the parent is to make sure your teen stays on task.

We used Chalk Dust video courses at home. Experienced math instructor Dana Mosley was originally contracted by D.C. Heath to produce companion video instruction for their highly rated line of college textbooks. This experience led Dana and his brother, Richard, to begin producing high-quality video instruction for high-school-level texts. The result is a full line of college-prep video courses aligned with textbooks written by Ron Larson. (You can save money by buying the texts used.) The lack of graphic animations make this choice less desirable for many students, but this shortcoming is offset by video of a live teacher explaining each lesson to the student, which will be of more value to certain types of learners.

Master teacher Tom Clark uses computer-generated graphics to demonstrate step-by-step application of math concepts in the VideoText interactive algebra and geometry courses. Available in VHS and DVD format, each multimedia program includes the student workbook and solutions manual. The multimedia presentations emphasize math concepts and mathematical reasoning and assume that parents will view the lessons alongside the student and then reinforce the lesson through discussion and illustration. This resource is an ideal choice for a small co-op class, with one parent taking responsibility for overseeing students' progress. The algebra program is advertised as including pre-algebra, algebra 1, and algebra 2. Geometry is advertised as covering geometry, trigonometry, and pre-calculus. Each is said to be equal to two high school math credits. For this to be comparable to what is legitimately expected to be covered in two full-year courses, I think a parent would need to supplement the video lessons quite a bit with additional instruction and practice work. VideoText has been adding additional problem sets to their websites for parents to download.

Of these choices, Teaching Textbooks are written in a more engaging style, with a conscious effort to show the application and history of the math they are covering in the textbook. Tom Clark of VideoText is a gifted instructor who conceptualizes the math exceptionally well. Chalk Dust's textbooks, though, are published in full color and are conscientiously aligned with national math standards developed by a leader in the educational market.

All three of these choices require a significant investment, but you are paying for the technology. The good news is that none of the programs' components is consumable, so you will be able to resell your material easily or use it over and over again. Considering the importance of math skills for any high school student and the need for visually presenting abstract concepts, the expense is justifiable.

COLLEGE-LEVEL WORK

Math requirements vary greatly from college to college and major to major, so you need to be checking the websites for colleges your teen may be considering to ensure that his or her college-level work at home will count.

Students planning to major in the humanities will likely have one math requirement for their major: college algebra. Other non-science majors, such as business and education, may have more specific math requirements. College algebra is not available as an Advanced Placement course, but there are CLEP tests that may exempt a student from these requirements. College algebra is equivalent to algebra 3 and should not be undertaken until the student has completed algebra 1 and 2, geometry, and some core trigonometry topics. Students who have completed calculus may be able to test out of college algebra, but this often does not exempt them from their general education math requirement. This just means they get to take a higher-level math course to earn the necessary credits.

Your student may be able to complete college algebra through your local community college or university if he scores high enough on the institution's placement test. College algebra is a difficult course, and many students will find trigonometry and pre-calculus easier to grasp. Remember, algebra is the language for higher math, so this is pretty advanced language study in those terms.

AP Statistics is an exam that may fulfill a general education or major requirement for many students planning to obtain a Bachelor of Science degree. A course of study that prepares you for this exam can be found online, or you might consider enrolling your teen in an Introduction to Statistics class at a local college. There is no CLEP exam for statistics as of this writing.

Students inclined towards the sciences can consider AP Calculus. There are two tests: AP Calculus AB and AP Calculus BC. Calculus AB is equivalent to calculus 1, so if your teen completes a thorough calculus course at home, she can consider sitting for the AB exam. A score of 4 or 5 should exempt her from one semester of college calculus. The BC exam includes topics from calculus 1 and 2. A score of 3 will likely exempt your teen from one semester of calculus, while a score of 4 or 5 should exempt her from two semesters of calculus. A well-designed, yearlong AP Calculus course should prepare students to sit for either exam.

213

Taking AP Calculus is a one way for scholarship-seeking students to demonstrate high aptitude and a willingness to challenge themselves. But testing out of calculus 1 and 2 places science and engineering majors directly into calculus 3 in their freshman year—not always a blessing. I still recommend taking AP Calculus for any high school student ready for it, but parents should be ready to help their kids reevaluate their placement without recrimination once they get started in college.

Establishing a solid GPA freshman year trumps all other considerations. Among other things, most renewable scholarship awards are tied to maintaining a solid GPA.

THE GIFTED MATH STUDENT

If your teen shows a high aptitude for math and is self-motivated, you aren't trying to figure out how to just get through this daunting task. You want to know where you can find an appropriate challenge for your kid. Not only is there a great resource available, but also there's an entire online community of math geeks just waiting to welcome your teen into the fold. Art of Problem Solving, founded by formerly frustrated math whiz kids, is just the place to find challenging textbooks, problems, competitions, and competitive training, as well as online classes. Visit www.artofproblemsolving.com.

15 HIGH SCHOOL SCIENCE

You must be careful to lay a solid foundation in writing and math in your high school program, so that your teens will be prepared should they ever need to change academic or career directions quickly. In the fine arts, history, and science, your range of teaching options is broader. Therefore, adapt your curriculum in these subjects to suit your teen's interests and learning style. Use these areas to teach your student *how to learn*, not what information to master, and teach in such a way that your teen develops an appreciation, even a passion, for the subject.

Science is especially important in this regard. Science is the study of God's creation and the intricacies and mysteries of His design. You have a unique opportunity to use your child's study of the sciences to inspire greater awe of our Creator. Many traditional science materials are more focused on reducing creation to a series of facts for kids to memorize and leave young learners with a sour taste in their mouths.

CHOOSING SCIENCE CURRICULUM

You can use textbooks for your science studies, or you can use science journals and selected trade books from the science section of your local library. You can complete in-depth reading in the sciences online, or you can watch educational videos. Most students will learn best with a mixed approach.

In selecting science resources, first consider the writing style used. Read a few pages yourself. Is the text interesting? Are the concepts understandable? Science is a challenging discipline with complex ideas, but a good high school text should demystify science, not obscure it. This is one reason we used Apologia Science as our core resource for all the high school sciences. Dr. Jay Wile is a teacher at heart, and this comes through in his writing. He knows how to communicate difficult concepts, and he employs numerous examples and illustrations so students will see how science affects real life. And now Apologia also offers online classes for all their high school science courses. Learn more at www.apologiaacademy.com.

We always supplemented the text with outside sources: Having a topic explained from different perspectives and through different media will help your student to master the material. Science is probably the high school subject that most requires visual representation. Educational videos, fieldwork, and science centers are a must if you want your teen to really learn the material in a way that lasts.

Possible course titles for high school science include biology, physics, chemistry, astronomy, geology, anatomy, environmental science, and even marine biology. Additionally, any college-level work your student completes can fulfill high school science requirements.

Before you settle on a plan for science, don't forget to work

> **Before you settle on a plan for science, don't forget to work backwards from any major(s) and institutions your teen may be looking to enter after high school.**

backwards from any major(s) and institutions your teen may be looking to enter after high school. Many of these will specify science work that must be completed. For example, most engineering schools will require high school physics, and depending upon the type of engineering, they may also specify chemistry. Pre-med students will need chemistry.

The Importance of Lab Work

Most colleges expect to see at least two hard sciences on a high school transcript along with related lab work—more if your teen wants to be considered for a scholarship. Distinguish this by listing the course title as "Biology with Lab" or "Physics with Lab." Traditionally, lab work is set apart on a student's schedule as an extra class period. For example, at our homeschool co-op we offer thirty weeks of classes. Science classes meet every week, with an additional fifty-minute period every other week to complete a lab. Students in our science courses complete fifteen different labs—a respectable number by any standard.

This was the driving force behind the founding of our co-op. Parents wanted to provide rigorous laboratory experiences for our college-bound kids, but none of us wanted the responsibility or cost of setting up labs in our homes. Pooling our resources meant we could invest in quality laboratory equipment, such as high-powered microscopes, and one or two parents could take responsibility for knowledgeably leading a group of students through a set of labs.

Of course, initially set-up of the labs took a few moms a lot of time. Much of one summer was devoted to determining the labs to be done, ordering materials, and organizing them with instructions for students. While the lab materials must be replenished at the beginning of each school year—and we've added or deleted labs a few times—this does not consume a great deal of time due to the foundation that has already been

217

laid with that initial effort. Today, scores of co-op families have been able to provide quality science classes for all their kids. Indeed, many of our graduates have gone on to major in science-oriented studies at competitive colleges—really rather remarkable considering our shoestring budget. I know I never could have provided the same level of study for my children on my own.

Fortunately for homeschool families everywhere, there are now excellent sources for laboratory equipment and supplies available online. Check out Home Science Tools at www.hometrainingtools.com and Tobin's Lab at www.tobinslab.com.

Online Labs

If you just cannot pull off hands-on labs at home, then you can meet this need using virtual labs online. So far, the research suggests that students who prepare for the AP science exams using virtual labs perform as well as those who complete live labs. At Sciencecourseware.org, reasonably priced virtual labs can be purchased as a package or per lab. Developed by California State University, with funding from the U.S. National Science Foundation, these labs are modest but well designed.

The most celebrated virtual labs online are found at Y Science Laboratories at Brigham Young University (chemlab.byu.edu). These are worth the price for the serious science student preparing for AP exams.

M.I.T. and the Open Content Movement

Open content refers to the free distribution and development of intellectual property across the Internet, including software, music, and art. The free distribution of courseware (online classes) may well one day make homeschooling barrier-free. When M.I.T. (Massachusetts Institute of Technology) decided to distribute all their courses online for free (ocw.mit.edu), other universities felt pressured to do the same. The result is the OCW Consortium (Open Courseware) at www.ocwconsortium. org. Of particular interest will be the high-school-level content for AP Biology, AP Calculus, and AP Physics.

If you are interested in why these folks are doing this, or what trends are fueling the open content movement, check out two books the topic: *Disrupting Class: How Disruptive Innovation Will Change the Way the World Learns* by Clayton M. Christensen and *Crowdsourcing: Why the Power of the Crowd Is Driving the Future of Business* by Jeff Howe, an editor at Wired magazine.

Creation Science

The creation vs. evolution debate is no longer a subtopic in secular textbooks—evolutionary theory now forms the framework for most high school and college science courses. Unless you envision for your children a life that insulates them from any exposure to evolutionary thinking, you should prepare them to encounter the *best* arguments on both sides of the debate. I emphasize best because it is common for either side of any issue to build their arguments around their opponents' weakest defense. When my three older kids entered college, they found their peers and professors to be a lot smarter and well reasoned than they had expected. Fortunately, they all took this experience to heart and now devote more time to a thoughtful and intellectually rigorous consideration of cultural issues. They've

> Unless you envision for your children a life that insulates them from any exposure to evolutionary thinking, you should prepare them to encounter the best arguments on both sides of the debate.

219

also found being winsome more effective than being arrogant.

One of the most memorable traditions at our co-op is the Creation vs. Evolution Debates held during the years we offer biology. Conducted as a courtroom drama, students assume the roles of famous scientists on both sides of the debate, and teams of student lawyers defend or prosecute their assigned position. A jury comprises teachers and students outside the class. Some years the creationist team is judged the winner; other years the evolutionist team comes out on top. In preparation, all the students have compelling reasons for studying the best arguments on both sides of this issue and come away better prepared to defend their faith than at the start.

Recommended Resources

Darwin on Trial by Phillip Johnson

Darwin's Black Box: The Biochemical Challenge to Evolution by Michael Behe

Evolution: A Theory in Crisis by Michael Denton

Reasonable Faith: The Scientific Case for Christianity by Jay Wile

The DVDs *Icons of Evolution, The Incorrigible Dr. Berlinski,* and *Investigating Evolution* from Coldwater Media (www.coldwatermedia.com)

The Center for Science and Culture (www.discovery.org/csc) is the premier site for research and policy development on intelligent design

COLLEGE-LEVEL SCIENCE

If your teen is planning to attend college and major in science or engineering, I highly recommend he or she do college-level work in high school through Advanced Placement classes online or at a local university or college. This is the best way for your teen to determine if he is truly ready for the rigors of these types of studies. In my experience, homeschooled students are better equipped for college than most of their peers, but even they find the sciences and engineering studies at a competitive school to be challenging. Enrolling in an excellent Advanced Placement science course online is a great way to experience the kind of college work they can expect.

Your teen can take AP classes and tests in biology, chemistry, physics (three different topics), and environment science. To do this, she will need to have completed a high-school-level course in that science as well as algebra 1. In some cases, two high school sciences and algebra 2 should be completed. Check prerequisites with the instructor. Evolutionary theory will be incorporated into this college-level coursework and will appear on some of the AP exams, and you will have to decide how you wish to approach this. The AP teachers who teach through PA Homeschoolers handle evolution in a manner respectful of a Christian worldview, which is one advantage of their program.

16 HIGH SCHOOL SOCIAL STUDIES

Social studies is a catch-all category for the study of human society and includes history, civics, government, geography, economics, and cultural studies. Traditionally, high school students are expected to complete three courses in this subject area, but college-bound students are wise to do more. Frequently, diploma programs specify that these credits must include one American history course and one civics course. In some states, state history must be covered somewhere in the curriculum between the seventh and twelfth grades. In our case, we covered Pennsylvania history concurrent with completing a U.S. history course, as state law doesn't designate a set amount of time to be spent on the subject. It's generally fine to combine other subjects in this way and designate a half credit of study to each—for example, U.S. government and economics or world geography and cultures.

Possible course titles for high school social studies include American cultures, ancient history, anthropology, church history, civics, economics, geography, history, modern history, political science, psychology, sociology, U.S. history, U.S. government, world cultures, world geography, and world history. This is a good place to cut a wide berth if your teens are uncertain about their future direction. They may not have had enough exposure to certain topics to recognize a particular interest. On the other hand, for the science- or engineering-inclined student, this may be your best chance to lay a solid foundation for biblical thinking, as the rigorous course of study they will follow in college will leave little time for taking the liberal arts seriously.

For the Christian family, there are two high-level approaches to consider. The first is to follow a classical Christian approach and study these topics as they emerged and developed from within the Western tradition. Consider curriculum from Tapestry of Grace, Veritas Press, and Well-Trained Mind for this path. The second option is to connect your studies to a concern for world missions and outreach. Sonlight and My Father's World, both developed by former missionaries, are perfect for this approach. Neither one of these options is mutually exclusive—all of the aforementioned companies merge the two concerns at some level. But with so much ground to cover, it is helpful to consider your primary motivations before choosing which courses you will complete and the curriculum you will use.

> **You can gain time in this subject area by combining your reading for an English course with some of your reading in social studies.**

As mentioned earlier, you can gain time in this subject area by combining your reading for an English course with some of your reading in social studies. For example, *The Scarlet Letter, Uncle Tom's Cabin, The Adventures of Huckleberry Finn, Up From Slavery, The Jungle, The Great Gatsby, All the King's Men,* and *Native Son* can all count toward both American literature and U.S. history. You can also count research papers and other types of writing completed in social studies toward a credit for high school

223

composition. I integrated coursework everywhere I could, not because I wanted to take a minimalist approach but because I wanted to allow time for each of our kids to study their passions and to cover topics they weren't going to see in college.

Making the Case for Setting the Bar Higher

College definitely went well my first year. I found the transition to classes very easy—I took eighteen credits my first semester, twenty my second, and earned straight A's all year. Taking classes at the community college in high school probably helped, but I honestly would attribute most of my preparation to the way my parents handled my homeschooling.

The assignments they gave me were difficult and graded fairly. (My parents would give me bad grades if I deserved them!) My mom was not lax about due dates, so by the time I got to college I was accustomed to writing five- to ten-page papers and doing long sets of difficult math problems.

My parents also taught me to learn independently, to be able to research things myself and to work hard. And, really, that's made all the difference.

Jesse Gunsch
Student at the University of Arizona

COLLEGE-LEVEL SOCIAL STUDIES

Advanced Placement exams that may exempt students from common general education requirements in the humanities include AP U.S. History, AP European History, AP World History, AP U.S. Government and Politics, AP Macro Economics, AP

Micro Economics, AP Human Geography, and AP Psychology.

CLEP exams include American Government, Human Growth and Development, Introduction to Educational Psychology, Introduction to Psychology, Introduction to Sociology, Principles of Macro Economics, Principles of Micro Economics, Social Sciences and History, U.S. History, Ancient History, and World History.

Before you plan to take any of these tests, you must determine which of them will actually exempt your teen from specific course requirements at the colleges they are considering. This will depend upon the school's policies regarding AP and CLEP credit and the major they're pursuing. You will find a list of potential AP and CLEP credits on each college's website.

Some of these courses, such as U.S. history, presuppose the prior completion of high-school-level coursework in the subject. If you've laid a solid foundation in middle school, then take the subject in question as an AP course as soon as your teen demonstrates that he's ready for college-level reading. Other AP social studies courses—such as psychology, sociology, and economics—assume this is the student's first exposure to the material and thus no prerequisites are necessary.

Recommended Resources

I'm recommending here only a few worthwhile resources you may not be aware of. There are many quality resources you might form coursework around.

Church History in Plain Language by Bruce Shelley. All of my kids completed their senior year with a course in church history. They invited several of their friends to participate, and we met twice a month in our home. Shelley's book was our core text and aligned neatly with the *History of Christianity* DVD series narrated by Dr.

Timothy George. The DVD course includes a leader's guide and student study guide, and includes six half-hour segments. The DVDs are available at www.visionvideo.com.

Drive Thru History: American History and *Drive Thru History: Ancient History* use a slick combination of live-action camera work and entertaining narration by Dave Stotts to provide crisp analysis of the historical and biblical currents at work in human events. You will find these and other productions of interest at www.coldwatermedia.com

Western Civilization Series by Jackson J. Spielvogel. These marvelously engaging and exhaustive books are college-level texts often used for AP World History.

Teaching Company (www.teach12.com). Even though we've completed our homeschooling years, both my husband and I like to listen to these audio courses. I made use of their history courses extensively during high school. And they're now available in MP3 files!

17 ARTS & LANGUAGES IN HIGH SCHOOL

The traditional high school diploma program requires at least two credits in this category, which includes foreign languages, drama, art, and music. But how do you know whether to award credit for a program or count it as an extracurricular?

Private studies in music and art can be converted to high school credit. Participation in dramatic performances can also be reflected as an extracurricular activity or credit. I chose to award credit if a qualified instructor or tutor led the activity and the program led to a greater proficiency in skills or covered theory or history. In general sixty hours of instructor-led activities translate to a half credit, while 120 hours add up to a full credit. I recommend that you do not repeatedly convert music and art activities to credit on a transcript if what your kids do from year to year does not increase in complexity and proficiency. For example, I counted the first dramatic production we did with our high school co-op as a drama credit and an extra-curricular, whereas subsequent productions were listed on my children's transcripts as extracurricular activities only. However, during Kristen's senior year, our drama group produced a full-scale musical in which she had the leading role. I counted this as a half credit for music and a half credit for drama because she took private voice lessons in preparation and the production required a whole new level of skill.

I've seen high school transcripts for homeschoolers with as many as twelve credits for one year of study. Using the 120 hours rule of thumb for determining credits makes this a bit unbelievable to prospective colleges. Many credits are better listed as extracurricular activities. Suffice to say, this is a judgment call for your family. The truth is that, aside from foreign languages, most college admissions officers don't really pay much attention to credits in this area unless they're related to the student's intended major.

Advanced Placement exams are available for music theory, art history, and studio art. There are no CLEP exams in these areas.

FOREIGN LANGUAGES

Foreign language studies are an important component of a college-prep high school program for several reasons. Many colleges and universities are now requiring proficiency in a second language for many of their majors. Make sure you look into this when investigating colleges and majors, as this requirement will vary from institution to institution. Students who have studied a language in high school may be exempted from this requirement, but a placement exam will likely be necessary to prove proficiency. College-level language studies are frequently more intensive than high school, and students who have not begun language work earlier often struggle to meet the requirements for graduation.

Language studies in high school, in some form, are advis-

> Many colleges and universities are now requiring proficiency in a second language for many of their majors.

able. If achieving proficiency seems beyond what you can accomplish, then focus on vocabulary and conversation. This will at least lay some important groundwork for your student, as many professors practice the immersion approach, which means the course is conducted extensively, if not completely, in this second language.

Another great reason for doing language studies at home is to allow your teen to study abroad at some point during her college years. There is no easier time to see the world than in college, and the cost can be unbeatable. (I will go into the ins and outs of studying abroad in a later chapter.) When choosing a language for study at home, consider where your kids may want to travel. Mike and Kayte studied French because it is an official language in many countries in Africa and the Middle East, whereas Gabe studied Spanish because it made sense for pursuing a business degree.

Proficiency in a second language significantly increases your child's marketability, and several years of studying the same language in high school is viewed positively by both companies and scholarship committees.

What Language Should You Study?

As always, you will need to work backwards from your child's educational or career goals in order to choose a language for study in your program. Latin is emphasized in the classical Christian curriculum, and many liberal arts colleges like to see Latin on a student's transcript. Other colleges will specify that the language studied must be a living language—that is, currently in use in the world today. Latin is not going to help you fulfill that requirement, nor will classical Greek, even though it has value in the realm of biblical studies.

If you want your child to use a foreign language outside of school, then you need to anticipate the possibilities. For ex-

229

ample, Spanish speakers are in demand everywhere, especially in business and education. International businesses value Mandarin, Japanese, and other languages spoken in the Pacific Rim. The U.S. government will actually pay your child to learn "critical languages"—those now in demand by the State Department where speakers are in short supply. Arabic, Mandarin, Japanese, Russian, Hindi, Korean, Persian, Turkish, and Urdu are high on their current needs list. However, the government is looking for a commitment to federal service in exchange. For more information, see the NSEP David L. Boren Undergraduate Scholarships at www.iie.org.

> Our ability to speak foreign languages is a significant way to communicate our good will and concern for a people group.

If your student has a heart for world missions, then this will also help you choose a language for study. Even though English is conveniently spoken in almost every part of the world today, we still must be able to communicate the gospel and the Bible into the mother tongue of every people group if we expect to convey the full scope of the Christian faith. Our ability to speak their language is a significant way to communicate our good will and concern for a people group. If we expect them to interact with us strictly in English, it reinforces the image much of the world holds of Americans as arrogant.

Recommended Resources

Rosetta Stone is a great option if speaking the language is the primary goal. The Peace Corps and business travelers use this program for crash courses in order to hit the ground running. Our kids used Rosetta Stone in the same way prior to studying abroad. However, the program is cient for preparing to pass an AP or language proficiency test. For that you need a traditional approach that covers writing, speaking, listening and reading skills.

Annenberg Media at learner.org provides free streaming videos for full college-level language courses in German, French and Spanish. If you purchase the accompanying texts and work through everything, your teen will have completed four semesters of college-level language studies.

Free open courseware is available online. Programs offered by M.I.T. and the BBC are highly rated, though you will find a growing number of universities following suit. Visit ocw.mit.edu and www.bbc.co.uk/languages for more information.

College-Level Work in a Foreign Language

You are going to find a wide discrepancy among college institutions as to what constitutes fulfillment of foreign language requirements. Some universities will count a student's first four semesters toward a major or minor, while many others start counting credits toward a degree only after a student is studying above those levels. The latter are typically the universities that take their language studies seriously. So if your student's goal is to be exempted from foreign language requirements from a specific institution, then make sure what you do will accomplish this. In most cases, no matter what you do, a placement test will be necessary.

Community college language classes may be your weakest option for university-level studies, especially if the instructor is not a native speaker or is not a certified instructor. This may be a great option for getting started with the conversational aspects of the language, but placement exams are going to measure reading, writing, speaking and listening skills, and the writing is going to primarily be graded on grammar.

Because Kayte had a number of goals for her French studies, we paid a higher price for her to take French courses her junior year at a four-year college where her instructor was a full professor and a native-born speaker. During her senior year, she took AP French online with an American missionary living in Paris. That summer she studied abroad in Aix-en-Provence with her older brother, and this allowed her to complete the study-abroad component of her French major before beginning at Pitt.

Advanced Placement tests in foreign languages include Spanish Language, Spanish Literature, French Language, French Literature, German Language, Chinese Language and Culture, Italian Language and Culture, Japanese Language and Culture, Latin Literature, and Latin: Virgil.

CLEP Tests include French, German, and Spanish, levels 1 and 2.

Use It or Lose It

Finally, no one achieves proficiency in a second language without authentic opportunities to use the language in context. We hosted French exchange students for a number of years, thus opening an opportunity for Kayte to travel to France several times during high school. We offered a French club at our co-op and one year took a trip to Montreal, where we stayed in the French quarter. As you consider a language for your student to study, be sure to consider the various options at your disposal for immersion opportunities.

No one achieves proficiency in a second language without authentic opportunities to use the language in context.

232

18 HIGH SCHOOL ELECTIVES

We have focused thus far on the components of your program that are going to matter most if college is your child's next step. If your teen plans to enter the job market after graduation, or enroll in a trade or technical school, you can be more flexible in building your high school program. There are many options for electives, including physical education, vocational courses, home economics, computer science, and journalism. Also, conscientious Christian parents will want to cover a number of other subjects before their kids move into adulthood.

Again, the rule of thumb for assigning credits is as follows: 60 to 90 hours of instruction and study equals a half credit; 120 to 180 hours of instruction and study equals a full-year course or one credit. Most colleges expect to see twenty-one or more credits on an applicant's high school transcript, so four years each of English, science, social studies, and mathematics will leave you with at least five electives to complete. Typically, these will include foreign languages, art, music, health, and physical education, but these subjects may not be required and others may be more germane to your teen's post-graduation plans.

HEALTH AND PHYSICAL EDUCATION

Most diploma programs will have some kind of minimum requirement in this area, and it's an important subject from a lifestyle perspective, if nothing else. If it's your family's practice to exercise regularly and to educate yourselves about healthy lifestyle choices, then these activities can be bundled to fulfill one or more credits on the transcript, depending on the time and study devoted to the subject. If time and priorities permit, then Total Health from the Association of Christian Schools is an excellent resource. There is a course of study for both middle school and high school, and these include a textbook, student workbook, teacher's guide, and test bank.

All four of our children participated in at least one scholastic sport every year during high school, and I counted this as partial fulfillment of a yearly physical education credit.

DRIVER'S EDUCATION

One of the happiest days of my life was the day our youngest daughter passed her driver's test and I could say good-bye to my driver's training days. I found it very stressful coaching our teens through the process—something just didn't seem right to me about letting novice drivers on the road as part of learning to drive. I appreciated that most of the homeschool parents in our community set higher standards than the state requirements for their teens' driving privileges, and this set a good precedent to follow.

Teens tend to think they

> I appreciated that most of the homeschool parents in our community set higher standards than the state requirements for their teens' driving privileges, and this set a good precedent to follow.

234

need a lot less training and supervision than they actually do. One timeworn strategy for addressing this is to begin instruction long before your teens get a permit. My sons were eager to drive and asked lots of questions, and they talked their dad into teaching them how to drive the car on our property long before they were allowed out on the road. Because our boys learned so quickly, I was not prepared for the complete lack of background knowledge that Kayte possessed about driving. It was quite a scary adventure to sit in the passenger's seat next to someone who did exactly what she was told to do without fully evaluating the situation. Initially, she did as I instructed immediately, even if there was other traffic in her path. Her father and I were sharing instruction but not really communicating about her skill level. This set up a regrettable state of affairs that ultimately led to a serious accident. Fortunately, no one was hurt, but two cars were totaled. And Kayte and I were so shaken that we simply shelved driver's training for some time. Finally Kermit taught her and Kristen the basics of driving, and I joined in only when the foundation was established.

We were very fortunate to have my father, a retired driver's education teacher, provide the six-hour behind-the-wheel instruction required to qualify our sons for an insurance discount. One enterprising mom arranged for the AAA course to be taught at our homeschool co-op at a very reasonable rate. I would highly recommend that every homeschool group arrange something similar with AAA or other agency.

235

Recommended Resources

Driver Ed in a Box (www.driveredinabox.com) is a full-length course of study developed by a veteran driving instructor. A certificate of completion is issued at the end of the course, and most states and insurance companies accept this course as fulfillment of their driver's education requirements.

Driver-Zed is an inexpensive, interactive computer game that allows teens to simulate more than a hundred live-action situations on their PCs. Available from www.aaafoundation.org.

National Driver Training Institute (www.usdrivertraining.com) provides a full-length course of study that includes access to a large library of online videos related to driving safety. Completion of the course will also qualify your teen for a reduction in insurance costs and credit for driver's education in some states.

BIBLE AND THEOLOGY

Presumably, you are encouraging your teens to devote a portion of their day to Bible study and private devotions. If you want to treat this as an academic subject, then you will want to take a more systematic approach.

My sons asked for time to devote to theological studies their senior year, and I wasn't going to deny the request. They had few requirements left to complete for their diplomas, and colleges would be using coursework from ninth through eleventh grades to evaluate their applications, so I figured senior year was a great time to think outside the box. I ran a church history class in our home using Bruce Shelley's *Church History in Plain Language* and several videos produced by Vision Video. (*The History of Christianity*, narrated by Timothy George, was our core resource.) The Christian History Institute's excellent website

> **If you want to treat Bible as an academic subject, then you will want to take a more systematic approach.**

(www.chitorch.org) was also a mainstay of the class. In addition, Mike and Gabe worked through a list of titles we compiled beforehand covering a range of topics related to apologetics and systematic theology. They earned a final English, history, and theology credit for the reading and writing they did in this area.

I also highly recommend you consider studying the Bible as literature. For this, I suggest the wonderful materials developed by Leland and Phillip Ryken, including *The Literary Study Bible*, *Realms of Gold* and *Words That Delight: A Literary Introduction to the Bible*. You might add to this list books by Gene Veith and Peter Leithart. These are some of the materials I've used to award an English credit during high school.

19 INTERNSHIPS AND APPRENTICESHIPS

As a homeschooler, your teen has access to opportunities beyond the reach of most public school students. Yes, the academic requirements of a rigorous high school program at home can seem like a lot to get done, leaving little time for outside activities. However, in terms of preparing for the future, I would rank hands-on experience in the teen's field of interest right beneath reading, writing, and math skills in terms of importance. I don't mean that history and the arts are not important, but you need to keep working backwards from what comes next. You and your teen are about to make some huge life decisions together, perhaps even purchasing a big-ticket item known as a college education, and you do not want to waste time or a dime.

Whether they will be pursuing a job or choosing a major, teens need context and real-life knowledge in order to make informed choices. Just because a kid finds science fascinating doesn't mean he's cut out to work in a laboratory. Young people tend to romanticize their futures, and their career interests are highly influenced by what they see in popular television shows, best-selling novels, and blockbuster movies. As parents, we don't need to burst their bubble, so to speak, but we do need to help them ground their financial decisions in realism. But given their aversion to the phrase "trust me, I know," this is where internships and apprenticeships come in.

An internship is a short-term opportunity at a place of business or profession in which the employer provides experience and/or training in exchange for the student's labor. An internship may be a paid or unpaid position. The expectation between both parties is that the intern will be moving on to another place of employment in the near future.

An apprenticeship, on the other hand, is a protracted period of training, usually in a trade, in which the apprentice gradually increases his or her skills and value to the employer. The expectation is that the apprentice will eventually become a long-term employee, though the apprentice will eventually move on to self-employment in the trade. An apprenticeship can often replace formal education (such as a college degree) as a route to qualifications for a profession.

Our sons both had internships during high school that grew into financially beneficial arrangements and helped to clarify their direction in college and as adults. Both became business majors, though Mike chose international business and Gabe chose finance and economics. Mike worked at our homeschool supply store and eventually became a manager, while Gabe worked for a conservative political lobby in the state capital. Today Mike is an entrepreneur, and Gabe is headed to law school.

Now how does one go about finding internship and apprenticeship opportunities? Unfortunately, there is no national repository of internships and apprenticeships for homeschooled teens. You must make these happen. Whom do you know in your town, homeschool community, or church who has a profession or skill in your teen's area of interest? After making sure your teen is up for a work experience more related to discerning the future than making some quick money, consider approach-

239

ing this individual about a possible internship or apprenticeship relationship.

A good first step is to request that your teen be allowed to "shadow" the individual at work for a day to learn more about the profession. This test run will allow you and your teen to find out if the individual would be a good mentor. Is he a natural teacher? Is she interested in passing on her enthusiasm for her occupation to another? Is the work environment compatible with your Christian convictions? If the shadow day is a positive experience for your teen, then inquire about a more protracted relationship.

> A good first step is to request that your teen be allowed to "shadow" the individual at work for a day to learn more about the profession.

Here are a few tips for making these relationships work well for both parties:

* Define everyone's expectations up front. What is your teen hoping to gain from the experience? What is the mentor hoping to gain?

* Set a definite time period. This can always be extended if things are going well, but establishing this up front gives you a graceful way to end an opportunity that is no longer proving helpful.

* It is exceedingly common for the teen to be given jobs no one else wants to do. After all, an employer has little incentive to give a teen important responsibility if the teen plans to stay for only a short time. However, doing menial jobs well and remaining committed to the arrangement should lead to more opportunities. Remember, this is also a learning experience in how to work for someone.

* If you want a written evaluation or letter of recommendation from the mentor, make that known upfront. In some cases, you might want to provide an evaluation form. Keep the expectations on the employer simple.

* As soon as possible, your teen needs to negotiate the relationship alone. It might be helpful if you ask the mentor how things are going, but you want your teen to learn to navigate these waters independent of you.

GIVING CREDIT FOR A WORK EXPERIENCE

I gave credit to my sons for their internships during their senior year, but not before. By this point they had completed the minimal requirements for graduation and wanted to work. Their internships were now paying decent money, and they had been given a lot of responsibility on the job—much more than they would have been given while working at a typical teen joint. So we documented their internships and reported this as a full credit on the final transcript. This made sense because they were entering college as business majors and were already accepted on the strength of their work through eleventh grade.

This is where that four-year plan (FYP) can really aid you in your long-range planning. I had learned from other veteran homeschool moms that homeschooled teens are not immune to "senioritis." Time and time again I've seen homeschool teens struggle to remain motivated that final year, especially if a decision on college has already been made.

A good approach is to make the senior year look different with an internship, travel abroad, a service project, or early start to college. Any of these can inject some life into your program and create a worthwhile opportunity to round out the résumé.

In the case of an apprenticeship, it may very well mean bypassing college altogether and going straight into the job market with a significant head start. Several young men we know did this, and it has turned out college just wasn't necessary. They have become successfully self-employed as a result.

PART 6

HOW TO DO THE HARD STUFF

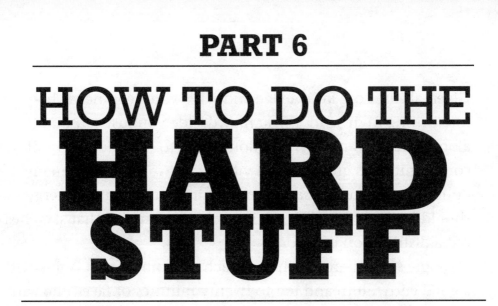

Bottom line: Doing high school at home is tough, and you may not be able to do it alone. And that's okay. It's in your teen's best interest to mix it up. She needs to figure out how she learns best, and a mixture of teaching approaches will help her develop flexibility and independence. In this section, we will look at different ways to lighten your load as the parent-teacher while still getting your teen through more difficult subject like physics, calculus, and foreign languages.

20 TUTORS AND MENTORS

Given all the core knowledge and skills your teen needs before exiting high school, you may decide you just can't do this alone. The good news is you don't have to. The homeschool community has grown into a vibrant network offering many options in any subject area. Your main investment of energy should be toward high-level, long-range planning that sketches out a distribution of labor.

Some subject areas you can teach on your own at home with a good curriculum and ten to twenty minutes of face time with your teen each day. For other subject areas, you may need to look to others for help to complete. How do you decide which subjects to teach and which to hand off? Start with your own passions and expertise. What subjects do you feel most competent to handle? What background experience do you bring to the table? Because I'm an English teacher by training, I didn't look for others to share the load in this area. Rather, I used this talent to barter with other parents for help in my areas of need.

If you don't have specialized training in any subject, do you have a particular area you find most interesting than others? Are you willing to become more knowledgeable in this area? Consider focusing your efforts to become more equipped to teach or lead an area so that you can barter with others for their expertise. I realized early on I was not going to be able to do it all well. So I invested my energy in developing several English courses and trusted God to provide people and resources to do the same in the other required subject areas.

HIRING A TUTOR

When it came time to hire a math tutor for my three older kids, I didn't start by at newspaper ads or visiting the local Sylvan Center. Instead, I jumped on a providential conversation with a friend of mine at church. In lamenting the difficulties I was having covering math with my then seventh-grade twins, my friend Carole mentioned that she loved math. Turned out she had majored in chemical engineering in college but switched to sociology her senior year because she wanted to finish quickly and get married. I asked if she had ever considered tutoring. Even though she had no experience, she was willing to give it a try. I offered her twenty dollars an hour for weekly tutoring for my twins together.

Together, Carole and I considered the available programs and selected Jacob's Elementary Algebra followed by Jacob's Geometry, which is today available with much better supplemental materials. Carole went on to tutor my sons through high school and also provide spot tutoring for Kayte, who didn't need as much support. She then provided tutoring for several other kids in our church using the same materials. She's still offering support in mathematics through our local homeschool co-op.

My daughter Kayte created a small business for herself as a tutor in math and French starting in tenth grade. She usually had one or two students each year. By the end of high school, she was being paid well for tutoring. She figured out how to set up a website and online forum and eventually offered her

247

services over the Internet. While in college, she tutored kids online, charging twenty-five dollars per half-hour session. With a great deal of effort, she could help a willing student work through an entire course of algebra 1 or geometry in a summer, but she doesn't recommend this approach—it's far too much math to master in so short a time.

If you don't already know someone who's qualified to tutor your teen, the best place to find a tutor is online or through your local homeschool community. Get plugged in. Post your need on local and state message boards. Ask others for their recommendations. Be the first to recognize a potential tutor in an older home-schooled teen and pitch him an offer he can't refuse. You may have to do a bit of hunting to find a good fit, but once you do, pay well enough to keep your tutor secured for all your kids.

> **The best place to find a tutor is online or through your local homeschool community.**

FINDING A MENTOR

Pairing your teen with a mentor is an arrangement less formal than that of hiring a tutor. You're not looking for a mentor to help your teen through a course of study or necessarily be paid for his or her services. Rather a mentor uses his or her training or area of expertise to support your teen's interest in a collaborative way. Is your daughter an amateur photographer? Then consider looking for a mentor through the local camera club, someone who might take her under wing and devote some time to helping her complete a special project. Is your son interested in software development? Is there someone in your church who does this on the job? Ask if he has an interest in developing a mentoring relationship. In my experience, many adults, especially homeschool parents, are willing to share their skills and passions with a teen that has a serious interest and a sense of appreciation for the person's time. In some cases, with some foresight on your part, a mentoring relationship begun early in high school can turn into a formal apprenticeship or a paid position for your teen.

To find a good tutor or mentor, start with a survey of your homeschool and church community. The best situation is a win-win arrangement, often possible with another home-schooler. Consider looking for someone who will tutor or mentor your child in exchange for your services—if you can't mentor or tutor their kids, can you clean or cook for them? Could this initial arrangement turn into an ongoing service for this homeschool parent as it did for our daughter? Don't hesitate to make this suggestion. And don't just look at adults. We routinely gave our older teens opportunities to tutor and teach in our homeschool community. Research has found that older students who tutor younger kids benefit academically from the arrangement as well.

21 HIGH SCHOOL CO-OPS

CHESS Family School was started in 1995 by my good friend Cindy McKeown, who was dissatisfied with her oldest son's high school experience at home. Essentially, he stayed in his room, working through difficult material alone while she worked with her younger children most days. His first year as an undergraduate in pre-med was very difficult as he just didn't have the necessary foundation in math and science. Fortunately, he had a work ethic and independent learning skills, so he still did well and today is a successful doctor.

Cindy wanted a better option for her remaining kids, so she recruited my help and we began investigating how other homeschoolers were sharing responsibilities through high school co-ops. We compared notes with others around the country who told us what worked and what didn't. The framework Cindy set in place continues to work exceedingly well today.

During the first year of the co-op, we offered only science and English because we had qualified teachers in those areas. Cindy knew from previous experience that we needed one mom just to handle administration, which she took on. We had fewer than fifty students at the beginning, and classes were over before lunch. Students had to go through an interview process with Cindy to be accepted. She was looking for a few things: Did the family's philosophy of education match ours? Was the student respectful and self-governing? And did the student— not just the parent—want to join classes? We still conduct an interview process, looking for this basic match.

We also ask that a family be sponsored by a current co-op family who knows the family well enough to provide a candid recommendation. We have far more families interested in joining than we can accommodate, so we find this screening system useful. As a result, discipline problems are rare and the list of written rules is minimal. I cannot emphasize enough how valuable this is to any culture—disagreements and disciplinary issues are almost always the primary cause of leadership burnout, and the fallout is often the disbanding of the co-op. If you want to be part of a co-op that will be there in the future, then take time to set up clear and appropriate standards for membership.

> **If you want to be part of a co-op that will be there in the future, then take time to set up clear and appropriate standards for membership.**

As qualified teachers joined our ranks—and we've learned from experience that the best teachers are homeschooling parents—we expanded our offerings to include a full day of classes in core subject areas for grades six through twelve. We have a scope and sequence in place so families can plan their high school work around our rotation. Our English classes cover grammar, composition, and literature. Our sciences include life science, earth science, physical science, biology, chemistry, physics, and advanced biology, all with a lab every other week. We also offer a consistent sequence of art, French, Spanish, math, computer science, and government courses.

251

Today we have nearly 200 students, twelve teachers, and two administrators. Students pay for classes, and teachers and administrators are paid. Volunteers head up our other programs, including yearbook, a graduation, girls' basketball team, and co-ed volleyball teams. Our drama club became so large that it is now its own entity. We provide a hot lunch every week, which parents take a turn providing. Teachers receive one free class per course taught and a lot of love and appreciation at our recognition night.

These kinds of co-ops around the country charge between $200 and $400 a course, plus materials, and CHESS is at the lower end of that scale. No one is making a living as CHESS teacher or administrator, but it's such a rewarding experience working with these students that a surprising number of teachers have stayed on after their own homeschooling years have ended.

The co-op required an enormous amount of time and effort at the beginning, especially for the founder, but now it runs like clockwork. And many families tell us that the organization is the main reason they continue to homeschool through high school. I know my kids believe they got a great education because of the quality of teachers at the co-op. All are passionate about their subjects and understand that the heart of homeschooling is to cultivate in kids a love for learning.

> If your homeschool community does not have a high-school-level co-op, consider what role you might play in starting one.

If your homeschool community does not have a high-school-level co-op, consider what role you might play in starting one. The co-op solved many challenges for me as a parent, providing a great place for my kids to socialize with their peers, fulfilling our need for quality science classes with labs, offering scholastic sports for our daughters, and motivating our teens to succeed because they were challenged by their peers and cared about pleasing their teachers. Plus, it practically eliminated the draw to attend public school.

The first two years of setting up the co-op proved very time-consuming. But because Cindy was thoughtful in starting small and building slowly, only adding classes when we had found the right teacher and putting an enrollment process in place that fostered a positive peer culture, I now anticipate the day when my own grandchildren will attend CHESS and my daughters or daughters-in-law may teach there. Cindy's sacrificial investment of her time on behalf of her own kids ended up providing a wonderful legacy for our entire homeschool community.

BLENDED SCHOOLING

The term co-op essentially implies equal degrees of cooperation and collaboration among member parents. However, in recent years, many high-school-level co-ops have become more structured and formalized, often meeting more than once a week. These "co-ops" combine aspects of homeschooling with elements of a traditional public school setting. Blended schooling—also known as the university model—is increasingly becoming the standard among cooperative efforts.

253

In my experience, such organizations begun by homeschooling families to meet their families' needs (and not primarily for profit) tend to retain the values of homeschooling—that is, they welcome involvement from parents and offer flexibility in choosing classes and activities. The advantage of blended schools is they provide structure and stability to your program. Disadvantages include an inability to modify classes to meet the individual needs of your teen, an overscheduled life, and perhaps more time with peers than is helpful to your teen.

The National Association of University-Model Schools (NAUMS) is an organization that has established a strong homeschool-oriented model as a blended-learning option at the high school level. Visit www.naums.net for more information.

Recommended Resource
Homeschool Co-ops: How to Start Them, Run Them and Not Burn Out by Carol Topp

22 DISTANCE LEARNING

Distance learning may be the most exciting development in home education today. It's opening whole new vistas, making home education possible for greater numbers of families. Online classes may end up costing more than traditional home-schooling, but it's still less expensive than private education. We used distance learning judiciously—as we did all the other methods suggested in this section—which helped us control our costs.

In the not-too-distant future, online learning will likely be a component of every course of study in high school and college. Almost all college textbooks now come with a supporting website with interactive work for students to complete without much direction from the professor.

Keep checking online and at your annual curriculum fair for the latest and greatest innovations in distance learning. You may find it a bit overwhelming culling through the many online options, so here are some recommendations and guidelines you might consider.

COMPATIBILITY

When considering an online course, the first thing you will need to determine is whether the format of the class is compatible with your teen's needs and learning style. Online classes may be delivered in synchronous or asynchronous time. They may be self-paced or scheduled. They may be highly interactive or not. They may make use of cutting-edge technology or be extremely basic in their design.

When considering an online course, the first thing you will need to determine is whether the format of the class is compatible with your teen's needs and learning style.

Synchronous means classes are held at a set time, with a "live" teacher leading the activities. This method allows for immediate feedback and a high level of interaction between learners and teacher. The disadvantage is your teen must be at the computer during the specific meeting time. This means a loss of flexibility in your scheduling, but some students do much better with this kind of set time commitment and direct access to the teacher.

Asynchronous time means students take the class at their convenience, checking the website for updates or feedback on class assignments. Students may be allowed to work through the material at their own pace, with instructor feedback provided as they submit work, or the instructor may set weekly deadlines for work to be submitted. I use asynchronous time for the online AP English classes I teach. I communicate weekly with students via e-mail and an online forum where students can post questions and discuss the literature we are reading. I also provide podcasts and video lecture. On the website I provide many helps and a class syllabus with due dates for weekly assignments. Feedback is not immediate, but typically I complete grading within a week and respond to e-mail questions within forty-eight hours. Student who thrive under this format tend to be more self-directed and want more flexibility in managing their schedules.

Online courses can also be *self-paced* or *scheduled*. In a self-paced course, the student can start a course online at any point during the year and work through a set curriculum at his own rate. A scheduled class, whether asynchronous or synchronous, is completed according to a prescribed schedule set by the teacher. The self-paced course is best for a student who needs maximum flexibility, does not care about interacting with other classmates, and is responsible enough to stay on task without enforced deadlines. A scheduled class provides a higher level of accountability and usually allows for interaction not just between teacher and student but also among the students themselves, so an online community of learners is created.

The course can also be *highly interactive* or relatively low-tech. Consider the kind of technology you will be using at your end. If you do not have high-speed Internet access and a powerful computer, then signing up for an online class that makes use of streaming media will prove counterproductive—you will be crashing your computer regularly or waiting forever for course content to download. On the other hand, if your equipment is up to date but the class interface is significantly behind the times, this may create an obstacle to learning.

257

TEACHER-STUDENT INTERACTION

Despite the advanced technology in use, this is still a teacher-led class, so explore these questions before you sign on: How often will the student receive feedback from the teacher? How quick is he or she to respond to e-mails? Is the instruction and feedback from the teacher concise and understandable? Can you expect commentary on assignments? How often will a grade report be sent? Considering the cost of the online class, is the availability of the teacher reasonable?

STUDENT-TO-STUDENT INTERACTION

Does the course website provide a means of communication among students, such as a forum where they can talk about the assignments and get to know one another? During class, can they see their peers' interaction with the instructor through a dialogue box or instant messaging? If students are able to interact with one another, then there is an opportunity to collaborate and the potential for learning is expanded. However, if these communications are not monitored or directed by the instructor, there is definite potential for problematic social exchanges.

WHERE IS THE CONTENT?

Where is the content in the online course you're considering? Is it on the website or in a textbook? Do students download materials and work on them with pen and paper? Or are they sitting at the computer to do all their work? Reading text online is very wearying if not presented well—and much of it isn't. I'd much rather see my kids print off their weekly assignments and work away from the computer screen. If kids do everything online, then where is the record of their work kept? Do you have hard copies or just a report of student scores? This is often not conducive to student learning. Kids need to take notes, review the text, make graphic organizers, and have tactile experiences. Online learning can be very flat and counterproductive to the retention of information. Take this into consideration when choosing a course, especially if you are signing up for several that will be conducted exclusively online.

AFFORDABILITY

Distance learning can be very expensive, and often the cost does not equate with the value of the course. If you are taking an online class that gives college credit, then it should be no more expensive than what you would pay to earn course credits at a physical institution. Unfortunately, the convenience of completing the work at home has driven up the prices of online classes in recent years. Interactive high school courses now run close to $400 or more for a full-year course. You will find college-level work in the $500 range and above. Before making a commitment, remember to add the cost of textbooks and other course material to the listed tuition. These can add another $100 or more, unless they are widely available in used condition. And if you are completing the work for college credit, be sure the credit will transfer if you need it to.

ACCOUNTABILITY

It's been my experience (with my own kids) that even responsible teens can become less responsible in an online environment. When taking a distance-learning course, kids can fall pretty far behind before a parent becomes aware of the situation. Online teachers cannot provide the same level of

> **When taking a distance-learning course, kids can fall pretty far behind before a parent becomes aware of the situation.**

259

accountability as an instructor in a live classroom or co-op. So what level of accountability are you willing to provide?

Even if the course in question provides access to your teen's coursework or an online grade book, you still must remember to stay current with this information if you are concerned about your teen's diligence. If you register your student for online classes through a college, you will not have access to the course unless your teen allows you access through his account. Therefore, you should work this out in advance.

If the ease of distance learning beckons, I suggest putting some safeguards in place to ensure that students keep up with their work.

SUITABILITY

Is your teen's personality suited for distance learning? All of my kids completed several distance-learning courses in high school, but only Kayte preferred this format. An autonomous and self-directed child, she didn't require a lot of interaction with her peers, and in collaborative situations, she often found that the others would let her do all the work. Kayte enjoyed interacting online with an enthusiastic instructor and would stand out as one of the more motivated students, whereas in a live class-room she was quieter than her fellow students and faded easily into the background. My other three children participated in online courses in high school and college because of the conve-nience, but they all performed better in a live classroom or in collaboration with peers. Gabe and Mike, for example, found it easy to miss deadlines and procrastinate with online assign-ments—something they never did in a classroom environment and rarely at home with me. The impersonal nature of online learning seemed to de-motivate and frustrate them.

Likewise, I have found that the outstanding students in my online courses are often quiet and reserved by nature. Their parents have reported that these teens seem to come alive online, and that my online class was among their favorite

> My observation has been that online learning often works best for kids who don't stand out in more conventional settings.

high school experiences. My observation has been that online learning often works best for kids who don't stand out in more conventional settings. Distance learning also works well with students who are underachieving and unmotivated in other environments.

That said, I urge you to jump in and try distance learning. Eventually all modes of education will have an online component, whether it is a supporting website, forum, e-mail, or test bank. Therefore, kids may want to get used to this rapidly evolving aspect of learning if they plan to continue their education after high school. Check the refund policy for the online classes you're considering, and then try one that seems promising. If it's a disaster, you can always drop it.

Recommended Distance Learning Providers

Write at Home (www.writeathome.com) provides writing classes in asynchronous time. Every student has a personal writing coach.

The Potter's School (www.pottersschool.org) provides a full range of high-school-level classes in synchronous time led by qualified teachers. Courses meet weekly for ninety minutes and include whiteboard demonstrations and live chats. To accommodate families with low bandwidth, video instruction is kept to a minimum. The original heartbeat of Potter's School was to meet the needs of missionary families living abroad, and it continues to have this flavor, which I think adds to the value of the experience for all kids. And for a teacher-led online course from a Christian worldview, Potter's School's price structure is very reasonable.

261

Apologia Academy (www.apologiaacademy.com) is the online learning branch of Apologia Educational Ministries. Apologia Academy offers college-preparatory science (including advanced science), Bible, apologetics, and Christian worldview courses through a dynamic, virtual classroom experience that combines outstanding curriculum, experienced teachers, and the latest Internet technology.

NorthStar Academy (www.northstar-academy.org) provides a full range of teacher-led high school classes in asynchronous time, as well as a diploma program. Families can elect to register for a full year of classes and work toward the accredited diploma, or just take a few courses as needed to augment their homeschool program. NorthStar Academy is organized as an online Christian school, but it was founded by a homeschooling family and is willing to work with families in a flexible manner. The refund policy—a full refund anytime during first three weeks of classes—is about the best you will find on the Internet.

Apex Learning (www.apexlearning.com) provides self-paced college preparatory high school courses and Advanced Placement review classes. The curriculum is presented digitally without a teacher. The courses are expensive, but state-of-the-art presentation of material and depth of content make it worth considering.

Pennsylvania Homeschoolers (www.pahomeschoolers.com) provides SAT essay prep and an extensive slate of AP classes with qualified teachers exclusively for homeschooled students. On the website you will find enthusiastic reviews of their teachers from past students.

Escondido Tutorial Service (www.gbt.org). Fritz Hinrichs has been providing Great Books tutorial services since 1993 and has expanded to allow other tutors to offer classes with a classical Christian emphasis through his site. ETS has recently added whiteboard, audio, and video capabilities. Classes meet at a scheduled time for two-hour blocks. Visit the site for the best listing of classical Christian instruction on the Internet.

23 SELF-INSTRUCTION

Self-directed kids can work independently of a teacher if you provide them with well-designed resources that guide student learning. Video courses and interactive software programs are the most obvious choices in this area, though some curriculum embeds instruction in the student materials, as in those from Saxon Math and the Institute for Excellence in Writing.

Of course, you will need to provide a measure of accountability for most students, as it is easy to just slide by with this approach. You can position your teen for success by using self-instructional material by helping her set up a year-long plan with deadlines and clear rewards for staying on pace. Go back to the chapter on how teens learn and implement some of the strategies covered there, such as preparing for a SAT II subject area test as the end goal or completing a research project or paper that will be presented to a group. You need to plan to monitor progress weekly to make sure your teen does not fall behind.

I tended to look for self-instructional materials my older kids could use while I was working with a younger child. In doing my high-school-level planning for a year, I'd pencil in what I was doing during each time block, just to make sure I wasn't scheduled to work with Kristen on reading at the same time my sons might need me to explain their math lesson. The best place to use self-instructional material is in a subject area of strength for your teen.

Recommended Resources

The Teaching Company (www.teach12.com) has found the most engaging professors on college campuses today and packaged their lectures on DVDs, CDs, and MP3 files. Workbooks are provided for high-school-level courses. You will need to add assignments or other resources to round out the coursework, but you can use these fascinating lectures as your core content. The Teaching Company runs monthly sales offering significant savings, and everything is on sale at least once during the year, so get on their mailing list and wait for the courses you are interested in to be offered at a discount. You need to exercise discretion in some subject areas, such as modern literature and psychology, as these can contain mature content.

Chalk Dust video courses on DVD feature Dana Mosley's lectures accompanying Ron Larson's highly regarded high school mathematics courses. Visit www.chalkdust.com.

Teaching Textbooks by the Sabouri brothers have improved upon Chalk Dust's idea by developing self-instructional mathematics courses that include a textbook and companion CD with step-by-step instruction for all the lessons and problems. Visit www.teachingtextbooks.com.

Rosetta Stone offers foreign language instruction in a box. Courses assume students are primarily interested in learning to speak the language, though they also include listening, reading, writing and some grammar. Every language is available in Level 1 through Level 3, and all

265

student work is completed online. Visit www.rosettastone.com.

Learner.org is the web portal for Annenberg Media, which has made many of their video courses available free online. Some of these are now dated, but the content is still accurate. I use these segments in my online courses and other teaching situations. You will find streaming video for many courses you will want your teen to cover in high school. Use these to design an entire credit course or as a supplemental resource.

PART 7

COLLEGE CREDIT @HOME

24 EARNING CREDITS DURING HIGH SCHOOL

If your teen is ready to do college-level work during high school, then this may be the wisest investment of his and your time. The key to determining your teen's readiness is assessing his reading level. Hand him a college textbook and see if he understands what he's reading. Talk with him about the content to make sure. Note how long it takes him to complete a chapter and you should be able to determine if he's reading quickly enough to complete the course within the allotted time. You can expect a college-level course to require a time commitment of about ten hours a week.

> If your teen is ready to do college-level work during high school, then this may be the wisest investment of his and your time.

If your teen has tested beyond high school on a standardized test in reading or math, or scored 1100 on the verbal and quantitative portions of the SAT or 26 on the ACT, this too can be an indicator that your teen is ready to do college-level coursework.

College work performed in high school may result in earning either credit or advanced standing. Credit is worth the most as it actually counts towards a particular degree at an institution. Advanced standing does not award credit, thus does not bring you closer to a degree, but it allows the student to register for upper-level classes in the same subject area. This has some value in providing a student greater flexibility in scheduling. Kayte received junior standing in French (usually reserved for students with 60 undergraduate credits completed) and this gave her access to a greater number of courses on the schedule. This allowed her to put together a schedule that enabled her to complete a pair of degrees—French and mathematics—in four years. She completed a minor in Arabic as well.

There are several ways to earn college credit or advanced standing during high school:

* Take classes at a local college that admit high school students.
* Take equivalency exams, such as the AP or CLEP exams.
* Achieve the baseline for exemption on the College Board exams.

Each of our four children earned college credit during high school, which gave them the flexibility to study abroad, complete dual majors, or graduate early (thus saving thousands of dollars in tuition). Kayte earned forty college credits during high school. She sacrificed a significant part of her social life to do so, but she was highly motivated—she had a lot of ambition and a small budget. Here's how she did it:

271

Source of High School Work	Credits Awarded by Pitt*
AP French Exam—score 4	3 credits (1 class)
AP European History Exam—score 5	6 credits (2 req. courses)
AP U.S. History Exam—score 5	6 credits (2 req. courses)
AP Psychology Exam—score 5	3 credits (1 req. course)
AP English Literature Exam—score 5, plus exceeding 700 on verbal section of SAT	6 credits (2 req. English courses)
French 1 & 2 @ four-year university**	6 credits transferred into Pitt
Exceeded 700 on math section of SAT	3 credit exemption
Studied abroad in France ***	6 credits transferred into Pitt
Score on Pitt's French placement exam	Exemption from a 4-credit required course

* Each institution determines what credit or advance standing it will award for work completed during high school. This varies greatly. Once we knew the University of Pittsburgh was a top choice for Kayte, she used the list available on their website to select her AP courses.

** Completed at half-price tuition rate offered to area high school students.

*** This was the most expensive decision. During her studies abroad during college, Kayte was allowed to apply her scholarship awards to the fees. Here we had to pay full price out of pocket, but it got this requirement out of the way so she could study abroad elsewhere (Cairo) during college.

THINK OF YOUR CHILD FIRST

Before you dive into a plan to knock off college coursework during high school, you need to think first of your child, not the potential savings to you. Our other three kids each transferred in six credits of college work from their high school studies—a manageable amount of advanced work that didn't make them miserable in the process. Kayte, however, asked to take a shot at the SAT in eighth grade. Her brothers had taken them in seventh as part of a talent search program, which seemed unnecessary and too expensive in hindsight. But she asked, and I agreed. I was pretty surprised by how well she scored, and I realized she was a good test-taker. Kayte actually had to work quite hard at her studies, but these scores showed me she was capable of hitting the benchmarks necessary for scholarship consideration. I talked to Kermit about this, and he endorsed a plan that allowed Kayte to build a résumé in high school that resulted in full-tuition scholarship offers from the universities she applied to.

Keep in mind:

1. Your teen needs to have a work ethic and must be willing to tackle advanced work.
2. College credit is never free of charge. You will have to spend some money in high school.

In the following chapters I will show you how to exercise your student's options for earning college credit during the high school years.

273

25 DUAL ENROLLMENT

In many places universities and community colleges are now actively recruiting homeschooled teens. When high school students take a college-level class that counts towards their high school diploma *and* earns them credit towards a college degree, this is referred to as *dual enrollment*. In some states—Florida and Minnesota, for instance—tuition is even waived for high school students who exercise this option. This is a growing trend, so keep an eye on your state legislature's activity in this regard. Researchers are finding that students who complete dual enrollment work have higher college graduation rates, so there is a push to make this option available nationally.

The first step toward planning for dual enrollment classes is to find out what the policy is for institutions in your area. And if you don't think their policy is affordable or homeschool-friendly, then begin a campaign to get that changed. If you are amiable and informative, you might be surprised by the response. Initially, colleges in our area were reticent about admitting homeschooled high school students, but once a few institutions began offering free or discounted classes to home-schooled students, others quickly followed suit. Most institutions still will not admit high school students prior to their junior year, but it's not unheard of.

If your teen has her eye on an institution with a favorable dual enrollment policy, then script this into your four-year plan. If she's had little experience in a classroom setting outside the homeschool community, it might be best for her to take just one course the first time around, perhaps enrolling with a friend. Some culture shock is inevitable, and a full slate of classes right from the start may be too much of a transition. If you know other homeschoolers who have exercised this option, then solicit their guidance. They may already know which courses and professors are worth seeking out.

If your teen has a choice between taking classes at a four-year university and a two-year college, and money is not an issue, choose the university. The credits will transfer more easily, and a top grade from a course there will be weighted more favorably by scholarship and admissions committees than a top grade from a two-year school. However, you want to select the option where your child will be able to do his best.

If cost is a factor—that is, if the community college is free and the four-year university is not—but your teen wants to build a scholarship-ready résumé, then he should take just one course at the four-year institution, preferably in a major area of interest. Take any others at the community college. Make sure your child understands that he needs to make getting a top grade (and perhaps a recommendation letter from the university-level instructor) his highest priority.

The hardest lesson I had to learn in regard to dual enrollment work is that *homeschool*

> The hardest lesson I had to learn in regard to dual enrollment work is that homeschool parents must neither be seen nor heard. The student must do all the interfacing with the instructor.

275

parents must neither be seen nor heard. The student must do all the interfacing with the instructor. It was fine if I wanted to talk to admissions or, more importantly, pay the bill. But professors consider students to be autonomous individuals with no human attachments of significance. The attitude irks me, but in the end, it is probably best for teens to learn how to navigate their own academic issues, with their parents advising loudly from the sidelines.

Dual Benefits

One concern most parents of college-prep students have is making sure their children will be prepared to adjust to college life. A study was done that showed students who went away for their first year of college were significantly less likely to ever finish college than those who lived at home their first year. Apparently the sheer quantity of stuff kids have to learn, from classroom lessons and scheduling their day to how to get their laundry done and stock up on shampoo, can be overwhelming and they just give up.

Lots of kids manage to stick it out and graduate, but this survey impressed me with how helpful it's been for my son to take dual-credit classes at a community college. While still living at home, he has nothing "new" to conquer except the actual class material. In order to experience multiple subject classes before going off to college, my son took one community college class the first semester, then two the second semester. Taking a variety of classes taught him to balance the requirements of different coursework, which is part of a successful college career.

Sylvia Starger
Moderator of the Yahoo! group homeschool2college

TRANSFERRING CREDITS

If your teen is not planning to complete a degree at the school where she is taking dual enrollment classes, then you need to consider which classes will transfer most readily to the institution she does plan to attend. If you have a good idea where this will be, then e-mail the school's admissions office for advice in course selection.

If you don't know where you will need the credits to transfer, your student's best bet is to take the most common general education requirements—English composition, literature, history, economics, psychology, speech, lab science, and college algebra. Or if you know the major your teen will pursue, have her take introductory classes in that subject. The more your teen can narrow her list of possible colleges or possible choices of majors before taking courses, the better.

Each department within an institution decides for itself which transfer credits they will accept, so your teen should *always* keep the syllabus from any college coursework completed while in high school. This is how colleges determine

> **Your teen should always keep the syllabus from any college coursework completed while in high school.**

whether or not the class a student has taken correlates with a course they offer. Even so, this may not be foolproof. Kayte did everything she was told to do by Pitt to transfer credits from her summer studies in France, but in the meantime, Pitt's French department dropped one of the courses she was seeking exemption from. Pitt accepted those three credits as an elective, but the French department did not count it toward the completion of her major. Therefore, it didn't really help her gain any ground.

You have to remember that when a university accepts trans-

277

fer credits, they give up the fees you would have paid them for these. They don't have a lot of incentive to generously accept another institution's credits. Yet everything is negotiable. Just because credits are initially rejected for transfer doesn't mean you should not continue to press your case (or have your teen press his case) with a department head or higher governing body at the university.

Some institutions give you the option of completing an associate's degree concurrent with completing your teen's junior and senior years of high school. This is a tremendous opportunity, especially if you live in a state where dual enrollment is free or discounted. Your teen can then transfer to a four-year institution and be able to complete a B.S. or B.A. with just two more years of work. And the fact that the legislature has worked out this arrangement for you means credits should transfer without incident.

I've often had questions from parents worried about earning too many credits at home and risking scholarship opportunities. Your teen can earn as many credits as he wants through any means possible *before* graduating high school. Kayte transferred in forty credits, while a good friend of hers completed more than sixty college credits in high school. The key is to check "Incoming Freshman" on the application, not "Transfer Student." There is considerably less scholarship money available to transfer students than to incoming freshman. Most universities consider a student a transfer student if the student earned credits at another institution *after* high school graduation.

26 ADVANCED PLACEMENT (AP)

Advanced Placement is the rapidly growing brainchild of the College Board, offering exams in thirty-seven subjects corresponding to the most commonly offered college courses. The exams are given at set dates and times in early May and must be administered by an approved AP proctor, typically a high school guidance counselor. The exam schedule can be found at the College Board's website, www.collegeboard.com.

REGISTRATION

As of this writing, each exam costs $86. You may have to pay an additional fee to the proctor for her time and service. To register for a particular test, you will need to find which schools in your vicinity are offering that test and request permission to take the exam at their site. The College Board urges, but does not require, exam sites to allow students not enrolled in their school to sit for the exam. The College Board will supply you with a list of schools in your area offering the exam your student is interested in taking. My online students have found private schools more accommodating than public schools.

SCORING

AP exams are scored on a scale of 1 to 5, with 3 considered a passing score by most public institutions. A score of 4 or 5 may be required to receive credit at the more elite universities. The institution determines what the passing score will be for credit, if any, in a given subject area. Information about various institutions' AP policy can be found on the school's website or at http://apcentral.collegeboard.com.

SELF-STUDY VS. TAKING AN AP COURSE

Your teen does not have to complete an AP course in order to take the exam, but studies have shown that a higher percentage of students pass the exam after completing a yearlong subject-specific AP course. Exams are three hours long and rigorous, and the material is based on course content taught at top universities. Students who earn a high score on an AP exam through self-study have generally been working in that subject area at the college level already.

> A motivated student with the right resources can prepare on his own for these exams and score well.

With that said, a motivated student with the right resources can prepare on his own for these exams and score well. Course descriptions and past exam questions and essay prompts can be downloaded at the College Board's AP site for students. I recommend your student use a combination of review materials from Barron's, Princeton Review, and McGraw-Hill's 5 Steps to a 5 series. Plus, it's a good idea to actually work through the subject using a college-level text—you don't want your teen to place into a higher-level course in college without truly having a sound foundation in the subject.

More students, however, will benefit from taking a course

designed specifically to cover the Advanced Placement course outline. Keep in mind that, as of 2007–08, schools and home-schoolers may not use the AP trademark to identify a course on a high school transcript without first submitting the course syllabus to the College Board for approval.

The most established place for homeschooled students to find AP courses online is through Howard and Susan Richman at PA Homeschoolers (www.pahomeschoolers.com). These homeschool pioneers have been offering AP classes since 1995 and have figured out how to do this well. Most of their teach-ers have a master's degree or PhD in the content area, and the Richmans provide a great deal of support.

AP COURSES VS. COLLEGE COURSES

You may find that a local community college is offering a course whose content correlates with a subject-specific AP exam. If so, you will need to decide whether this is a better op-portunity for your teen than taking an actual AP course. The advantage of the college course is that your teen is likely to pass the class. The risk of an AP class is that credit will only be earned if your teen achieves a qualifying score on the exam. So why even consider taking an AP course instead of the college course? Here are a few reasons:

* High scores on an AP exam are weighted highly by schol-arship committees.

* AP coursework is considered more rigorous than com-munity college coursework and is viewed favorably by admissions committees.

* AP credit policy is clearly delineated on the school's web-site, so you know whether the credit will transfer or not, whereas transfer credits from another institution must be reviewed on a case-by-case basis.

281

* AP exams are relatively inexpensive compared to the cost of taking a college course.

* If an AP course is taken online, then it is probably more convenient than driving regularly to the local college.

* Your child may be academically ready for the advanced work, yet not be ready for a college setting.

As for comparing AP credit to transfer credits from a four-year institution, this is a toss-up. Admissions committees will view both of these favorably, especially if a student earns a 4 or 5 on an exam or an A in a college course. As far as scholarship committees are concerned, some view high AP scores with greater distinction, while others see an A from a four-year institution with a rigorous reputation as having greater distinction. Most weight them equally.

OTHER CONSIDERATIONS

Listing an AP course on the transcript really doesn't buy your teen much in terms of scholarship consideration. The student's exam score is what matters most. Because college applications are submitted fall of the senior year, only your teen's scores from exams taken in tenth and eleventh grade will be available. So your teen should take those AP exams he is likely to perform best on first, then save the more challenging subjects for his senior year. Also keep in mind:

282

* It's better to take just one AP exam and earn a 4 or 5 than to take several AP exams and not do as well.

* All exams are given during a two-week period in May, so don't load your teen with too many AP courses in one year. Look over the exam schedule in advance. Several

exams are given on the same day, so you need to be sure your teen will be able to handle the actual exam schedule. Taking two AP exams on the same day is not the ideal scenario. The schedule is relatively stable, so consider taking exams scheduled for the same day in different years.

* Students rarely find it profitable to take an AP exam prior to tenth grade. I accept only juniors and seniors into my AP literature course—younger students are just not ready to talk about the serious themes we discuss, nor have they had enough time to do the background reading expected. I do accept sophomores into my AP language course. These are tough courses, and emotional maturity is just as important as intellectual ability. Your teen must be willing to accept critique without offense.

* I have found highly motivated and capable teens can handle one AP course in tenth, two in eleventh, and three in twelfth. I've known teens that have tackled more, but only a handful in twenty years who achieved high scores consistently on all exams.

* Loading a student up with a full slate of online AP courses in a single year is probably not a good plan. It's really far more reading than is humanly possible for most students.

283

Recommended Resources

5 Steps to a 5 is a test-specific series from McGraw-Hill written by experienced AP teachers and AP readers who've scored past exams.

27 CLEP EXAMS

The College-Level Examination Program (CLEP) is another type of equivalency testing you can use to earn college credit inexpensively. The College Board creates both the CLEP and the AP exams. So what's the difference between CLEP and AP exams? Here's the bottom line:

* AP exams are more prestigious and should be used if you are looking for scholarship money.

* CLEP exams are less rigorous, shorter, and less expensive, currently costing $77 per exam.

* CLEP exams can be taken anytime at an approved test site, whereas AP exams are given on a fixed date once a year.

* AP exams can only be taken during high school, whereas CLEP exams can be taken during high school or college.

Here's a rundown on how to use the CLEP tests to your advantage. If your kid is potential scholarship material, then consider having her take AP exams in strength areas to show her academic potential. Once you've got what you need for scholarship consideration, round out her credits with CLEP exams.

If she's a solid student but not scholarship material, then forego AP exams and jump straight into CLEP testing. The beauty of CLEP exams, as compared to AP exams, is they can be taken anytime in your life. AP exams are only for high school students. For instance, my sons took a CLEP exam in marketing right before their senior year of college as part of a four-year plan that allowed for multiple study-abroad experiences and on-time graduation. With all the other business coursework under their belts at that point, they studied for a weekend with the Official CLEP Study Guide and earned a passing score easily.

> The beauty of CLEP exams, as compared to AP exams, is they can be taken anytime in your life.

Currently, CLEP exams offered in thirty-two subjects, a list of which can be found at www.collegeboard.com. Some of the English and mathematics exams will duplicate material, so make sure a CLEP exam correlates to a degree requirement at your teen's school of choice. Check out the college's website for its policies regarding CLEP exams.

CLEP tests are ninety minutes in length and can be taken anytime at a test center, usually on a college campus. The test is multiple choice and administered on a computer, except for the English Composition exam, which includes a hand-scored essay. Test results are immediately received at the conclusion of the session. If the student does not earn a passing score, he must wait six months to test again. Homeschooled teens I've known have had no trouble passing a CLEP exam after a good high school science or history course, but some students will benefit from taking the exam while enrolled in college.

Use the chart below to help you determine the best way for

285

your teen to accumulate college credits during the high school years.

	AP Credits	Synchronous Online Class	Asynchronous Online Class	Community College	4-Year College	CLEP
Cost						
Time						
Difficulty						
Maturity Required						
Prestige						

28 EARNING A COLLEGE DEGREE AT HOME

A growing phenomenon—and not just among homeschoolers—involves earning a college degree entirely through distance learning. I see two reasons why this is happening:

1. The rapid growth of the Internet has made learning much more accessible and interactive, so the quality of online coursework has elevated.

2. The cost of a brick-and-mortar college education has skyrocketed.

Students are looking for a fast track to earning a qualified degree while working a job and without piling up a lot of loan debt.

Twenty years ago, companies that offered distance education options were snidely called "diploma mills," and a degree through such an institution was often considered worthless, if not fraudulent. But that stigma is being left in the dust as more and more non-traditional students are exploring this avenue to a four-year degree. Fraudulent organizations are still out there, however, so it's important to investigate any organization's accreditation and authenticity.

Thomas Edison State College (www.tesc.edu) is one reputable school through which you can compile a four-year degree through a combination of CLEP exams, online coursework, and work experiences.

The best website for sorting through all your distance education options is eLearners.com. Another helpful site is College Plus! (www.collegeplus.org) which is run by homeschool graduates who have completed college via distance learning. You can now hire them to coach your teen through the process. They have worked out arrangements with several institutions, making the transfer of credits much smoother.

You will want to consider whether your child may want to transfer any of these credits later to a brick-and-mortar institution or use her distance learning degree to pursue further education. At this point, most colleges and universities accept AP and CLEP credits as well as distance learning credits from other brick-and-mortar universities, but they may not accept credit transfers from institutions (such as the University of Phoenix) that are solely virtual.

While homeschooling her teenage daughters and teaching a full slate of science classes at the co-op, my good friend Vicki earned a Master's of Science degree in biology online from the University of Nebraska. It took Vicki two and a half years to complete the thirty-six credits required for the degree. She watched course lectures on DVD or online while her girls were watching lectures for their own high school coursework. She often had to watch the lectures in segments, hitting pause when her girls needed help or the laundry cycle had finished. She wrote her papers while her girls were at field hockey practice. It's never too late to learn!

Home Colleging

One afternoon my brother, who was thirteen at the time, asked from the back seat of our car, "Hey Mom, can you home *college* us?" My mother wondered where this was coming from. After all, no one 'home colleges.' Our extended family thought we were strange enough. Now we were talking about keeping the kids home for an extra four years?!

Some years later a friend told us about a program through which a student could earn a Bachelor's Degree in eighteen months for less than $12,000. I was thinking, *Yeah right. That's going to earn you an accredited diploma that employers will accept?* As it turned out, my friend not only graduated high school and college in the same year, but he used his business degree to land a position as a tour manager for a national company.

Not long after, we enrolled in CollegePlus! and began our own collegiate trek. I simply can't say enough about this company. I have enjoyed every minute. When you enroll, you get assigned to a coach. The staff members pray about these assignments and match you as best they can according to major, personality, and stated life goals. Guys are assigned male coaches, and girls are paired with female counselors. These coaches were once CollegePlus! students themselves, so they can guide students from personal experience and offer godly counsel.

What's fantastic about this program is that your scholastic schedule can ebb and flow to fit job, family, and vacation schedules. I was able to accumulate 66 credits, direct a stop-motion animation film, teach a public speaking course, judge at multiple speech tournaments across the country, *and* take a family vacation—all in just a year and a half!

Jessica Rondina
Entrepreneur and 'home college' student
www.shatterpointentertainment.com

PART 8

RECORD
KEEPING

29 AWARDING CREDITS AND GRADES

While planning your high school program, you need to know your state's standards for awarding credit toward graduation for your teen. Keep these questions in mind:

* What required courses must be completed?
* How much work in each subject must be covered to earn a credit?
* How many total credits of work must be accumulated before I can award my child a diploma?

In some states the answers to these questions will be spelled out in a homeschool law or school code. In other states, there are no specific legal requirements, so you will have a certain freedom to make these decisions.

Again, you will need to work backwards from your teen's educational goals. Is he planning to attend college? Will she immediately enter the workforce? Does he plan to go to a trade school? Remember that many colleges and universities have a published list of coursework they want to see on an applicant's transcript, so don't forget to review websites for this information. And this coursework can vary from department to department, so check the requirements for the field of study your teen plans to enter.

The methods for determining high school credits can vary from state to state. For the purposes of discussion in this book I'm using the Carnegie Unit as my standard:

Full-year course, or 120 hours of instruction = 1 credit
One-semester course, or 60 hours of instruction = 0.5 credit

Keep in mind that in order to compile 120 hours of instructional time, your "class" must meet an average of five times per week for about fifty minutes each for a total of thirty weeks.

Here's a list of the most common high school requirements. Remember to check your state law, as requirements can vary:

* 4 credits in English or language arts
* 3 credits in social studies (these courses are often specified and usually include U.S. history and government)
* 3 credits in mathematics (algebra 1 and higher)
* 3 credits in science, including two lab sciences
* 2 credits in the same *living* foreign language (not Latin)
* 1 to 4 credits of physical education
* ½ credit of health
* 5 or more credits of electives (speech, art, music, or technology)

293

The total amount of credits needed for a high school diploma ranges from twenty to twenty-four now in almost all states. If you want your teen to be considered for merit scholarship awards, then completing *more* than the minimum requirements is essential. Each of our kids earned between twenty-four and twenty-six credits. If you award too many credits at home, admissions officers may question whether or not you devoted enough time to each subject. If the credits come from outside sources, such as a community college, this likely won't be a problem.

HOW MUCH WORK?

Decide with your teen how many credits will need to be completed in each subject before you will graduate him or her from high school. Then determine how much work will equal a credit. You can measure coursework in several different ways. Here are a few.

Count Hours

In using the traditional Carnegie Unit (120 hours of instruction = 1 credit) I counted 120 hours of time on task, as opposed to hours in the "classroom." For instance, the year our homeschool co-op mounted its first musical and Kristen had the lead role, she was involved in rehearsals and individual preparation for her role in excess of 120 hours, so I translated that experience into a half credit of drama and a half credit of music on her transcript. For the college-bound student, this is a good rule of thumb for non-core subjects, such as electives. In core areas, all but the brightest of kids will need more than 120 hours of time on task to make sufficient progress.

> In core areas, all but the brightest of kids will need more than 120 hours of time on task to make sufficient progress.

Count Days

Another method is to require a certain number of days of daily lessons, no matter how long a lesson may take. In the Pennsylvania homeschool diploma program in which we participated, 120 days (or more) of lessons could be counted toward one credit. I used this rule just to know when we really didn't need to be concerned further about meeting a minimum requirement.

Count Work

In the core subject areas crucial to college success, this method of tracking work is probably the best way to serve your teen's long-term interests. My advice is to establish a contractual relationship with your teen before the course begins, laying out the amount and quality of work necessary to earn the credit and a passing grade. Here are examples:

American Literature: Honors

* Complete two-thirds of BJU American Literature anthology, with selected assignments
* Read seven additional texts from the American literary tradition, including *The Scarlet Letter, Adventures of Huckleberry Finn* and *The Great Gatsby*
* Write three analytical essays
* Write one research paper of 2500 words or more, with a bibliography citing at least five sources
* Complete mid-term and final tests with scores of 80% or higher
* Complete one creative project, with a 10- to 15-minute presentation

American Literature: Standard

* Complete two-thirds of BJU American Literature anthology, with selected assignments
* Complete mid-term and final tests with scores of 70% or higher
* Write one research paper of 2500 words or more, with a bibliography citing at least three sources

World History

* Complete an independent study of seven eras/civilizations of human history, from Ancient Egypt, Ancient Greece, Ancient Rome, the Dark Ages, the Middle Ages, Renaissance, the Age of Exploration and Colonization, the Industrial Age, World Wars, the Space Age, and Globalization
* Maintain a bibliography of books read and websites consulted for study
* Watch at least five documentaries on related topics
* Write at least one overview of the major developments of each era
* Complete two creative projects, each with a 10- to 15-minute presentation
* Visit at least two museums with related exhibits
* Create a portfolio of work completed for final evaluation

Mix-and-Match

Choose three to five of the following options to create a credit-by-contract agreement for a given subject area:

* Read two-thirds of a selected textbook
* Read five to ten non-fiction books on selected topics
* Read majority of content at five to ten authoritative websites
* Watch five to ten documentaries on selected topics
* Visit two to three exhibitions on related topics
* Design five to ten graphic organizers on related topics
* Design two to three triptych displays on related topics
* Design one or two creative projects, each with a 10- to 15-minute presentation
* Create a map or timeline displaying course content
* Write three analytical papers on a related topic

* Write one research paper of 2500 words or more, with bibliography
* Write seven to ten reports on topics related to the subject
* Give a speech on a topic related to the subject

You could consider a course "Honors" if the student completes seven of these options.

DETERMINING GRADES

Grades need to be assigned on the high school transcript so that admissions offices have an assessment of the student's achievement in terms they understand. In order for grades to also be meaningful and motivational for teens, the standards for evaluation should be determined ahead of time, enabling the student to control the outcome. The easiest way to do this is to establish the grading scale and scoring rubric for major assignments ahead of time.

Grading scales can vary. Here's mine:

97–100	A+
94–96	A
90–93	A-
87–89	B+
84–86	B
80–83	B-
77–79	C+
74–76	C
70–73	C-
67–69	D+
64–66	D
60–63	D
0–59	F

In most cases, I require a passing grade on an assignment before moving on, so students need to retest or resubmit their work if they do not achieve a 70 percent or higher. This scale allows me to point out several areas in a student's work that need improvement, while still allowing a generous range for assigning a successful grade.

If only letter grades are reported on your transcript, and not percentages, then the grading scale should appear somewhere on the transcript as a key to how grades were determined.

CALCULATING GRADE POINT AVERAGE (GPA)

This is a number college admissions office will care a lot about, so it's important that your calculation accurately reflects your teen's achievement in the best light. Because high schools use a variety of methods for calculating the GPA, some colleges take the transcript and throw the data provided into their own GPA calculator in order to put everyone on the equal footing.

The first thing you need to do is convert letter grades to a numeric scale. Here is the scale commonly used to do that:

A+ 4.0

A   4.0

A- 3.67

B+ 3.33

B   3.0

B- 2.67

C+ 2.33

C   2.0

C- 1.67

D+ 1.33

D   1.0

D- .67

There are two types of GPAs—overall and academic only:

Overall GPA

1. Convert letter grades into numbers and add.
2. Add up the number of credits awarded
3. Divide the sum for grades earned by the sum for credits awarded.
4. This is the student's overall GPA.

Academic GPA

Follow the steps above, but only count the core classes. Do not include electives, such as art, music, and physical education.

You can find GPA calculators online to help you do this.

DO YOU NEED TO GIVE GRADES?

Not really. Grades are not a requirement for graduation in any state I know of. If you want to determine credit according to a pass/fail standard or any other method, that is your prerogative. However, if you are compiling a transcript primarily for college admissions, a lack of grades on the transcript will complicate the acceptance process. Any institution you apply to will ask you to explain how work was evaluated, and additional documentation will probably be requested. Some schools are progressive and will consider a portfolio of the student's work as an alternative, and they may even think it's pretty cool that you're philosophically opposed to grading. Others will simply overlook the ungraded transcript and focus solely on your teen's scores on the entrance exams. So consider the ramifications of going the no-grades route and decide if this is the proverbial hill on which you wish to stand your ground.

30 TRANSCRIPTS RECORDS AND DIPLOMAS

Before I get into the nuts and bolts of creating official documentation of your program, allow me to make a suggestion that will save you a boatload of time and frustration: *Create multiple copies of all important documents and keep all these items filed in a safe location. Do something to remember where this "safe location" is.*

This is a tip from my "things I wish I'd done" pile. Not only will you have to produce copies of these important documents if your teen undergoes the college application process, but you may also be required to resubmit these important documents at various times while your child is in college. And once again if your child decides to go to grad school, or goes back to school after a twenty-year hiatus, as I did.

Be sure to teach your teens what sort of things are "important documents" and get them started filing this kind of stuff in an organized and secure way.

TRANSCRIPTS

Whether your teen plans to attend college or trade school or enter the military, the most important record you will be asked to produce is his high school transcript. This is an overview of your child's coursework and accomplishments during high school, and it is the document that allows admissions directors to *quickly* assess your student's qualifications. Does this applicant have the required coursework completed? What is his GPA? How does he rank in comparison to his peers? What is the strength of his schedule? These qualifying questions need to be answered quickly and clearly because admissions staffs have a lot of applications to cull through.

The one thing all admissions officers want homeschool parents to know is this: *Please make your high school transcript easy to understand.* Your student's chances are not helped by a transcript that looks radically different from those of her traditionally educated peers. The document needs to make sense. In a recent article in The Chronicle of Higher Education, the trade journal for college admissions offices, counselors told some very funny stories about the reams of information they'd received from homeschooled applicants.

> **The one thing all admissions officers want homeschool parents to know is this: *Please make your high school transcript easy to understand.***

"In many cases their transcript is here, there, and everywhere," says Paul M. Cramer, vice president for enrollment at Elizabethtown College, in Pennsylvania. That's why the college "strongly encourages" all home-schooled applicants to go to the campus for interviews, he says.

Eddie K. Tallent, director of admissions at George Mason University, recently received one application that contained a page of explanation for each class listed on the transcript. "That was a bit much," he says.

> So your first step is to make your transcript stand out by choosing a format that is visually well organized.

So your first step is to make your transcript stand out by choosing a format that is visually well organized. Matthew Bass is a homeschool graduate who has created an online transcript builder for homeschoolers. You can develop one transcript for free, or you can build unlimited transcripts with additional functions for a relatively small fee per year. Creating a transcript doesn't need to be a stressful experience. You just need to clearly delineate what your student has done, and this site helps you do that in an elegant, step-by-step fashion. Visit www.teascript.com for more information.

Covenant College, in Lookout Mountain, GA, welcomes homeschooled graduates with "open arms," according to its website. They've created a GPA calculator and an editable transcript with examples for you to follow. Even if the college is not of interest, you will find their resources helpful. Visit www.covenant.edu/admissions/undergrad/home-schooled to learn more.

Janice Campbell, a veteran homeschooling mom, has written a definitive guide to homeschool record keeping, and it's available at a modest price as an e-book at transcriptsmadeeasy.com.

Sample transcripts are also reproduced for you in the appendix of this book, including one from Janice.

What Should You Include on Your Student's Transcript?

You need to include your grading scale somewhere on your teen's transcript. It's fine to use a generic 90% = A, 80% = B, 70% = C scale. However, if you do, then indicate the actual percentage your student earned for each course next to the letter grades on the transcript. If you use a more graduated scale, then just report the letter grade, with plus or minus (+ or –) qualifiers.

Another thing you might indicate on the transcript is any outside evaluation. If the student's grade for a particular course was assigned by someone other than you—for example, a college professor or co-op teacher—indicate this with an asterisk and footnote. A mix of grades from other instructors helps validate the credibility of the overall transcript. If you've assigned A's for most courses, then it will help evaluators to see that the student also earned A's from her outside teachers.

Weighted Grades or Credits

Some schools weight grades to reflect work done in honors or Advanced Placement classes, meaning some students have a GPA *higher* than 4.0, even though the school uses a four-point scale. However, many university admissions offices strip weighted credits and grades out of the student's records in order to standardize their internal formula for evaluating transcripts. You can ask admissions offices if they prefer advanced coursework to be weighted or not, and then determine how much effort you want to put into designating this on your teen's transcript.

If you choose to weight your grades, here's how it's done. An Advanced Placement course might be converted to 1.5 credits towards graduation because it is considered college-level work. Or an Honors English credit course might be worth 1.25 credits because the workload is 25 percent greater than what a student in a regular, college-prep English course is expected to complete. Weighting coursework is a good way for school districts to give students an incentive for selecting a more rigorous course of study. However, grade inflation has become a big problem in our culture today, and many school districts have

303

started weighting *all* their college-prep classes so their students look better than those graduating from the school district down the road.

Does this mean your homeschool graduate will be at a disadvantage if she doesn't have a GPA exceeding 4.0 from weighted grading? Ask the college admissions office via e-mail, but I'm confident you will find the answer is no. All admissions offices have a process for equalizing how students are evaluated, and in most cases this means stripping out weighted grades. And many colleges evaluate homeschool applicants separately, not in comparison to traditionally educated peers. This means a more holistic evaluation is taking place, not merely number crunching. However, this is all the more reason for paying careful attention to the documentation you submit. It needs to be neat, well organized and clear.

Did I say that already?

Naming Courses

Here is where you can indicate the "strength of schedule," i.e., the degree of difficulty of subjects studied. Admissions officers want to know how rigorous the coursework completed has been and to what degree the student has availed himself of the most challenging opportunities offered. If a student coming out of a top suburban high school has a 4.0 GPA and high test scores but has not taken any of the advanced coursework offered at his school, questions may be raised about the student's willingness to be challenged.

In years past, homeschooled students did not have access to AP work or dual enrollment options with local colleges, but now they do. So the transcripts of students looking for admission to top schools or scholarship money need to demonstrate that they have pursued a rigorous course of study.

If your teen completes AP courses or college classes at a

local institution, then indicate this in the course title or with an asterisk and footnote. Remember that a course may not be designated as AP without pre-authorization from the College Board. AP teachers must have their courses approved through the AP audit process outlined on the College Board's website. There is a provision for homeschoolers to complete this as well, but it requires submitting a course syllabus that shows all AP objectives for that particular course will be covered. Colleges requested this standardization because they were seeing so many courses designated as AP on student transcripts that the distinction was losing its meaning.

Feel free to title a course "Honors" if the student has indeed completed *quality* work in a particular subject area that *exceeds* minimum standards outlined in the previous chapter.

> College admissions offices are attracted to homeschooled applicants because they have found them to be inquisitive, passionate, and self-starting.

Don't let a concern for strength of schedule box you into a traditional approach to homeschooling. College admissions offices are attracted to homeschooled applicants because they have found them to be inquisitive, passionate, and self-starting. If your teen has an area of interest to which she wants to devote significant time, don't compromise her pursuit of learning for a straitjacket schedule of local college classes just because you think it's expected. Let her write her novel instead or travel to an archeological dig. These are the types of trump cards that will put her application on the top of the scholarship committee's pile.

305

Extracurricular Records

Carefully review college application packets and scholarship applications to determine whether or not additional records are required or permitted. Some schools make it clear they do *not* want additional documentation added to their required forms.

If a school's packet states that they don't want anything extra included in the application, then you will need to include on the reverse side of your student's transcript any extracurricular activities, leadership responsibilities, AP test scores, and unique opportunities. Create a list, not a narrative. You only want to pique interest in your application. There will be time in the college interview to elaborate on the student's high school record.

> Because most homeschooled students do not, as a rule, participate in traditional after-school clubs and athletics, you might want to create a form for qualifying the types of enrichment activities your teen is involved with.

Other applications will allow addendums and may even encourage them. If so, then this is something you should consider doing, as applications usually include a very small box for noting extracurricular activities. Because most homeschooled students do not, as a rule, participate in traditional after-school clubs and athletics, you might want to create a form for qualifying the types of enrichment activities your teen is involved with. However, don't pile on. Think quality, not quantity. If your teen wishes to submit a writing sample, he shouldn't send the entire two-hundred-page novel he wrote for National Novel Writing Month.

Attendance

An attendance record is not necessarily included in a college application, but you can indicate number of days logged in a corner of the transcript. This is only necessary if asked for, or if you have to compile this to meet state homeschool requirements. In Pennsylvania, we must log 180 days or 990 school hours each year. We traditionally passed this minimum long before the school year was over, so I indicated attendance as 180+ days or 990+ hours.

Social Security Number

This is a catch-22 for you to navigate as you feel best. You don't want to publish your child's social security number unless absolutely necessary. However, if he applies to a large university, the social security number on his transcript and other documentation is pretty much the only way admissions offices have of keeping everyone's files straight. If your teen has an unusual name, or is applying only to small schools where documents can easily be matched by name or address, then including his social security number on the transcript may not be necessary. (As a compromise, you might include the last four digits of the social security number on all forms.)

COLLEGE TRANSCRIPTS AND TEST SCORES

You also need to keep track of scores and grades your teen earns through outside evaluation. These may include College Board exams and transcripts from community college coursework or online classes. Official reports must be sent directly from these institutions to the schools where your teen applies—you will pay a fee for this—but you also need to report this information on college applications, so keep these records on file. Also keep the syllabus from any college coursework and be ready to offer this as additional documentation if the transfer of credits is de-

> **Get a portable file box for each of your teens and show them how to organize their hanging folders.**

bated. Every time your child is asked to supply a transcript in the future, an official transcript from these institutions must be provided. Even if her current institution has already awarded credit for this work, the original source will still be required if she's considering grad school, study abroad, employment opportunities, etc.

Because our kids were going to need to manage their own records during college, we found a portable file box the best storage solution. Get one for each of your teens and show them how to organize their hanging folders. Once our kids got to college, they had to produce the transcripts and AP exam scores several times as proof of having fulfilled a requirement. In my experience, colleges often misplace paperwork or do not share information across departments, so don't be surprised if you must provide the same documentation more than once.

Diplomas

The transcript is by far the most important piece of documentation you will generate, but diplomas are also of concern to most homeschooling parents. In our case, we had to submit proof of graduation before our kids arrived at their chosen colleges. We mailed a final, signed transcript plus a copy of the diploma issued by our homeschool organization, Pennsylvania Homeschoolers (www.pahomeschoolers.com). This option was particularly timesaving as the organization took care of officially sealing and sending all the documentation colleges asked for, and they did so within two business days. I found this helpful for several reasons:

* They maintained records and official authentication of these documents.
* They sent the transcript and diploma directly to colleges for me. I didn't have to create them or remember to submit them on top of all the other forms.
* They set a high standard that was recognized and respected by college admissions offices.
* Fees were very modest.

There is something of a debate in the homeschool community about organizations setting up diploma programs such as these because they may undermine the acceptance of parent-issued diplomas. I can only report that in our case the diploma program was a time-saver and a contributing factor to the opportunities and scholarships our kids received.

However, bottom line, you do not need a diploma issued by anyone other than yourself in all but a few situations, and the Home School Legal Defense Association (HSLDA) continues to work vigorously to change these as well. As the parent supervising your child's education, you have the right to determine what coursework and what quality of work must be completed for graduation, and this makes you the most qualified individual to verify his studies.

You should not hesitate to issue your child a diploma. This decision is not going to make or break your child's chances of getting into the college of his choice. The transcript and test scores will be weighted heavily. Who signs the diploma will not. You certainly do not need to enroll in an expensive accredited program just because they promise to issue a diploma. The diploma is a small concern. You can purchase an elegant diploma to sign and perhaps notarize—it adds an additional air of authentication—from HSLDA.

Many regional or state homeschool organization also offer di-

309

plomas and graduation ceremonies for their members, so check there first for an inexpensive and meaningful diploma option.

TO G.E.D. OR NOT G.E.D.—THAT IS THE QUESTION

Does your child need a GED? No. Because of the stigma attached to the G.E.D. as a device used by those who have dropped out of school, the Home School Legal Defense Association has diligently worked to eliminate this as a requirement for homeschooled graduates. Your teen does not need a G.E.D. to enroll in college, qualify for federal or state financial aid, or enlist in the military. If an organization or employers will only accept a G.E.D. as proof of completion of a homeschool program, then put your foot down and contact HSLDA for assistance.

On the other hand, make sure you have documentation that demonstrates your teen has indeed completed a bone fide high-school-level homeschool program. Refusing to pursue the G.E.D. means your teen has more than exceeded that standard and has evidence to substantiate that claim.

31 PORTFOLIOS

In some cases, compiling a portfolio of your teen's high school level work may be of value. In Pennsylvania, as is in a few other states, a portfolio is required for each child every year, so I now have more than forty three-inch binders gathering mildew in my basement. I didn't always enjoy the burden of compiling these tomes, but my adult children enjoy looking through them. (Now that I'm thinking of it, I should move these to higher ground—right after I finish this book.)

Despite the fact that our children applied to almost twenty schools and attended several college interviews, no one ever asked to see these portfolios. Samples of high school writing assignments and book lists were the only two things ever requested of us, but then we did not apply to top-tier schools. Students invited to interview with selection committees at elite schools may be asked to bring along samples of their work. In this case, your student should place samples of his very best work in a binder no more than three inches wide.

The purpose of the portfolio is to efficiently highlight the strengths of your teen's high school achievement. Think about what these areas are and then consider how best to represent this visually and comprehensively in simple fashion. You may choose to compile a digital portfolio online. This is especially advisable if one of your teen's talents is technological savvy or if your teen is going to pursue a technology-driven discipline.

Remember, your student will be given little time to make her case at an interview or during the application review process—we parents always have far more to say about our teens than others really have time to hear—so resist the urge to turn this portfolio into a creative memories project. This piece needs to convey seriousness of purpose, not scrapbooking finesse. If your teen wants to turn the portfolio into a statement of his or her individuality, then by all means allow them to do so. But if you are the one pulling this together, keep it simple and straightforward. Keep in mind that most college admissions officers are secretly concerned that mom is not going to cut the apron strings; scrapbooking the college application package will only confirm that suspicion.

Here are some of the things you might include in the portfolio:

Student writing

* Add this especially if the work has been evaluated or won awards.
* Include a mix of creative and analytical works.
* A research paper with a clear, insightful thesis and extended bibliography will be of interest, as schools are always looking for future researchers.
* Include only excerpts of long works of fiction, but the entirety of a research paper.

Reading lists

* Include the texts used for coursework, especially if they are college-level or works by noted expertise or academics in the field.
* Include substantial works of nonfiction.
* Include fiction works of literary merit.
* If you include popular fiction, such as science fiction, just a smattering will do—don't overwhelm the list with it. Keep it focused on the rigors of your program. Remember: quality, not quantity.

Noteworthy artistic achievement

* Include original art or photography, especially if it has achieved recognition.
* Document other artistic achievement with pictures or programs from recitals and plays. Highlight your student's credit on the program.

Scientific and math achievement

* Document a science fair project (no more than two pages).
* Include lab reports that represent college-prep or college-level work.
* Include advanced math work demonstrating mastery of the subject, as well as any math competition work.

313

Noteworthy extracurricular activities

* Include pictures of the activity with other students, especially if they show the diversity of your homeschool community in terms of ethnicity, age, and gender. (Some critics of homeschooling say we are not diverse and that this is intentional, but research says otherwise: 25 percent of all homeschoolers identify themselves as members of a minority group.)

* Include programs and awards that show the scope of these activities and the level of organization. For instance, CHESS volleyball tournaments span a tri-state area and use referees from the state athletic association governing scholastic sports. If this is not pointed out, college admissions officers will assume a much lower level of competition.
* Add any other documentation that shows the range of activities your teen has been involved in and the level of accomplishment he has achieved.

Okay, one more time: Keep the portfolio concise and clear. Think in terms of the information that might be conveyed in a five-minute perusal by an admissions officer or selection committee—that's why images are effective. Send your teen to the interview or college visit with portfolio in hand, even if it hasn't been asked for, and encourage her to offer it for review.

PART 9

NEXT STOP:
COLLEGE

32 CHOOSING A COLLEGE

If your teen has decided to go to college, then the next big question is this: Which college is the right one for your teen? The Bible tells us, "If anyone lacks wisdom let him ask of God who gives generously without reproach" (James 1:5, ESV). So the first step is to ask God to lead and direct your family's search and to supply the wisdom He has promised.

Throughout this chapter, I am going to walk you through the factors we considered as a family, not because I think all homeschool families should use our approach, but to provide you a real-life model of the choices you will face as a family. This is not a time to expect your teens to wander off alone. College costs too much money and is too sophisticated a decision to think your adolescent is ready to figure this out without your guidance. Without oversight, your teen could find herself a young adult with a boatload of debt and an unmarketable degree, and that's no place to start adulthood.

It's normal for teens to be overwhelmed by this decision and, therefore, put off thinking about it. It's a running joke in our circles that the quickest way to make a senior girl in high school cry is by asking her what she plans to do next year. Guys are equally frustrated by the question. Kids seem to think—probably because adults keep asking—that they should clearly and firmly know exactly what they want to do after high school, but the plain truth is that nine times out of ten they don't. They're under the impression that it's an irrevocable decision, which it isn't—a lot of people end up going to more than one school, changing their majors, and taking longer than four years to earn a degree. As parents, we are wise to remember this and take these possibilities into consideration during the decision-making process.

Your teen needs your help and emotional support during this difficult time, so strike a collaborative relationship with your child and gently guide her through the process. You don't want to be overbearing, but you don't take a hands-off approach either.

PUBLIC, PRIVATE, OR CHRISTIAN SCHOOL?

What types of institutions are your family willing to consider? The answer to this question will significantly narrow his choices right away. We were willing to consider large public institutions for two reasons. First, we had raised our kids with a view towards eventually getting out there and mixing it up with the world. Kermit and I both became Christians in college, and we still believe secular campuses are in need of a solid Christian presence. The whole focus of our homeschooling was preparation for an eventual launch into the broader scope of society. Because all of our kids were proven in their faith, we were comfortable with this choice. Had they not been up for the challenges they would face on a secular campus for the sake of the gospel, we certainly would have considered other options.

The second reason we focused our search on in-state public universities was the cost. My husband is particularly averse to debt, and the kids have all inherited that particular gene. Because our three older kids all headed off to school with gradu-

319

ate school already in mind, they had been wisely advised by a relative in higher education to pursue an inexpensive undergraduate degree and save the greater investment for graduate school, as this was the decision that would matter most.

I've worked with many homeschool families who would not even consider the public university route, and their reasons were quite valid. No one wants to waste money paying for the kind of worldly indoctrination common to campus life at a secular school. This reality should give you pause, especially if your teen is planning to pursue an area of study such as English or psychology, where some or even much of the content is likely to be antithetical to biblical teaching. Our sons were business majors, while Kayte studied math and French, and they did not find the content of their required coursework to be problematic. Kristen earned an education degree, where there was much more content that had to be chucked, but she handled it well.

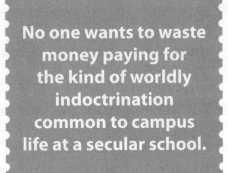

No one wants to waste money paying for the kind of worldly indoctrination common to campus life at a secular school.

HOW MUCH DEBT?

How much debt are you comfortable advising your teen to take on? This is going to narrow your choices quickly. For many families this ends up being the bottom line. They find a few schools that seem to be a good fit for their child and then wait for the final offers to come in. (The deadline for reporting most full scholarship and financial aid awards is in April.) And then they make a monetary decision.

The late Christian financial advisor Larry Burkett, who highly valued the earning power of a college education, advised students to take on no more debt than they can expect to earn as an average starting salary with that degree. This wisdom gave us a valuable benchmark. Our sons were able to get by at a state university with some scholarship money and a loan debt equal to half of their initial starting salaries. Mike elected to graduate a semester early in order to save money, while Gabe chose to stay to complete a double major and take a paid internship to help defray costs. Because they both ended up living at home for at least a year following college, they paid their college debt off quickly and began saving aggressively for graduate school.

We looked at debt somewhat differently for our daughters. For them we advised a debt load that wouldn't adversely delay marriage and motherhood. Kayte went to Pittsburgh on a full-tuition scholarship and took a position as a teaching assistant for the math department to help pay incidental costs. Kristen first attended community college and lived at home before transferring to a nearby state university. She also waited tables during college—probably the best-paying job a full-time college student can find.

Your teen can also control costs in college by moving off campus and/or obtaining a decent-paying job while in school. Our sons lived in the dorms for two years, then studied abroad for a full year in cheap places, then lived with families in their church during their senior year. Kayte moved off campus her sophomore year, studied abroad a full year, then lived with her pastor's family her senior year. Kristen only spent one year in the dorms, then moved off-off campus. A car generously supplied by a relative made that possible.

We didn't know enough to ask about job opportunities during college visits, but we are grateful these did materialize. Federal work-study, if your child qualifies, is only minimum wage. However, the advantage is complete freedom in working around a student's class schedule. At larger universities, there will be better paying positions for upperclassmen not tied to financial need. Kayte made good money grading exams for math professors and, later, as a teaching assistant. Gabe worked for his university on a software-conversion project. Other students I know have earned decent money as resident assistants, tutoring in writing or math clinics, and working as undergraduate researchers for their departments. These are more widely available at large universities, as their staffing needs are greater and they have more flexibility to hire students not on work-study. At smaller colleges, students qualifying for work-study have first dibs on college jobs, and departments have fewer students and less need for upperclassmen to help out with departmental needs.

WHAT'S YOUR MAJOR?

Every college has departments that are stronger than others. Attending a school with a solid reputation in your teen's area of interest can be very important in certain fields. If your teen plans to go into engineering, then a degree from a highly ranked school like Stanford or Purdue will make stepping into a position directly from college much more likely. Co-op experiences, available at some schools, will help your teen determine a lot about the type of company and position he'd be most interested in. And businesses will always seek applicants who have successful workplace experience, as experience invariably trumps GPA. A high GPA *plus* successful degree-related experience will result in the greatest number of job offers.

If your teen is interested in working for a Fortune 500 company after college, then attending a ranked business school with internship opportunities becomes important. If your teen will be satisfied working at a smaller firm, then it is not. My sons wanted to go to an AACSB accredited business school (fewer than 15% have this designation) because they saw this as important in anticipation of entrance into a top ranked MBA pro-

322

gram. A student interested in studying medicine will also need to be selective in choosing an undergraduate program. Don't be satisfied with knowing the acceptance rate for a college's graduates entering medical school; ask for a detailed report that lists the schools their students have gone on to attend.

If your teen is interested in eventually going to law school, then the major she pursues is not as important as the rigors of the program she chooses. Pre-law degrees that do not develop critical thinking skills aren't worth much. A reputable mathematics department or economics department that emphasizes analysis and quantitative reasoning may be the best place to prepare for success on the law school entrance exams (LSAT).

Strength of program is not going to be as important for other majors, such as education or nursing. You certainly want the best program you can afford, and the size of the department is one way of assessing this. But the job markets in education and nursing are so strong, stepping into a position directly from an undergraduate degree from any institution is relatively easy.

OPPORTUNITIES FOR CHRISTIAN FELLOWSHIP?

My kids all developed enduring friendships through the churches they attended during college, but friends who attended Christian campuses tended to maintain more relationships with fellow classmates after school. (And, yes, some came away with spouses, too.)

This is where our family took a different tact than many. While we were comfortable sending our kids to secular schools, a strong local church was a requirement, one with expository preaching and

323

While we were comfortable sending our kids to secular schools, a strong local church was a requirement.

biblical fellowship in a multi-generational setting. Our children took advantage of Christian fellowships at their colleges, but our concern with campus ministry as the sole source of fellowship was a reliance on peer advising and the risk of developing a self-centered approach to Christianity (as in, *I can only relate to Christians in the same season of life as me*). Our kids shared our convictions, and so they each willingly confined their college searches to those schools where a good church and transportation to and from were available. When visiting schools, we spent a weekend at the most promising campuses so the kids could attend a church near campus that was recommended. The side benefit of this approach was that it was relatively easy for them to find a family to live with when they moved off campus.

> **The availability of supportive Christian fellowship and solid biblical teaching should not be taken for granted as you select a school.**

The availability of supportive Christian fellowship and solid biblical teaching should not be taken for granted as you select a school. Assuming that a Christian college will provide fellowship enough does not always prove to be true.

HOW FAR FROM HOME?

324

Travel costs should be factored in when evaluating the total price tag of a particular school. In the end, both sons and Kayte had cars at school because, in part, we got tired of driving across the state to pick them up! They all started planning to only come home at break, but events like weddings and younger siblings' activities inevitably led to a few extra trips each year. I enjoy having Kristen at a college less than an hour away, as I get to see her more frequently and I can be there for her in any way she needs.

On the other hand, if your teens are adventurous enough to be some distance from home, you may find they receive better scholarship offers from schools that are out-of-state. One reason for this is that schools are attempting to bump up their diversity factor by offsetting the high number of in-state students with attendees from other regions of the country.

Among the biggest factors in considering location are the post-college job opportunities. Unless your child attends a top-tier school, the job opportunities for most schools' graduates will be regional. Companies within driving distance of a school will be more likely than national firms to show up for the school's job fairs. Our sons' business department had an active placement office that was eager to help them find positions, but their connections were all regional, and Mike and Gabe had come to realize they didn't want to settle in that part of the country. They ended up moving back home where they conducted their job search on their own. This certainly didn't make them regret their college choice; it was just a factor they hadn't anticipated.

As I surveyed where the homeschooled kids I know have ended up, a large percentage are now married and working near the cities where they attended school. So your teen may want to take a longer-term view of geographic location when choosing a college.

325

HOW BIG?

The size and setting of the college campus should come into play for most kids when making a decision. Kayte loves an urban setting and has studied in the U.S. and abroad in some pretty dicey places. But she thrives on diversity and opportunity, so she's been willing to deal with the accompanying safety issues. Many kids underestimate how size and location will affect them—some like the intimacy of a small campus and rural location, while others are easily bored with this setting.

If your student is considering a large university, he will need to be more proactive about seeking advice and figuring out options along the way. Smaller schools typically have good advisor-to-student ratios, which can prove a distinct advantage. Had our kids not been vigilant about managing their course schedules, none of them would have graduated within four years. University advisors just don't make this a priority.

WHERE TO LIVE?

Housing arrangements are an issue not to be overlooked. Is living on campus required for underclassmen? Is housing availability guaranteed? Can your teen choose honors housing? Are there study dorms? Alcohol-free living? It's common for colleges to guarantee two years of housing, while many small schools will guarantee four. Some even require students to live on campus all four years. Conversely, many urban schools have a shortage of student housing.

Kayte was guaranteed housing only for her freshman year at the University of Pittsburgh. This meant by November of her freshman year she needed to start figuring out where she was going to live her sophomore year and with whom. Because we didn't anticipate this situation, it became quite a distraction during a time Kayte was eager to establish herself academically. As it was, housing turned out to be the most stressful part of her experience during an otherwise terrific time at Pitt.

EXTRACURRICULAR ACTIVITIES?

Athletics and other activities will matter greatly to some students. My sons were sold on their school by the state-of-the-arts fitness center. This was their consolation prize for passing on a Division I school with a famous football team. (They couldn't afford that option.) For others, a broad offering of cultural activities offered at the school or in the city will factor into a college decision.

STUDY ABROAD?

For our three older kids, the opportunity to study abroad was a big part of their final college decision. They each chose schools with a well-established study-abroad office and departmental support for studying overseas, as well as a price tag that allowed for this possibility. Mike, Gabe and Kayte each had three different study-abroad experiences and still graduated on time.

NARROWING THE LIST

Early in your child's high school career, head for the College Board's website (www.collegeboard.com) and set up a free account. There you can search extensively for promising colleges and universities, review their admissions requirements, and receive test results online. Numerous helpful tools and articles are also available. This is where you start to get a feel for what is out there and what your teen needs to do to attend the school of his choice.

Once you identify schools of interest, track down formerly homeschooled students on campus—inside information from students who fit a profile similar to your teen's will give you a good idea whether or not the school should make it onto your short list.

Start making college visits during your teen's sophomore year. Don't invest in travel yet, just begin getting acclimated to the routine—visit the local ones at a convenient time and sit in on a couple of informational sessions. Very quickly they will all begin to feel alike. But this exposure is an important part of helping kids get comfortable with the process.

By the fall semester of your teen's senior year, you will have enough data (test scores, GPA, and interest inventories) to

327

> By the fall semester of your teen's senior year, you will have enough data (test scores, GPA, and interest inventories) to help your teen figure out what schools are potentially good fits.

help your teen figure out what schools are potentially good fits. Final visits should be made in September and October, because application deadlines for competitive schools and scholarship considerations can be as early as late November or early December. In my experience, it's a mistake to choose a college without making a visit—there really is a big difference between taking a virtual tour online and an actual visit. There are too many factors that will be important to both you and your student that a virtual tour is not going to point out, especially if it's an undesirable feature, such as a campus located near a high-crime area.

Why narrow the list? Why not leave your options open? For sanity's sake—your own as well as your teen's. College applications take a long time to fill out, and most teenagers tend to procrastinate. It's also typical for teens to have a much shorter attention span for this process than their parents. Conserve their energy for the hard work that must go into putting together a competitive application. Even if you use the Common Application—an online application that allows students to submit standard information, recommendations, and school records to any of 300 participating schools in a single shot—each school requires unique essays and paperwork that will be time-consuming.

One of my sons spent weeks on an application to a school where he couldn't afford to go, even if he was accepted. When he finally accepted the limitations of our financial situation, it was quite a drain to start over doing applications for appropriate schools. I've known teens that were highly motivated and willing to complete seven or more applications, but I find three applications is often a teen's limit.

Even though there are more than 4,000 colleges and universities your teen might attend in the U.S., by the time you finish listing the qualities that matter most to your family in selecting a school and you then list the core values of the schools that align with your requirements, you're going to have a pretty short list, certainly ten or less. What follows in these chapters is how your teen can get into his or her top choices and, perhaps most importantly, how to get the best financial offer.

33 WHAT ADMISSIONS OFFICES ARE LOOKING FOR

Higher education is big business, and you are a consumer purchasing a big-ticket item. This is the reality. If you want to figure out how the system works, follow the money and everything will make a lot more sense. In the end, colleges are most concerned with perpetuating their existence. If a college can develop and maintain a reputation for providing a better bargain or a better education than other schools, it will remain in business and perhaps even prosper. And it's not just about enrollment numbers—the top-ranked schools attract more funding for programs and research from the U.S. government, private foundations, and big business.

When looking at potential applicants, admissions offices consider how individual students might contribute to that end. Does the student's record strongly suggest she is likely to complete her degree? After all, graduation rates are important. Colleges don't want to offer a space to a student who's going to drop out during her junior year—they've already counted your tuition check toward the budget. Will your son's ACT scores help bump up their averages and, thus, their reputation? Has your teen demonstrated strong leadership potential? If so, then it's a good bet that she'll be a leader in her chosen profession and bring recognition to her alma mater, or better yet, be successful enough to be an annual contributor to the alumni fund.

Bottom line: Admissions offices are looking for students who will increase their ranking against their competition, whether their competitors be small Christian colleges, large public universities, or the Ivy League. Your teen will be most competitive when applying to institutions where he or she beats their averages on the ranking scales.

THE RIGHT KIND OF APPLICANT

Every school has an identity it wants to project. Think of "branding" as a business concept, and you'll see where this is going. In considering an individual applicant, the admissions team evaluates how the student will fit into the picture they're creating for the public and for their contributors. You can know what particular identity a school is hoping to convey just by scrutinizing the welcome page of its website or the introductory information in their promotional materials. The school's core values will be clearly communicated here through the images used, quotes from students and faculty, and school slogans. Colleges want to attract the right kinds of applicants, so this information will be readily apparent. Your teen's application will be considered in light of the school's core values and the degree to which your child fits snugly into the big picture.

For insight into how this works, let's look at the websites for two different Christian colleges seeking to attract home-schooled students, Baylor University (www.baylor.edu) and Grove City College (www.gcc.edu). I've chosen these two because both have informational videos on their site. Watch these and see if you can identify the core values at each school. Note the order in which values are implicitly or explicitly expressed and what traits are repeatedly emphasized.

Here's what I picked up:

331

Baylor	Grove City
Ethnically diverse—emphasized in image	Academically rigorous—the video shows one student defining it as "grueling," while others emphasize working hard
Students note that they applied to upper-tier schools, implicitly putting Baylor in this category	Good value for the cost—laptop computers are given to all incoming freshman as part of package
Large—emphasized in images.	
Academically challenging—the school's ambition is to reach the upper echelons of schools while retaining its Christian values	"Authentically" Christian—the faith of faculty and students is highlighted throughout.
	Academically challenging—the school's ambition is to reach the upper echelons of schools while retaining its Christian values
Supportive faculty	
Big-time athletics	
Study abroad	Athletics, clubs, Christian ministries, and hanging out are emphasized
Research institute	
Outreach to community and world. Christian faith is more implicitly than explicitly expressed.	Not terribly diverse—look at the students in the video
	Study abroad
Grad school is the goal of several students featured	Friendliness of students makes for a close-knit community
Students are destined to make impact on society	Faculty helps create family environment
	Pristine setting shows the aesthetic appeal of campus
	Students have the opportunity to contribute to campus life

332

Though both schools are potentially attractive options for homeschooled graduates, these are pretty divergent choices, and the profile of the student who will do well at each school is quite different.

I'm most familiar with Grove City, as quite a few students from our homeschool community have enrolled there. It's a selective school, with an admit rate of only 45 percent. Grove City has turned down many outstanding applicants with high SAT scores and GPAs. The make-or-break process is the on-campus interview, in which students must demonstrate their compatibility with Grove's core values. This is a close-knit, conservative Christian community looking for students who will bring leadership and academic tenacity to the campus. Campus life is Grove City's heartbeat.

Baylor is the better choice for a student seeking adventure, a demonstration of his faith through outreach, diversity of student body and ideas, and graduate school or professional impact as his next step.

I once heard an admissions officer advise, "Parents think schools are looking for the well-rounded student, but that's not true. Schools are looking for a well-rounded student body, and that's why they like kids who demonstrate unique strengths and focus." This statement has a mountain of truth in it and should help you and your teen figure out what to emphasize on an application. The one caveat I'd throw in is that the definition of "a well-rounded student body" looks different from school to school. The key is figuring out where your child is most competitive in relationship to the school's core values and then highlight that edge for the admissions committee.

Examine the website and promotional materials of colleges that interest your teen most. Sit down with a marker and highlight every adjective or qualifier the institution uses to define itself. From this a clear profile will emerge. Remember, they aren't trying to mislead anyone. What the school emphasizes will likely turn out to be real advantages of that university. Pay attention to what they don't say to get a clue as to the disadvantages of the school. Did you notice that Baylor's video never mentions cost?

The University of Pittsburgh's website highlights major distinctions about Pitt that can't be ignored. If your student is considering Pitt, the city of Pittsburgh confronts you at every corner. Students are constantly dealing with it, and either they love it or hate it. The university considers its urban setting to be a huge advantage that they integrate into their students' experiences in many ways. It's a real mistake to attend Pitt if your teen isn't enthusiastic about city living. The website also emphasizes the "experiential learning" component of Pitt's identity, which includes studying abroad and field-related experiences through co-ops, internships, teaching assistantships, research, etc. Students who want to capture the scholarship committee's attention will show they have strong interest in both urban living and experiential learning.

Grove City College

Ten percent of are students at Grove City College were homeschooled in high school. A fair number of our faculty are themselves homeschooling parents.

GCC offers, compared to some schools, a small number of majors. This is one of the means by which we keep our costs down. As a result, some students will not find the program they are looking for. If you find a match, however, you will discover quality academic programs at GCC. Because of the academic rigor at GCC, students who are not serious about their academic training should look elsewhere.

Students with an excellent academic history who are not admitted through the early-decision program should not give up; many will be admitted during the second round. The application process is designed to seek out students with strong academic credentials. (Evidence from standardized tests like the AP, SAT, and ACT is helpful.)

However, we are also looking for well-rounded students. Your student can build outstanding credentials through involvement in church, music, athletics, competitive speech and debate, and missionary programs, just to name a few.

Gary L. Welton
Assistant Dean for Institutional Assessment
Grove City College

335

34 NAILING THE HIGH-STAKES TEST

Even though the use of test scores as a criterion for college admissions has been falling out of favor for traditional applicants, test scores are still crucial for homeschooled students. While GPA and strength of schedule have been shown to be better predictors of college potential, admissions officers believe these measures are compromised for homeschool applicants due to the lack of direct peer competition. Colleges want to know how your student will perform when measured against other students, so they must rely on standardized test scores as predictors of future success.

The Educational Testing Service, also known the College Board, creates almost every high-stakes test your teens will take during their high school years. What a racket! (I wish I had thought of it first.) The good news is, the tests' common heritage makes prepping for them a bit less confusing, whether you teen is taking the AP, PSAT, SAT, SAT II, or CLEP. The ACT, the other widely used college entrance exam, is independent of the ETS, yet many of the study strategies to prepare for the test are similar.

Here then is a primer for the major tests your teen may elect to take.

ADVANCED PLACEMENT (AP) TESTS

These subject-specific tests can only be taken while the student is in high school. A passing score will exempt students from college coursework and may also earn credits toward graduation. Each university sets its own policy for what constitutes a passing score and what credit will be awarded. Most AP tests include critical reading in the subject area, and many require essays. All tests are three hours in length and are administered at a specific date and time during the first two weeks of May. You must arrange to take these tests at a local high school designated as an AP test site. Most students take the test following a yearlong course in preparation, but the course is not mandatory. As of this writing, the fee for taking each test is $86.

COLLEGE-LEVEL
EXAMINATION PROGRAM (CLEP)

The CLEP tests are subject-specific tests that can exempt students from college coursework and may earn credit toward graduation. These differ from AP tests in several ways: 1) They are less rigorous; 2) they can be taken anytime, even during college; and 3) they consist of multiple-choice questions only. These tests can be taken at will at a CLEP test center—usually a computer lab on a college campus—and currently cost $77 each.

337

SAT SUBJECT TESTS

SAT subject tests are used to demonstrate high-school-level achievement in specific subject areas. Because grade inflation is rampant, colleges use these scores to standardize applicants' achievement for evaluation purposes. Many elite schools require at least two SAT subject tests: math and a foreign language. High scores on these tests do not result in college credit, but they can qualify a student for exemption from introductory coursework. Students should take these tests if the schools where they plan to apply require them, or if they want to increase their competitiveness for scholarship consideration. Your teen should take the specific test the year the coursework is completed—for example, she should take the U.S. history subject test following a rigorous U.S. history course.

Many students do not realize that universities may require subject tests, and they end up taking several at the last minute. So do your homework early and decide which tests your teen should take and when. The tests are multiple-choice and one hour in length. They are administered at College Board test sites, though not all tests are given on all test dates. Each test costs approximately $20. You may not take the SAT Reasoning test (the "big one") and SAT subject tests on the same day, although you may take up to three subject tests on the same day.

PRELIMINARY SAT/NATIONAL MERIT SCHOLARSHIP QUALIFYING TEST (PSAT/NMSQT)

This test used to not count for much, but now it's a high-stakes test in its own right. The PSAT was originally intended to help tenth- and eleventh-graders prepare for the SAT test. Today it is also used to determine National Merit Scholarship winners and for colleges to identify prospective students for recruitment purposes.

338

The PSAT is a shorter version of the SAT Reasoning test, and the extensive report you receive on your teen's performance will be helpful in identifying his academic strengths and weaknesses. Taking the test will also put you on mailing lists. Students fill out a brief questionnaire before testing that provides colleges a profile. You might want to discuss with your teen the interests he or she wants to identify on this questionnaire, but if that's too much to think about on test day, a more detailed profile for colleges can be filled out and submitted through the College Board's website.

The PSAT/NMSQT is given at your local high school to their students, so you will need to first request permission from the school to have your homeschooled teen tested and then register and pay for this test. Do so in early September of your teen's junior year. The test is given only once in October at each school, either on a Wednesday or Saturday. Scores are used to determine National Merit standing, so teens with potential for scoring well should take the test for practice during their sophomore year, then again in their junior year.

National Merit Scholarship

The granddaddy of prestigious scholarship competitions, the National Merit Scholarship identifies the top 4,700 high school juniors and assigns them commended, semi-finalist, or finalist status. Each state is guaranteed a set number of finalists, so qualifying scores vary from state to state and from year to year. The 1,300 finalists are determined by their scores and subsequent strength of application. These students receive automatic scholarship offers from many colleges and universities, and a select few receive a scholarship from the National Merit Corporation.

339

SAT REASONING TEST

Formerly known as the Scholastic Aptitude Test and Scholastic Assessment Test, this is the college entrance exam most widely used, though both SAT and ACT scores are accepted at almost all U.S. colleges and universities. The reasoning test is long—almost four hours—and opens with a twenty-five-minute essay as part of the writing test, followed by critical reading and math sections.

In recent years, the degree of difficulty on the math section has increased, so students should complete algebra 1, algebra 2, geometry and some of trigonometry or pre-calculus in advance of testing.

Each of the three sections is worth 800 points, with 500 (more or less) representing the mean score. Most state schools will be looking for a composite score of 1500 as a benchmark for admissions consideration, while elite schools may set their floor at 1800 or higher.

This test is offered on seven Saturdays during the school year. Any high school student may take the test by registering online at the College Board's website. You do not need to seek permission from the school proctoring the test. The cost is currently $45, but registration deadlines fall at least one month in advance, and late registration fees are steep.

There is no limit to the number of times a student may take the test, and some colleges allow students to combine their best scores on the three sections to create an overall high score. With all the other high-stakes tests students may take in high school, two to three times is the most a student ought to take the SAT Reasoning Test. It's typical to take the test in the spring semester of junior year, after the student has taken the PSAT in the fall of junior year.

ACT TEST

Billed as the most widely accepted college entrance exam, this test is most popular in the Midwest and South, but teens elsewhere should consider taking it as well. Whereas the SAT claims to measure reasoning ability, the ACT measures achievement in English, math, reading and science. The essay-writing portion is optional and is administered at the end of testing. Because the

Acing the SAT

I think the best way to prepare for this test is to start early, so you have time to identify your weak spots and improve in those areas through repetition. Last-minute cramming might be helpful, but unless you have a photographic memory, it will take a while for you to absorb and remember everything you'll need.

My most challenging area on the SAT was math, so I studied—a lot. Princeton and Kaplan have excellent test prep books, so I took full advantage of them, taking countless practice tests and rehearsing key concepts over and over again. Chalk Dust, a company that produces math instruction videos, has a great series for SAT prep. I found these quite helpful because of their emphasis on timesaving strategies.

Whether you're studying math or vocabulary, I can't emphasize the value of repetition. Practice really does make perfect. If you need help with essay writing, find a tutor who can point out your weaknesses and make specific suggestions. When you get into a stressful timed situation, you will need the confidence that comes from careful, thoughtful preparation.

Rebekah Wilhelm
Earned a perfect score on the SAT

341

ACT measures achievement, advance preparation is likely to improve your student's ACT scores.

Students may decide which scores to release and which to suppress. The ACT is shorter than the SAT, approximately three hours in length, and costs a bit less. A composite score based on the four subject area tests will range from 1 to 36, with 21 representing the mean score and 30 being a good target for scholarship consideration.

You will find sites online showing equivalent scores for the SAT and ACT. For example, a 30 on the ACT is equivalent to a composite score of 1980 on the SAT. It's common for students to perform better on one entrance exam than the other, and colleges will use the higher results for admissions consideration. You will find a useful discussion of these tests and their strengths and weaknesses at www.collegeconfidential.com.

Year	Test(s)	Register	Why
Grade 7–8	SAT I	Online	Talent searches
Grade 10 (Oct)	PSAT	At high school in your district	Practice for NMSQT junior year
Grade 11 (Oct)	PSAT	At high school in your district	If student is competitive for National Merit, then take this exam; or use the results to prepare for SAT in spring
Grade 11 (Spring)	SAT or ACT	Online	Take first round of college entrance exams
Grade 12 (Fall)	SAT or ACT	Online	Take second round of college entrance exams to improve score
Grades 10–12 (as scheduled)*	AP/CLEP/ SAT II Subject Tests	AP—through local AP test site; CLEP—at CLEP test center; SAT II—online	College course exemption and/or credit

*Take early enough to report scores on college applications.

STRATEGIES FOR IMPROVING TEST SCORES

You've probably figured out by now that the teen who plans to apply to competitive schools or hopes to receive academic scholarships will need to take several high-stakes tests during high school. However, don't put your child unnecessarily through all this testing—make an honest assessment of your teen's potential before determining a course of action. Teens who do not test well will only be discouraged by numerous tests that repeatedly confirm this fact. To avoid this negative spiral, make sure your teen is well prepared before signing up for any testing.

What's the best preparation for doing well? The top strategy requires the most forethought: strength of academic schedule. Students who have completed work in a rigorous high school program, one that requires a lot of critical reading and advanced math work, have the best shot at doing well. These tests have undergone many revisions and are pretty bulletproof to prep programs that merely mask a lack of rigor in the student's regular studies. Expensive programs produce only very modest gains—the highest mean improvement I've seen is 60 points, which is not worth the thousands of dollars invested.

Students with challenging coursework under their belts can prepare to do their best on tests using the following plan:

1. Complete a self-study preparation program at least six weeks in advance of testing. Spend thirty to sixty minutes a day on this. We always grabbed a copy of Princeton Review's prep book for any particular test. For the SAT, try the most recent edition of *Gruber's Complete SAT Guide* by Gary Gruber or *Rocket Review Revolution: The Ultimate Guide to the New SAT* by Adam Robinson. For AP Exams, check out the 5 Steps to a 5 series from McGraw-Hill. Each program has different strengths and

practice exercises. The best approach is to use more than one test-prep resource. If the test will be taken on a computer, then find a prep program online that allows your teen to practice this.

2. If release exams (actual previous tests) are available from the College Board or ACT, use at least one of these and simulate actual testing conditions. Simulation will reduce test anxiety come test day. Not knowing what to expect usually lowers scores for most novice test-takers.

> **Not knowing what to expect usually lowers scores for most novice test-takers.**

3. If possible, test at a site where your teen has some familiarity with the setting. Context is a factor, and test conditions can be unpredictable and disruptive. Prepare your teen to stay focused even if the proctor is disorganized or other test-takers are goofing around (a common complaint).

4. Sample tests by Princeton Review, Barron's, and Kaplan are similar to the actual exams though not authentic, but they are still helpful for practice testing, especially if they give students a method for predicting a potential score.

5. Math scores are easier to improve than critical reading scores. That's because math achievement can rise more dramatically with instruction and practice in the general classroom, whereas critical reading skills grow slowly over time with lots of reading. Kids who have been reading broadly and ahead of grade level since elementary school will have strong critical reading skills, while kids who do not read will not. So the quickest way to improve overall test scores is to focus on math achievement. We

used the Chalk Dust Company's *ACT-SAT Math Review* program for this.

6. Critical reading questions often hinge on a student's understanding of vocabulary and grammatical construction. *Vocabulary for Achievement* is the program I like best, as it teaches words in context, includes reading comprehension questions, and is aligned with the SAT. *Gruber's Complete SAT Guide* has a good vocabulary list to work through if time is short. I'm not a big fan of intensive grammar programs, but here is where knowing the basics of sentence analysis (diagramming) will pay off. *Shurley Grammar* (www.shurley.com) certainly addresses this well, as does the free online tutorial at www.englishgrammar101.com. We also used the practice exercises for the writing section of the SAT as our actual grammar work. (I like Barron's for this.)

7. Schedule each test well in advance and control your teen's schedule that week. Don't choose a date when other commitments are draining your teen of energy and interrupting her normal routine. (If you figure out how to do this, e-mail me, because we never got this right.)

8. On test day, serve your teen a protein-rich breakfast— avoid sugar and carbohydrates. These tests are long, and protein will generate energy for a longer duration. The sugar and carbs in muffins and cereal are going to give them a quick burst, and then fatigue will set in, compounded by the natural anxiety of taking a test. Send along a high-energy snack to be eaten at the break.

9. Use a checklist on test day to make sure your teen has everything he needs: photo ID, calculator, admission's slip, etc. If your teen does not have a driver's license or passport, you will need to either go with him to verify

his identity by showing your own driver's license, or you need to obtain an official ID in advance. AAA can provide one, and some homeschool organizations are now providing these as well.

10. Use the follow-up reports you receive to strategically prepare for the next round of testing. If critical reading scores are low on one test, they will likely be low on other tests, so bump up the rigors of your program, starting with vocabulary work and practice sets that integrate critical reading strategies into your regular schedule. Do the same thing if the problem area is math or writing.

CAN RETESTING IMPROVE SCORES?

Yes, usually it does. A familiarity with the test and testing conditions typically helps kids increase their scores the next time around. After teens have tested once, they may also be more motivated to prepare more thoroughly the second time around.

What kind of improvement is typical? Test scores are relatively stable over time. Any test prep program that guarantees significant gains is advertising falsely (look closely and you'll see there's a loophole). In my experience, a hundred-point jump is common with additional preparation, and a twenty- to thirty-point gain is likely through retesting alone.

However, if your teen simply does not turn out to be a high-scoring test-taker, it's not the death of a dream. Forget about investing a lot of time in improving his scores and work on the other graces in his life. There are other ways for teens to distinguish themselves to colleges and future employers.

346

> In my experience, a hundred-point jump is common with additional preparation, and a twenty- to thirty-point gain is likely through retesting alone.

35 LETTERS OF RECOMMENDATION

Recommendation letters will be required for admission to a competitive school and for meritorious scholarship decisions. So if you think either of these is in your teen's future, you should anticipate this early on.

Letters of recommendation can heavily influence admissions and scholarship offers if written by individuals who are highly qualified and discriminating (able to evaluate your teen against prior students or employees) and can provide thoughtful and detailed insight into your child's noteworthy qualities. These kinds of letters take time, something the most qualified individuals you know may not have a lot of. So your teen needs to do his or her best to be the deserving student a qualified professional will want to recommend.

This is where you can provide helpful foresight and guidance. Think through in advance what teacher, employer, or professional in your church may have contact with your teen. Find a context for your teen to work with this individual, perhaps in a class, a job, a mentorship, or volunteer activity. Timing is important—if you can delay an opportunity until your teen is mature enough to make a commitment to do his or her best, do so. It also shows maturity if the student (not Mom) approaches the individual for a letter of recommendation.

It's perfectly acceptable and even advisable to *offer* to provide the letter writer with the criteria for evaluation and to supply anecdotal evidence of how your teen meets this standard. When former students request a letter of recommendation, I ask them to refresh my memory by writing down their best projects and papers completed in my class and the grades they received.

However, it is not acceptable to ask to see the letter of recommendation—if it's signed and sealed, don't open it. When requesting the letter, your teen should ask first if the individual is willing to provide a *strong* letter of recommendation. That's the point where the person should have the honesty to say yes or no.

People writing letters of recommendation should have things to say that are striking and unique about your student. This is one way to offset less-than-impressive test scores. If your child has shown leadership in a field of service, that's going to mean just as much to admissions officers as any test scores. Future leaders make distinguished alumni.

> People writing letters of recommendation should have things to say that are striking and unique about your student.

So whom should your student ask to write a letter of recommendation?

* Individuals who will be able to make a valid comparison between your teen and the teen's peers.
* Professionals who are successful or make hiring decisions.

* Experts in the field of study your child intends to pursue—you may be required to provide at least one recommendation from a teacher or mentor in the declared major, especially for a competitive field of study such as engineering or the sciences.

* Unbiased individuals who can highlight your teen's work ethic or character traits—a coach, employer, or youth pastor, for example.

If the letter writer is qualified but unsure what types of things to mention, here are some of the areas I typically touch upon when writing a letter:

* *My own qualifications.* I'm an English teacher with thirty years' experience working predominantly with gifted and talented high school students

* *The context in which I know the student.* I identify the course and the criterion for acceptance, and I explain the college-prep orientation of our classes to show that it's a fairly competitive environment.

* *I recap the student's achievement in my class and how that student compares to others I've taught.* If the student has ranked near the top of my classes in a particular dimension—e.g., writing or creativity—I highlight this fact.

* *If I've been given the criteria for consideration, I work through the list, providing illustrations.* If I don't have a list, I focus on the student's academic achievement, leadership, service, persistence, willingness to accept input, and initiative.

* *I zero in on what is unique or memorable about the student.* I will mention it if the student is a first-generation college applicant or has overcome difficult odds, as well as anything that illustrates character. I highlighted one

349

student's devotion to the foster children her family cares for; for another, I mentioned his heroism in acting quickly to save a sibling from harm.

* *I provide the letter of recommendation on letterhead.* CHESS family school and Encore! Home School Productions created letterhead, in part, to have official-looking documents to use in situations like this.

350

36 THE TOP-NOTCH APPLICATION

Okay, so your student is working through a rigorous academic schedule and has received her scores from the appropriate tests. It is now summer prior to your teen's senior year. It's time to start working on college applications.

Divide the prospective schools into a "dream" pile and "safety" pile. Select a school from the safety pile to complete first as practice; this will give you a good idea what kind of time and effort is required. Then work on the most important applications next so they will be ready to submit by fall deadlines. Work on the application over a period of several days.

If your teen has the qualifications to attend a select school and wants to apply many places, then use the online Common Application for this (http://app.commonapp.org). There are more than three hundred participating schools using this application process, which will save you both time. This also indicates to admission offices that your teen is motivated to get into competitive schools and will likely receive competing offers.

Divvy up the work between you and your teen. Your teen

351

needs to assume responsibility for this process, but you need to save most of her energy for filling out the application and generating an essay. I suggest you perform all the record-keeping tasks and ordering of official transcripts and test scores.

Come up with a plan for submitting an application that is organized, neat, and focused. Based upon your research about the particular college and department, what qualities do they appear to be looking for? What evidence is there in your teen's program and extracurricular activities that demonstrates these qualities? How and where can these be highlighted?

> I suggest you perform all the record-keeping tasks and ordering of official transcripts and test scores.

A few guidelines to keep in mind:

* Applications should be typed unless the student's handwriting is striking. It's fine to answer questions in a Word document and then neatly cut these to fit and use rubber cement to secure in place. If photocopying is permissible, then do that. Make sure all signatures, though, are original on the final document.
* The transcript should be printed, not handwritten. Include the information outlined in chapter 29.
* If an addendum is used to list extracurricular activities, organize this on a single sheet of paper in résumé format or on a grid. Attach the addendum only if it's permitted. Call or e-mail the admissions office if you're not sure.
* Make sure every page of the application and addendum includes your teen's full name (and social security number if you are not averse to this) in the header. This is especially important when applying to larger institutions.
* Submit your applications online if possible, but make

sure you save copies. If you mail the application, pay extra to request delivery confirmation from the post office.

* About ten days after mailing the application, your teen should e-mail to ask if the application has been received and if the institution has everything needed for acceptance and scholarship consideration.

NOW, ABOUT THAT ESSAY . . .

The college application essay is the student's opportunity to do two things: 1) introduce himself to the selection committee in lieu of a face-to-face meeting, and 2) demonstrate how capable he is of expressing himself in writing. The goal is simple: Get committee members to say, "Hey, I'd love to have this kid in one of my classes. This person is intellectually curious and fascinating."

The essay prompts given by the college are designed to help the student do just that. If the prompts are generic and wide-open—e.g., *Describe a significant experience that has had an impact upon you*—then they want to see if your teen can think reflectively. In other words, to what degree does she take what life sends her way and learn from it?

If the prompt that is more targeted, or less personal—e.g., *Describe a current global problem and how you suggest addressing it*—they want to see evidence of critical thinking. In other words, to what degree is the student able to think deeply about the causes behind large-scale problems, and how innovative and persuasive can he be in expressing his position.

In either case, the student is introducing her "intellectual" self to the committee. And what she conveys in the essay is essentially a statement of what she can bring to the party. What is this person going to add to the campus culture? And how does that fit with the college's core values?

The essay is a very important part of the application, so it

353

should go through several drafts. The teen should solicit input from outside reviewers, especially if the essay is being submitted to a top-choice school.

Content is important, but so is tone—the attitude that comes through in what the student writes. Does he sound arrogant? Or confident? The selection committee is looking for *deserving* students, not *entitled* students. How it will sound to the selection committee may be difficult for your teen to gauge, which is why it's important to solicit feedback from others.

Recommended Resources

How to Write a Winning College Application Essay by Michael Mason

Conquering the College Admissions Essay in 10 Steps: Crafting a Winning Personal Statement by Alan Gelb

37 MAKING THE MOST OF VISITS AND INTERVIEWS

Early in high school you and your teen should attend college fairs and make a few visits to schools in your area. This will get her acclimated to the admissions process. Then as she narrows down her list of target schools, work into your schedule time to attend the open houses at the schools highest on her target list. You want to attend an open house, if possible, because the key people you need to talk with will more likely be available here. This is when you can get answers to important questions about financial aid, scholarships, study abroad, campus living, advising, and programs.

After you attend a few open houses and listen to the presentations, as well as the questions other parents raise, you will better understand what the important issues are. In the appendix of this book, you will find a list of potential questions to consider asking. Remember, this is a consumer decision. The more time you spend now researching potential schools, the better the final fit will be.

When you make visits together during your teen's junior or senior year to schools on his short list, it's time for your teen to engage and raise more questions than you. At these final visits, the admissions officers present are taking notes as well. It will make a strong impression if your teen appears more thoughtful and personable than the average bear just out of hibernation.

I'm not sure why it happened, but Mike and Gabe actually made their final visit to their target school without me. They drove themselves across the state to meet officials at the business school after being accepted into the university. They ended up meeting with the department chair instead of an administrator because of a scheduling conflict. This turned out to be fortuitous, and they started at that university with the head of the business school knowing them on a first-name basis and taking an active interest in their progress. This positive first impression, I'm sure, was a contributing factor to the internal scholarships and other opportunities they received once they entered school. Be ready for these serendipitous moments—coach your teen in advance to step up to the plate when the opportunity arises.

If your teen is invited to a college interview, then you can expect a positive experience. Typically, the college views the interview as an opportunity for the college to sell your teen on the school. If the interview is for a scholarship competition, all interviewees commonly walk away with something. After all, the university would like all candidates to matriculate there, since these students represent the top tier of applicants. Kayte was a finalist for the Chancellor's Award (a full-ride scholarship) at Pitt, and even though she was not selected, she was still offered an additional year of full tuition remission if she double-majored and was invited to a scholars' retreat for a small group of incoming freshman. Half the time in the interview was spent on selling *her* on *Pitt*.

Preparation for the interview will always improve the outcome. Many colleges highlight their outstanding students and

Making the Most of Your College Visits

First, know why you're going to college, and then look for a school that fits your goals and desires. You may need to make a few compromises, of course, but do not settle for a program you aren't really passionate about—you will only end up wasting money. Also, don't be content with reading the college literature. Most schools put their best foot forward in print, so you will need to seek more honest answers from a visit. Speak with the professors and students there, and ask specific questions. Also, make sure there are like-minded people in the student body. After all, you will spend the next four years in this community, and you won't enjoy the experience if you cannot find friends.

Rebekah Wilhelm
Student at Hillsdale College

award winners on their websites. Spend some time studying these to further understand what qualities and values the institution esteems. Help your teen think through which of his prior experiences and future goals *and* ambitions fit best with the college's profile. The interview will be an opportunity for the selection committee to assess your child's *potential*. Where is this kid headed and will that bring honor and distinction to his alma mater? Are there programs or research underway on campus for which this student is a great fit? Universities want to keep talent in the pipeline for the programs that are already winning them recognition. Your teen should be familiar with what's going on in the program he is applying to. If you know someone on the inside at the school, be unashamed to ask for any helpful information this person might provide.

If your teen has little experience with interviewing, then a mock interview can only help. While driving to college visits, I

357

would ask my teens questions in the car and let them get comfortable generating responses. (See the appendix for practice interview questions.) For Kayte's high stakes interview at Pitt, she put on a new suit and drove to a mock interview with a good (but intimidating) friend from church who had done a lot of hiring. Even though it felt like overkill at the time, she maintains it helped her manage her nerves during the real deal.

As a follow-up to a campus visit or interview, it's appropriate for your teen to send a thank-you note, especially if a department chair or other key decision-maker met with your teen.

38 SEEKING AND FINDING FINANCIAL AID

In the end, if you have a bunch of kids to ship off to school, you're going to wind up with a shelf of books on financial aid and a filing drawer full of financial-aid folders. I found buying a house to be a simpler financial transaction to understand than many financial aid programs!

The least complicated financial arrangement is that you and your child pay the tuition as she goes, in which case you can just ignore this chapter and all those applications for loans and grants and scholarships. The best deal is a full ride, meaning tuition, room, and board are covered by the school or scholarship foundation; you just have to spring for the books, which *will* cost hundreds and hundreds of dollars. But only a handful of incoming freshmen receive that kind of deal.

The more common situation is that the student with above-average stats for a particular institution is offered a partial scholarship and a mix of loans and grants. Some of these come from the federal government, while others come from private organizations. Some will be one-year grants, while others will be renewable, requiring new applications every year to be submitted by the deadline.

There are a lot of financial aid categories to keep track of, and you will need to help your navigate the many options in these complicated waters.

GRANTS

Grants are awards given based on financial need, not academic merit. You do not have to pay grants back, but you need to submit your applications by the deadlines each year or you don't get them. Grants can come from the federal government, your state government (often limited to use at in-state institutions), or the college itself. These financial awards are based on the parents' prior year's tax return, so that must be filed in a timely manner. Here's a tip: File your tax return as early as possible and then start filing your FAFSA (Free Application for Federal Student Aid) for the next school year.

STUDENT LOANS

Loans may come from the federal government, a bank, a private organization, Mom and Pop, Grandpa—whoever's willing to loan your student money for her education. A few loans are issued directly to the student, while others are available to the parents.

Stafford Loans from the U.S. government are the easiest to secure and are issued directly to students. The amounts rise incrementally as the student accumulates college credits, but the loans are relatively small—less than $5000 a semester—so students will likely need other sources of income to cover their costs. Perkins Loans are also available to students with financial need. Both loans have low interest rates, and repayment does not begin until six months after graduation or withdrawal from school. Keep this in mind should your teen decide to "take a semester off."

Other loans are available at higher interest rates. Signature loans, available through Sallie Mae, are issued to the student, but the interest rate is lower if there is a co-signer (you). Repayment on these loans is also deferred until after graduation. With loans issued to students, interest can be deferred as well until after graduation, if they demonstrate financial need. For other students, the interest is accumulating even though repayment has not begun.

Each year your teen must take out a new loan(s) to cover that year's bills—even if the loans come from the same source. In the end, students can have several loans from several different places, and you will be receiving constant mail about available loans. The craziness surrounding the process is one reason we encouraged our younger kids to choose the least expensive options, pay as they go, and borrow less and less.

> The craziness surrounding the process is one reason we encouraged our younger kids to choose the least expensive options, pay as they go, and borrow less and less.

If you will be using loans for some of your child's college education, then it's a good idea to make personal contact with the financial aid office at the target university during an official visit. Find out whom you should call or e-mail in the future if you have questions. Get a feel for how organized this office is—if your questions are fielded by student workers, be careful, as this may mean advice will be inconsistent.

361

SCHOLARSHIPS

Scholarships are awarded based on merit, either academic or athletic. Most merit scholarship offers will come from the schools where your teen applies. There are private sources of scholarship as well, but your teen will need to hunt these down, submit an application, and write a killer essay to get them.

Scholarship money comes from endowments, and nobody has bigger pots to draw from than the colleges and universities themselves. In the same way Division I athletic programs use scholarship offers to attract the best high school sports stars, colleges and universities use scholarship offers to attract students with academic potential (and whose stats will boost their rankings). Scholarships can come from various sources within the university: the department, the Honors College, the alumni association, and these offers may roll in slowly over several months. Schools have until April to make their final financial aid offers.

The best scholarships are renewable. If a student maintains his GPA at a certain level, the money will be applied to his bill every year for eight to ten semesters. Warn your student that scholarships are easier to lose than he may think. An inexperienced student may take a heavy course load freshman year—for example, a four-credit math course in a rigorous engineering program—and struggle. Help your teen make good scheduling choices that allow him or her to establish a solid GPA. A C grade in the junior year has a lot less impact on the overall GPA than a C in the freshman year. Keep in mind that grades earned at other institutions, such as a community college, will not count toward the GPA at the next school, so transfer students are starting from scratch.

A FEW IMPORTANT TIPS

Applying for scholarships and other financial aid is usually a fairly complicated procedure for most families, and the learning curve can be steep. The best idea may be to give one person in the family responsibility for learning the ropes and trust that you will get back your time investment on subsequent children. As you've probably inferred, I don't think this person should be the student. His job ought to be keeping those grades up.

Here are some of the best strategies for lining up the best offers:

* Time your kids' matriculation, knowing that the more kids you have in school, the more aid you qualify for. (I realize this may be a hard sell in some quarters.)
* Get your taxes done as early as possible for the year preceding your child's entrance into college.
* To get an idea what schools will expect your total annual contribution to your child's costs to be, run the numbers using FinAid's quick EFC (expected family contribution) calculator at www.finaid.org. The official number is generated when you file your FAFSA online at www.fafsa.ed.gov. Remember, you need to file those tax returns first.
* Politely let the admissions offices know if your teen receives a better offer from another school. It's not unusual for a college to then match or better the offer.
* Apply early. This indicates serious interest and organization on your teen's part. Colleges believe these applicants yield better students who will stay with the program. Also, many universities offer scholarships on a rolling basis, so there are fewer funds for late applicants.
* Your alma mater and universities where older siblings are already enrolled will often extend the best offers. Schools are interested in establishing a strong alumni network of future donors, and keeping it "all in the family" is one strategy they use to achieve this goal.

39 GETTING IN AND GETTING THE DOUGH

How do admissions committees ultimately decide when they have far more applicants than space? Most will tell you it's a holistic review, but the factors discussed in prior chapters will form the core of the decision-making process. Test scores are used to determine the student's basic potential, and high scores will at least put your teen's application in the pile for closer review. Some schools say the SAT/ACT scores are weighted equally with the student's GPA, while others say the GPA is given two-thirds or more weight in the equation. Again, with homeschooled students, scores count quite a bit more because the GPA may be viewed as less than objective.

When reviewing your student's transcript, selection committees will look for the strength of schedule I mentioned earlier. It is better to have a lower GPA and show numerous hard sciences, advanced mathematics, and Advanced Placement work than it is to play it safe, taking only the average high school classes, and get the 4.0. This won't set your student apart.

Those are the two criteria that get the most weight—how much they contribute to the overall decision will vary from school to school. Students must first demonstrate they know how to work hard and present evidence of having done so.

Selection committees will next consider any evidence of character, distinction, quality of fit, and uniqueness that emerges from a student's essays, letters of recommendation, and extra-curricular activities. These should combine to create a portrait that is compelling and relevant to the institution's core values. It's hard to say just what might jump out at the selection committee as compelling. They are, of course, reviewing your student's application in light of all other applicants in the pile. I know one student with exceptionally high scores and GPA who won the top scholarship award because the selection committee liked that he also juggled! They thought that was unique. Go figure.

Here's a checklist of qualifications that can influence merit scholarship offers and acceptance into competitive programs:

* High SAT/ACT scores will open the scholarship door most readily. You should expect some merit funding for SAT scores in excess of 1800 or an ACT over 27. You should expect substantial merit funding for SAT scores over 2100 or an ACT above 32. Individual math or verbal scores exceeding 700 can also yield merit scholarship offers if the student is majoring in a related field.

* Select challenging courses in high school. Advanced Placement and college level courses carry the most weight with committees.

* Teach your student to write essays that are engaging and reflective and show potential for intellectual growth.

* Your teen should pursue unique opportunities that demonstrate initiative and broaden her perspective of the world. She should also learn to write and talk about these experiences in an engaging and reflective way.

* Travel.

* Pursue cross-cultural experiences.

* Have your teen volunteer regularly over an extended period of time for the same organization. He should be able to write and talk about these experiences in an engaging and reflective manner.

* She should assume responsibility and leadership whenever possible.

* Have him start something—a business, organization, a ministry, etc.

* Allow her to devote herself long-term to a hobby or field of study. She can demonstrate her proficiency through completed projects, awards, and other recognition. In-depth devotion to one or two areas is better than short-lived interest in many things.

* Your teen should solicit recommendation letters from a variety of professionals who have observed him in a number of contexts, such as church, school, athletics, work, or volunteering.

> **Your teen should solicit recommendation letters from a variety of professionals who have observed him in a number of contexts, such as church, school, athletics, work, or volunteering.**

* Encourage your teen to spend her summers in an intellectually stimulating way, such as reading, volunteering, or participation in special academic programs, especially one offered by the target university.

* Arrange for him to intern or apprentice somewhere interesting. In other words, he shouldn't waste his time working at a burger joint.

* Know your audience—colleges and scholarship committees are looking for specific types of deserving students who will eventually bring honor and recognition to their organization. Discern the qualities they value by reading between the lines of the literature they publish about their program.

* Teens should express gratitude for opportunities extended to them. The folks behind scholarships and programs believe they are offering something of value, and they hope to select students who will appreciate the opportunity and make the most of it.

* Important character qualities that should be evidenced in your teen's recommendations, essays, and application include intellectual curiosity, initiative, thoughtfulness, openness to new ideas and experiences, leadership, responsibility, service, and/or creativity.

367

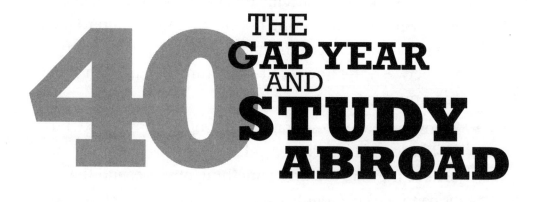

THE GAP YEAR AND STUDY ABROAD

We conclude our overview of the college decision-making process with a brief look at two experiences that your teen may want to consider.

A *gap year* refers to the practice of taking a year off after high school to travel prior to going to college. This practice is quite common in Europe and is becoming a frequent option for American students. Your family might consider taking a gap year for one of several reasons:

* Your teen isn't really sure he is ready for college and would like more time to explore his options.

* Your teen would like to work and save money for the big expenditure.

* Your teen would like to pursue experiences that will strengthen her résumé and perhaps increase scholarship offers.

All of these are viable reasons, and admissions offices will not look unfavorably on applicants who take a gap year if the purpose is clearly explained. A student who delays applying to colleges for a year will still be considered a freshman and qualify for scholarship consideration. It's also possible once your teen has been accepted to defer matriculating for one year. Acceptance and scholarship offers will be held. You just need to work out the details with the institution where your teen has committed to attend.

Another possibility to consider is inserting a gap year in the high school program, but only if homeschool regulations in your state are flexible enough to allow this. If your child is beyond the compulsory attendance age, then inserting a break will not be problematic. Or if your child only needs a few more credits for graduation, perhaps these can be completed while your teen is traveling or volunteering overseas. Several students I know spent a portion of their final years of high school serving missions overseas, and these opportunities invariably became life-shaping events that affected their college plans.

If the primary purpose of a gap prior to graduation is to earn money, try to plan this experience to also be academically or socially beneficial for your teen.

STUDYING ABROAD DURING HIGH SCHOOL

Studying overseas offers some advantages during high school. Our daughter Kayte took several trips to France during her teen years, and this is primarily why she was able to achieve fluency in French in advance of applying to colleges. Her first opportunity arose out of the exchange program we were involved with. We had a French exchange student one summer who invited her to visit in return. We were comfortable with Clemence and our interactions with her family, so we allowed Kayte to spend two weeks in Paris. From there we arranged for Kayte to spend time with two different missionary families in France who were also homeschooling. Kayte joined in with outreach activities and helped with homeschooling the missionary's children while there. Facilitating this type of arrangement is much easier

369

for homeschoolers today with the connectivity provided by Skype, Vonage, and other online telecommunications options.

Following these successful independent travel experiences, Kayte enrolled in a study abroad program in the south of France. Her brother Mike was already enrolled as part of his college program, and I reasoned she could fulfill her own upcoming college requirement to study abroad in France while traveling safely with her older brother. Kayte was able to earn college-level credits through this experience that transferred to the University of Pittsburgh.

There are many opportunities for high school students to study abroad. Of course, you will want to consider the academic and life value of the study, as this type of study is not going to be without concerns and cost. But the experience can prove life defining for many. I have seen many a self-focused adolescent return from a cross-cultural missions trip with his faith seasoned and character matured. There is nothing like seeing the suffering many face daily in much of the rest of the world to give young people a broader perspective on the meaning of life and their role in it.

> There is nothing like seeing the suffering many face daily in much of the rest of the world to give young people a broader perspective on the meaning of life and their role in it.

Here are a few tips for guaranteeing a positive study-abroad experience:

* Your own church and homeschool communities are the most reliable source of overseas opportunities and contacts. If you decide to go with an organization that regularly sponsors cross-cultural trips or study for teens,

make sure you check out their credentials and obtain recommendations from people you trust. A lot of these are also profit-making ventures, and the oversight they provide or the character of the students they accept may be problematic.

* If you are open to independent travel at this stage—for example, back-packing through Europe—make contact with a missionary or expatriate community on the ground in advance for the inside scoop. We found that English-speaking international churches in any international city are typically the hub of the expatriate community. Google "English-speaking churches," plus the city in question, and send e-mails galore.

* Be sure your teen has insurance coverage while out of country. You'll likely need to purchase a policy. It's common for first-time visitors to any country to get sick due to exposure to new viruses and germs. We also sent along with our kids a signed document giving the adults on the other end authorization to make emergency medical decisions.

* If your teen plans to spend an extended period of time in one place, she should register with the U.S. consulate or embassy in the region. This is so she can be quickly informed should a political situation arise which requires caution or evacuation. Also, the consulate often keeps a list of doctors and other individuals who specialize in service to the expatriate community.

371

* Make sure you have legal access to your teen's financial information and other personal data while he is abroad. If he is eighteen or older, you will need to have Power of Attorney in order to do this. Access to banking information requires both of you to appear in person and sign an

authorizing document.

* Negotiate with your teen in advance how she will document this experience. If you want her to complete a journal or study project as part of the privilege, get that in writing. If you expect anything from the hosts on the other end, that should be discussed up front.

* Finally, be at peace when things do not turn out as planned. This is a big part of getting outside the comfort zone, both for your teen and you. There are going to be snafus with travel arrangements, housing, itineraries, and cross-cultural communications. It's part of the learning experience. You can minimize the impact of these unexpected interruptions by being educated and plugged into the community of Americans living and traveling abroad.

Recommended Resources

Go Abroad (www.goabroad.com) is the *site* for finding the right program and getting helpful advice from seasoned travelers. It's well established and does not advocate any particular program over another. A great search engine for planning your teen's trip.

IIEPassport (www.iiepassport.org) is the non-profit administrator of the prestigious Fulbright Scholarship program. Their site provides a thorough understanding of the opportunities abroad and the safest, economical ways to achieve your goals.

Study Abroad 101 by Wendy Williamson. This book covers the nitty-gritty details you and your teen need to sort through before choosing a program. Read this and then surf the aforementioned websites.

Lonely Planet guides are a great source of information for

independent travelers, though the hostels they recommend may not meet your personal safety standards.

The Gap-Year Advantage: Helping Your Child Benefit from Time Off Before or During College by Karl Haigler and Rae Nelson. There are several good books out there about making the most of the gap year, but this is the only one written to parents. And if your house is like my house, then you are the one who will do the background reading necessary to make an informed decision.

RESOURCES FOR DOING
HIGH SCHOOL
AT HOME

TOP WEBSITES FOR
HIGH SCHOOL
AT HOME

Academic Earth

This site is your gateway to numerous free video courses from world-class scholars available on the Internet. Of particular value is the rating of these courses by users. Visit www.academicearth.org.

College Confidential

Here you will find excellent articles and active forums where individual colleges, acceptance rates, essays, and financial aid are openly discussed. Visit www.collegeconfidential.com.

Flexbooks

CK-12 is heading up an effort to create open textbooks on the Internet. In the online world, open = free. The initial effort is focused on textbooks for STEM courses—science, technology, engineering, and math. Course completed as of this printing include geometry and algebra. Visit flexbooks.ck12.org.

Homeschool Buyers Co-op

This site, run by a homeschooling family, pools the purchasing power of the homeschool community and negotiates deep discounts with retailers to qualify us for educational pricing. They also seem to have their finger on the pulse of homeschool desires, as you will find many popular resources offered here at special rates. They also post the most up-to-date list of scholar-

ship and contest opportunities for kids. Visit
www.homeschoolbuyersco-op.org.

Home School Legal Defense Association

Becky Cooke and Diane Kummer, veteran homeschool moms, have
built the "Homeschooling Thru High School" area of HSLDA's website. Very well organized and up-to-date. Visit
www.hslda.org/highschool.

Homeschool 2 College

You'll first need to request permission to join, but this is a very
active group with excellent archives. You'll find a lot of personal-
experience stories here as well as seasoned advice. Go to
http://groups.yahoo.com/group/homeschool2college. I regularly
follow the discussions on this board and that of its sister group,
Conservative Homeschool 2 College, at
http://groups.yahoo.com/group/conservativehs2c.

Discussion Forums at The Well-Trained Mind and Sonlight

Visit www.welltrainedmind.com and www.sonlight-forums.com.
While the discussion topics are most germane to the products these
companies sell, both have very active forums about homeschooling
through high school.

Learner.org

The top-end educational video courses produced by Annenberg
Media are now available free. Yes, I said free. These include courses
in literature, composition, algebra, statistics, Spanish, and more.
Visit www.Learner.org.

The Rebelution

Alex and Brett Harris, now college students, run this site that encourages teens to do the hard things. Visit www.therebelution.com.

Homeschooling Teen E-zine

This blog that features the adventurous lives of teens schooled at home, such as Zac Sunderland, who circumnavigated the globe solo at the age of seventeen (and took his schoolbooks with him). Visit www.homeschoolingteen.com.

TEN TERRIFIC ONLINE TOOLS

1. Moodle

Free content management system you can use for organizing online classes. Visit http://moodle.com.

2. Webspiration

Free web-based concept-mapping tool. Visit http://mywebspiration.com.

3. Google Docs

Free tool for collaborating on documents and spreadsheets. Visit http://docs.google.com.

4. Teascript

Free transcript generator. Visit http://teascript.com.

5. Google Groups

Free networking site where groups can collaborate, upload files, run discussions, and create pages.
Visit http://groups.google.com.

6. BrainPop

Hundreds of short animated video clips, available by subscription. Especially appropriate for junior high students and reluctant learners. Visit www.brainpop.com.

7. Rubistar Rubric Maker

Free rubric maker for setting the criteria for success in advance. Visit http://rubistar.4teachers.org.

8. WatchKnow

A collaborative effort to organize the best educational videos on the Internet. Visit www.watchknow.org.

9. Google Earth

Unbelievable! Just about any place on earth has been visually recreated in 3-D using satellite images. Plus, individuals can upload photographs of sites on the ground. You can virtually "fly over" your destination before you actually visit it. With version 5.0, you can see the images of that area from the past, tracking the course of recent history. Download at http://earth.google.com.

10. Wikipedia

I'm a convert. The wisdom of the crowds beats the elitism of academia in my book. Whether they will admit to it or not, virtually every serious researcher starts here. Go to http://en.wikipedia.org/wiki/Main_Page.

TEN GOALS EVERY TEEN SHOULD REACH BEFORE LEAVING HOME

1. Be able to manage a checkbook

2. Acquire a working knowledge of basic etiquette in a variety of social contexts

3. Create an organizational system for handling important papers and bills

4. Acquire some training in worldviews

5. Acquire some training in inductive Bible study

6. Read *Rich Dad, Poor Dad*, attend Dave Ramsey's Financial Peace University, or complete similar materials related to sound financial planning

7. Be educated in defensive driving

8. Read trusted books on choosing a spouse

9. Complete a career/interest inventory and/or shadow someone working in a field of interest

10. Experience another culture and volunteer among those who are less fortunate

SAMPLE STUDENT
TRANSCRIPTS

Sunnydale Home School

High School Transcript

Full Name: Gender:

Address: Place of Birth:

Date of Birth:

Parents: E-mail Address:

Telephone: Graduation Date: May 2008

SS Number: Class Rank: N/A

Freshman: 2004–05 School Year

SUBJECT	GRADE	CREDIT
Algebra II/Trig	A	1.0
World History & Geography	A	1.0
Public Speaking	A	1.0
*Programming Logic (CIS 130)	A	0.5
Graphic Art	A	0.25
English 9	A	1.0
**Latin 101 & 102 (MUS 111)	A	1.0
Physics w/Lab	A	1.0
*College Band (MUS 111)	A	0.25
Physical Education	A	0.50

*Apache Community College Course, Dual Credit

**Apache College Class, Dual Credit, taken in seventh grade

GPA: 4.0   Year Credits: 7.5

Cumulative GPA 4.0

Cumulative Credits: 7.5

Sophomore: 2005–06 School Year

SUBJECT	GRADE	CREDIT
Pre-Calculus	A	1.0
U.S. History & Geography	A	1.0
Biology w/Lab	A	1.0
American Literature	A	1.0
Composition 10	A	1.0
**Latin 201&202	A	1.0
* College Band	A	0.25
C++	A	1.0
Bible	A	0.25
Intro to US/AZ Govt.	A	0.50
Physical Education	A	0.50

*Apache Community College Course, Dual Credit

**Apache College Class, Dual Credit, taken in eighth Grade

GPA: 4.0   Year Credits: 8.5

Cumulative GPA: 4.0

Cumulative Credits: 16.0

382

Junior: 2006–07 School Year

SUBJECT	GRADE	CREDIT
AP English Literature & Composition [AP Score: 5]	A	1.0
AP US History [AP Score: 4]	A	1.0
*Calculus I	A	1.0
Chemistry w/Lab	A	1.0
**Intro to Networking (CIS 150)	A	0.5
Art (Yearbook Art Director)	A	1.0
Physical Education	A	0.25
**Racquetball & Weights (HPE 118)	A	0.25

*Continuing Education & Academic Outreach: Arizona State University, Dual Credit

**Apache College Class, Dual Credit

GPA: 4.0   Year Credits: 6.0

Cumulative GPA 4.0

Cumulative Credits: 22.0

Senior: 2007–08 School Year

SUBJECT	GRADE	CREDIT
AP Psychology	A	1.0
*Calculus II	A	1.0
*Calculus III	A	1.0
AP Physics B w/lab	A	1.0
AP Chemistry w/lab	A	1.0
Physical Education	A	0.5
AP Music Theory & Comp	A	1.0
Art (Yearbook Editor)	A	1.0
**British Lit/World Lit		1.0

*Continuing Education & Academic Outreach: Arizona State University, Dual Credit

**Apache College Class, Dual Credit

GPA: 4.0 Pending Year Credits: 8.5

Cumulative GPA: 4.0

Cumulative Credits: 30.5

383

OFFICIAL HIGH SCHOOL TRANSCRIPT

Student:
Address:

Social Security:
Telephone:
Birth Date:
Gender: Male

School:
Address:

Graduation Date: 05/29/2009
Credits Earned: 40.0 as of 05/31/2008
Cumulative GPA: 4.0 on a 4.0 scale (unweighted)
Class Rank: 1 out of 1

Courses and Grades			
Grade 9 – Academic Year: 2005-06	**1ˢᵗ Sem**	**2ⁿᵈ Sem**	**Credits**
English Literature: 19ᵗʰ & 20ᵗʰ Cent (H)	A	A	1.0
AP Calculus BC	A	A	2.0
General Biology – BI 101/102 *	A	A	2.0
Modern History: 1815-2000 (H)	A	A	1.0
AP German Language	A	A	1.0
Conversation et Composition Française (H)	A	A	1.0
Latin III	A	A	1.0
Music – Piano, Violin, and Orchestra	A	A	1.0
Grade 10 – Academic Year: 2006-07	**1ˢᵗ Sem**	**2ⁿᵈ Sem**	**Credits**
English Literature & Composition (H)	A	A	1.0
Multivariable Calculus (H)	A	A	1.0
AP Computer Science AB	A	A	1.0
Introductory Physics – PY 203/04 *	A	A	2.0
AP U.S. History †	A	A	1.0
AP U.S. Government & Politics †	A	A	1.0
Le Français à travers les âges (H)	A	A	1.0
Russian Language I	A	A	1.0
Music – Piano, Violin, and Orchestra	A	A	1.0
Grade 11 – Academic Year: 2007-08	**1ˢᵗ Sem**	**2ⁿᵈ Sem**	**Credits**
AP English Literature & Composition †	A	A	1.0
Differential Equations – MA 213 *	A	-	1.0
Linear Algebra – MA 218 *	-	A	1.0
Elem Statistics Probability – MA 207 *	A	-	1.0
Modern Physics III – PY 205 *	Summer Term: A		1.0
General Chemistry – CH 101/102 *	A	A	2.0
AP European History †	A	A	1.0
Russian Language II	A	A	1.0
Music – Piano, Violin, and Orchestra	A	A	1.0
Grade 12 – Academic Year: 2008-09	**1ˢᵗ Sem**	**2ⁿᵈ Sem**	**Credits**
Senior Honors English (H)	A	A	1.0
Intro. Partial Differential Equations (H)	A	A	1.0
National Cancer Institute Internship (H)	A	A	3.0
Elements of Microbiology – BI 203 *	A	-	1.0
Cell Biology & Tissue Cult. – BI 220 *	-	A	1.0
AP Macroeconomics †	A	A	1.0
AP French Literature	A	A	1.0
Music – Violin and Orchestra	A	A	1.0

Standardized Test Scores			
Test	SAT	SAT	PSAT
Date Taken	03/2008	04/2006	11/2007
Critical Reading	730	660	80
Math	720	800	80
Writing	800	770	80

SAT Subject Tests		
11/2004	French with Listening	800
11/2005	Mathematics Level 2	800
11/2005	German with Listening	760
05/2006	Biology-M	790
12/2006	Latin	660
05/2007	US History	750
10/2007	Physics	790
05/2008	Literature	780
05/2008	Chemistry	790

Advanced Placement Tests		
05/2005	AP French Language	5
05/2006	AP Calculus BC	5
05/2006	AP Biology	5
05/2006	AP German Language	5
05/2007	AP Computer Science AB	5
05/2007	AP Physics C – E&M	5
05/2007	AP Physics C – Mech	5
05/2007	AP U.S. Government	5
05/2007	AP U.S. History	5
05/2008	AP European History	4
05/2008	AP Chemistry	5
05/2008	AP English Literature	5
05/2008	AP Statistics	5

Total Credits Earned				
	9ᵗʰ	**10ᵗʰ**	**11ᵗʰ**	**12ᵗʰ**
English	1.0	1.0	1.0	1.0
Math	2.0	2.0	3.0	1.0
Natural Science	2.0	2.0	3.0	5.0
Social Science	1.0	2.0	1.0	1.0
Foreign Lang.	3.0	2.0	1.0	1.0
Arts	1.0	1.0	1.0	1.0
Total	*10.0*	*10.0*	*10.0*	*10.0*

Footnotes and Grading/Credit System

*   College courses taken at George Community College, Maryland
†   Online AP courses taken from Pennsylvania Home Schoolers
(H) Honors courses that require higher level of critical reasoning
AP College Board Advanced Placement courses

Courses: See attached sheets for course descriptions & grading.
Grading System: A 4.0, B 3.0, C 2.0, D 1.0, F 0.0, Passing = C.
Credit System: 1.0 credit = 180 hours (5 hours/week x 36 weeks)

I certify that the information in this transcript is complete and correct.

_____   _____
                                 Date

High School Transcript

www.Everyday-Education.com

Admission: 8/2005
Graduation: 06/2009

Basic Information

Grading Scale
A—Superior 92-100 (4 grade points)
B—Good 84-91 (3 grade points)
C—Satisfactory 76-83 (2 grade points)
D—Below average 68-75 (1 grade point)
P—Pass
* Indicates AP-level course with weighted grade points.

Unit
Represents 120 hours of guided study per 36-week school year.

Credit by Examination
(AP) or (CLEP) follows Course Description. Weighted grade is assigned based upon percentile ranking of test results.

Dual-Credit Courses
(ELACC) follows Course Description. Grade and course descriptions issued by East Los Angeles Community College. Weighted high-school quality points are granted for these classes.

Awards/Achievements
2006- Adventure Gamers Essay Contest: 1st place
2007- HTML Certification

Certification of Official Transcript

NAME
Date of Birth:

Fall 2005

Course Description	Grade	Units Earned	Grade points
English I	A	.5	4
Algebra I	A	.5	4
American History	A	.5	4
Computer Fundamentals	A	.5	4
Art: Graphic Design	A	.5	4
Physical Education: Volleyball	A	.5	4
Total		3	24

Spring 2006

Course Description	Grade	Units Earned	Grade points
English I	A	.5	4
Algebra I	A	.5	4
American History	A	.5	4
Earth Science	A	.5	4
Art: Graphic Storytelling	A	.5	4
Physical Education: Basketball	A	.5	4
Total		3	24
School total		6	48

Fall 2006

Course Description	Grade	Units Earned	Grade points
English II	A	.5	4
Algebra II	B	.5	3
World History I	A	.5	4
Web Design I	A	.5	4
Art History	A	.5	4
Physical Education: Swimming	A	.5	4
Total		3	23

Spring 2007

Course Description	Grade	Units Earned	Grade points
English II (CLEP—Eng. Comp.)	A*	.5	5
Algebra II	A	.5	4
World History II	A	.5	4
Web Design II	A	.5	4
Health & Fitness	A	.5	4
Physical Education: Tennis	A	.5	4
Total		3	25
School total		12	96

Fall 2007

Course Description	Grade	Units Earned	Grade points
American Literature	A	.5	4
Geometry	B	.5	3
United States Government	A	.5	4
Biology I (ELACC)	B	.5	4
French I	A	.5	4
Choir	A	.5	4
Total		3	23

Spring 2008

Course Description	Grade	Units Earned	Grade points
American Literature	A	.5	4
Geometry	A	.5	4
Economics	A	.5	4
Biology II (ELACC)	B	.5	4
French II	B	.5	3
Journalism	A	.5	4
Total		3	23
School total		18	142

Fall 2008

Course Description	Grade	Units Earned	Grade points
British Literature	A	.5	4
Pre-Calculus (ELACC)	B	.5	4
French III	B	.5	3
Fundamentals of Programming	A	.5	4
Speculative Fiction	A	.5	4
Art: Drawing & Painting	A	.5	4
Total		3	23

Spring 2009

Course Description	Grade	Units Earned	Grade points
British Literature	A	.5	4
Public Speaking (ELACC)	B	.5	4
HIS 101 West. Civ. (ELACC)	A	.5	5
French IV	A	.5	4
Creative Writing	A	.5	4
Health & Driver's Education	A	.5	4
Total		3	25
School total		24	190
Final Grade Point Average			**3.95**

SAMPLE COLLEGE APPLICATION ESSAYS

These are actual, unvarnished essays by former students who received full or substantial scholarships to the schools where they applied.

ESSAY #1

The prompt asked the applicant to describe a significant experience and how the student was affected by it.

It is the end of the first week of (name of pre-college academic camp) and anger prevents me from falling asleep as I lie on dirty dorm room sheets. Every time I close my eyes I see bloody body parts in the streets of Cambodia and hear Dr. John yelling about America's lack of involvement. For six days I have been bombarded with global problems: irreconcilable income charts, disturbing images of fleeing refugees, and the recurring theme of America's inaction ricocheted about my brain. This unasked for confrontation leaves me exhausted and agitated, challenging my preconceived beliefs.

I have been brought to a crossroads between apathy and involvement. The unsettling knowledge I have acquired leaves me with only two alternatives: The temptation to forget and "move on" provides an easy way out, but requires the silencing of my conscience. Or I can react, invest time and energy and actively work for change. The idealism surrounding this position scares me, and I question the solidity of its foundation.

Perhaps when inspiration and motivation are extinguished, I will be left further disillusioned. I am searching for a more realistic bridge, testing my resolution before I set out.

Apathy leaves me with little to applaud; the word itself describes merely a "lack". It holds no power, action, or purpose. Yet, this lack allows an effortless response and appeals to a high school student burdened with commitments and a packed extracurricular schedule. I can further plead that international issues should be secondary to more domestic issues. I need to prioritize and perhaps South African AIDS victims are too difficult and distant a problem for my limited time and energy.

This strategy parallels America's international policies in many situations. Take for instance the United States' response to the ethnic strife in Rwanda during the 1990's. The African country was dislocated from our political agenda and national interest; therefore, we didn't get involved. In the same way the fact that Croatian refugees are not in my self-interest should free me from obligation.

But the counter argument questions our moral obligation. Rwandans were being slaughtered, human rights violations were rampant, and the United States was appallingly idle. Does not basic morality require us to act? In the same sense, am I not as a human being obligated to help the poor and suffering? And on a more personal level, does my inaction as a Christian conflict with the principles of my faith? If I am to preserve my integrity and remain rational in my response, I must answer these questions.

On a national level I have concluded that moral obligation cannot serve as the determinative for action. There are two reasons for this: First, I do not think our citizens have a consistent belief system; and therefore, could not agree on what entails a moral obligation. Rapid, uniform action would be nearly

387

impossible. However, if we base our foreign policy on national interest, decisions are far clearer. Second, as a prudent realist I think it is idealistic to assume that the United States' involvement will solve global problems. Even if we are effective in our operations in a specific area, other atrocities are going to occur at the same time. This statement is weighty and may be judged heartless, but we have to accept that there is cruelty throughout the world and the United States is not able to be the global policeman.

These beliefs about our government's role in the world do not translate to my individual dilemma. I have not been able to excuse myself from moral obligation for two reasons. The problems with national involvement are not present on an individual level. I have a consistent belief system and therefore can act upon this moral code. Unlike the United States, which must have an objective application of its foreign policy, I can be subjective in the causes I choose to undertake. Honing in on one problem, I can focus on making a small difference in a few situations. Furthermore, I cannot ignore my moral obligation because I am compelled as a Christian to be merciful and active in caring for the needy. If I refuse to apply these commands to international issues, I compromise my system of belief.

Apathy is eliminated as a legitimate option so I am left with the daunting task of involvement. Arriving at this logical conclusion, I am relieved that I now can channel my convictions and empathy into action. Yet, where do I focus my energies? Even if I choose only one issue; for example refugees, the problem is so large and complex that it will be difficult to know where to start. And even if that is overcome, actions by one individual seem powerless and insignificant. My answer to this is cooperation with other convicted and passionate individuals.

For Shadow Day at (name of camp) I saw this method working first hand as I folded Nike seconds and boxed them up for Africa. I visited World Vision, an NGO active across the undeveloped world. Their donation centers process school supplies, surplus clothing, food, and financial donations, shipping them to the most destitute regions of the globe. Because they are a well-established organization, they have an influential amount of collective energy and resources. World Vision is able to be unbiased in their donations and consistent in their financial support. Individuals acting alone and randomly would not be able to accomplish such a widespread impact; but with cooperation and synergy, it is possible.

My time at (academic camp) is waning and soon the painful images and sticky global issues will fade. How am I going to respond to all I have learned in these past five weeks? What will be my first actions? Before anything else I will remember the cost of involvement and the reasoning that brought me to it. Recalling my moral obligation I will search for one global issue to focus on, perhaps refugees. There are many organizations in (name of hometown) region that are helping with assimilation. Cooperating with these groups will be the most effective use of my time. Because these actions are the result, I am now grateful for the assault of information that at first offended me so deeply.

ESSAY #2

The following essay was submitted in response to the question
"Who Are You?"

Since middle school, people have seen me as a smart, geeky kid. I was a walking dictionary, a human calculator, a living spell-checker. I won both the local MATHCOUNTS and spelling bee competitions for several successive years, earning a reputation for my achievements. I would use a rich vocabulary, exhibiting the quality reading I performed in my free time. Even when I was having fun with friends, I would often play chess or other strategy games, critically thinking to constantly exercise my brain. I persevered through the activities I took on, spending up to three hours a day studying for the spelling bee. However, despite my academic success, people see me as a responsibly well-adapted person, a confidant to whom my peers can come for advice.

My life has been a constant pursuit to better myself in any way I can. Even outside of my prior academic competitions, I continued this pursuit in other areas. When I began teaching myself to play percussion, I bought myself a drum set to practice as much as I could, then played drums or percussion at every opportunity I got, whether in wind ensembles, orchestras, or church bands, to improve. When I took up my first athletic endeavor in playing volleyball, I'd never played sports or exhibited athletic ability before. I worked hard, regardless of my lack of experience, even playing during the off-season to improve my skill, and eventually earned a leadership role as the team's captain my senior year.

A big aspect present in bettering myself has been perseverance. Persevering through learning the subjects I have not understood, through the competitions I did not win, through the athletic ability I did not have, and through rough circumstances I did not predict: this perseverance has been a huge aspect of my life and has helped me to succeed. One large trial I encountered last year was as Art Director of the yearbook; our adult advisor quit early in the year, and it was left to the Editor and me to lead the staff and finish the yearbook. Though it took countless hours of trying work and leadership, in addition to carrying an already-full course load, we still managed to create a yearbook that surpassed the quality of any year's before it.

As an excelling student, I realize that I have naturally become seen as a leader and a role model by those around me. With that in mind, I've taken the way I live seriously, knowing that people not only see my accomplishments, but my behavior and attitude besides. I try to be encouraging, both to my peers and to those students younger than I am. I try to be responsible, whether in helping my family at home or around my peers and in public. I try to live kindly, respectfully, according to my belief in God's standards.

ESSAY #3

Here is an example of an essay responding to a prompt designed to reveal a potential applicant's critical thinking skills.

Faced with real-life dilemmas, the choice between saving young children or saving the elderly has always been difficult. Medical and social factors both play a part in determining solutions. These dilemmas have been discussed many times over in varying forms; various cultures, generations, and social classes tend toward different answers. Eastern, collectivist cultures will protect their elderly out of respect for age and wisdom. Western, individualistic cultures often defend their youth, seeing more potential in their years to come.

Given a situation with only a hundred vaccines for a deadly

virus, where a hundred elderly and a hundred children need it, each culture clashes when finding an effective compromise. However, the comprehensively best solution would involve giving the vaccines to the weakest in the group. In this solution, children who are already sickly have an opportunity to survive, while the elderly receive the majority of the remaining vaccines. From a medical perspective, this leaves the healthiest people with stronger immune systems to either avoid catching the virus or to fight the virus off. Providing immunity to the sickest and weakest people allows for the greatest possible number of lives to be saved.

The biggest non-medical factor in this situation is an unclear value of human life. Modern schools of thought often suggest that the youngest and healthiest should be vaccinated to breed a stronger generation. This thinking desensitizes us to the people around us. When our only measure of a person's humanity is placed in their strength, youth, or abilities, we are discouraged from recognizing the elderly and weak as fellow humans and from therefore being willing to participate in encouraging and otherwise bettering their lives. When we fail to see value in the people surrounding us, regardless of their age or physical state, we lose every sense of community we may have once had and move toward self-centeredness, aiming to be the smartest and fittest to help and improve no one except ourselves.

This difference between finding value in those around us and having a self-centered perspective can be seen on a cultural level. On one side of the world, modern Western culture dictates individualism, teaching its adherents to be unique, self-sufficient, and, therefore, regardless of the people around them. However, older, and especially Eastern, cultures revolve around the opposite idea of collectivism. Society functions well when people work together, identifying their individual place in the world to progress toward common goals. Standing out discordantly from the crowd may provide individuals with a sense of uniqueness, but this egocentric approach towards life detracts from the potential of what people can do when they put aside their differences to function harmoniously.

With a proper view of human life's inherent value, a practical perspective towards both youth and elderlies can be attained. Each group has its place in society, helping culture to progress to greater ideals. Socially, the elderly should be respected and preserved, their wisdom heeded and their physical needs attended to. This earned respect is a simple application of the Golden Rule, rewarding their prior contributions to society as we would desire for our future selves. The youth, on the other hand, hold the future of society, as the limited lifespan of the surviving elders draws to a close. The youth are those who will continue improving the world, then pass on their knowledge and their earth to the next generation. Both are valuable.

At the end, the inherent value of human life solves this dilemma. Save as many humans as possible by vaccinating the weakest, understanding that people are valuable regardless of age, social status, or physical ability.

ESSAY #4

The following two examples were written by a homeschool applicant who subsequently was admitted to Harvard.

If I squint my eyes and use my imagination, I can almost see a fire in this wide stone hearth. I stand still for a moment, listening to its soft, pleasant crackling. Although it is late August, it is not uncomfortably warm inside, even with the fire: the thick stone walls of the house provide a natural air-conditioning. I can feel my long, full skirt swish against the rough floor-boards as I move toward the fireplace. I lift the lid of a large iron kettle, and a savory smell of German potato soup makes me smile. Almost done! Time to set the table and call the men in from the fields. Oh yes, and I'll need to fetch some more water from the well . . .

I laugh at myself and stop imagining things. The huge stone fireplace is as cold and dark as the solemn iron pots hanging in it. The table is decked with an assortment of chipped, dusty dishes. Under my feet enormous floorboards creak and groan with age. Most of the paint has chipped off the walls, revealing layers of ancient plaster. Instead of the crackling hearth and the occasional whinny of a horse outside, I hear only noisy motors and honking horns. I am not an eighteenth-century farmwife.

I am a twenty-first century museum docent at Schifferstadt, a farmhouse built by German immigrants two and a half centuries ago. Now, sandwiched between two busy streets in downtown Frederick, Maryland, it must seem as out of place as I do, standing in its antique kitchen in my capris and flip-flops.

I walk into the front room and glance out the window. No visitors yet. Watching car after car race by, I wonder how many of these busy drivers even notice Schifferstadt.

Does the sight of the house make any of them wonder what life was like in this city centuries before they were born? I catch sight of the building across the street where I attend orchestra rehearsals, and my thoughts turn to my new responsibilities as Concertmaster and the difficult trills and tremolos in Sibelius' Second Symphony. I remind myself to practice violin for another hour when I get home this evening. I'll have to finish my AP Economics homework first, though. Will I have time to grade my five Latin students' worksheets before swim practice? With a laugh, I suddenly realize that I am as busy as those hapless drivers rushing by. The sound of a doorbell interrupts my thoughts. I turn away from the window and greet a group of visitors with a cheerful smile. "Welcome to Schifferstadt! Would you like a tour?"

After giving them a brief historical overview, I lead the guests into the parlor and begin pointing out the unique architectural features of the house. I enthusiastically show them the five-plate stove, the wishbone chimney, and the huge "summer beams" that run the length of the ceiling. Enthusiastically, because I love this job.

Some people can't understand that. How can giving tours of a musty old house be "fun"? More people than I can count have told me that history is boring. But to me, history is not just lengthy lists of kings and queens and wars. It is also the study of how ordinary people lived their everyday lives in the past: what they ate and drank, what clothes they wore, how they worked and played, in what ways their lives were similar to ours, and in what ways they were different. I find this fascinating.

Through my archival work at a local historical society, I have been able to explore life in Frederick a hundred years after Schifferstadt was built. I have been re-housing, organizing, and creating an inventory of about four thousand documents from the McSherry family, who lived in Frederick during the nineteenth century. Civil War bonds. Letters from a son in the Confederate army. Receipts for everything from food and furniture to horses and buggies. Telegrams, wills, hundred-year-old newspaper clippings. It has been exciting to explore these bits and pieces of the McSherrys' lives.

Although I will miss these high school activities next year, I am excited about college and its wealth of new opportunities to enhance my knowledge of history both inside and outside the classroom. As I prepare to major in history and pursue a career as a history teacher, I am looking forward to a lifetime of learning and teaching what I love.

ESSAY #5

The room is filled with the sounds of young musicians warming up their instruments. Metallic trills from a flute. The deep, mellow voice of a cello. A few squeaks from an oboe. Occasionally a trumpet adds a few bright, brassy notes.

With my violin in one hand and sheet music in the other, I walk over to the forty chairs arranged at one end of the room.

"Hi Sarah!" I call to a friend. She smiles, lifts her bow from her cello and waves it. I take my place at the front of the orchestra and set up my music stand. As I tighten my bow, I feel a tap on my shoulder.

"Hey Anna!" My friend Kathleen sits down at the front of the second violin section and gets out her rosin.

"Hi Kat! How's everything going?"

"Alright, I guess. I've been so busy getting ready for a baton competition." She winces. "Do you think rehearsal will end early tonight? I've got tons of chemistry homework to do when I get home. And ten years' worth of English homework." She gives her violin strings a loud, frustrated pluck.

"Do these teachers think you don't need any sleep?" I give her a sympathetic pat on the shoulder.

She shrugs. "How's your internship going, Anna?"

I recently began working as a museum docent at Schifferstadt, a farmhouse built by German immigrants in the eighteenth-century. "Great! It's a lot of fun!" I reply enthusiastically. "At least, for history lovers like me," I add with a smile. Social Studies is not exactly Kat's thing.

"How in the world do you find time to do all this stuff, Anna? I know you've got at least one other internship, right? And two jobs? And orchestra rehearsals and swim practice every day and all the other stuff you do . . ." She laughs. "I don't get it!"

Good question. Why is this crazy schedule not a problem for me, while poor Kathleen struggles to find a few minutes of precious free time between school, homework, violin and baton? The reason why occurs to me almost immediately.

"I think it's because I'm homeschooled. That's the best thing about homeschooling. You can get so much more done in so much less time!"

"I wish I was homeschooled," says a boy behind me, his face envious behind his big round glasses. "I'd sleep in till noon every day!"

"I'd probably fight with my parents all day," says his stand partner. "Do you like being homeschooled?"

"Oh yes, I love it! It's so flexible. It gives me time to do more, and it also gives my parents and me more freedom to design a curriculum that fits me perfectly. I want to major in history and be a teacher someday, you know, and I've found so many great opportunities to gain experience in history and teaching. Since I'm homeschooled I have time for them, and I can also do things I probably would not be able to do if I were in public school." I think of my volunteer position at the local historical society, which is only open during school hours, and my job teaching Latin to six younger homeschooled students.

Kathleen nods slowly. "You know I want to study marine biology, right? I'd love to intern at the aquarium or something like that, but I just don't have time. But Anna, there are lots of great things about public schools, aren't there?"

"Yes, of course! All the sports and clubs and organizations that anyone in the school can participate in—that must be really great! Thankfully I've been able to find some good extra-curricular activities that are open to homeschoolers—like this orchestra!—but regular high schools have so much more."

"And you can't see your friends all the time," Kat adds. "That must be hard."

"Yes, it is. Thankfully I have swim practice every day and soccer practice and orchestra rehearsals and I take some community college classes, so it's not like I'm shut up in my room with a stack of books all day. I get together with my friends a lot too. It's really not that bad."

"But you can't go to homecoming!" cries a dark-haired girl in a half-shocked, half pitying voice. "And what about prom? I'd die if I couldn't go to prom!"

"I've survived so far," I reply with a grin. "Yeah, I guess if my 'school' did have a homecoming it would be really lame. Just me and my siblings. One of my little brothers for a date? No thanks!"

Kathleen bursts out laughing and we all join in.

Noticing that the orchestra members are all in their places, I wave to the oboe player. He blows a long, piercing B-flat, and the other wind and brass players join in. While they tune their instruments, I think of other reasons why I love homeschooling. Because I work much more independently than I would if I attended a regular high school, I have learned to discipline myself. Homeschooling has taught me to work hard and push myself in order to succeed. More importantly, I have grown up in an environment where learning is valued and encouraged not just six hours a day but all the time. My family and I can frequently be found watching a German movie, discussing current events in the car on the way to a swim meet, or using field guides to identify birds and flowers on a hike. My parents have always encouraged me to love learning and incorporate it into every aspect of my life.

The sound of wind and brass instruments fades away into silence, and I hear an A from the oboe, the signal for the strings to begin tuning. I lift my violin and slowly draw the bow across the A-string, my left hand adjusting the tuning pegs.

Sure, homeschooling has its disadvantages, but I wouldn't trade it for anything.

SAMPLE ACADEMIC
RÉSUMÉS

HONORS & ACTIVITIES

SOCIAL SECURITY #XXX-XX-XXXX

MICHAEL BENJAMIN BELL

	ACTIVITY	9	10	11	12	POSITION/ OFFICE
1.	I led a youth Bible study of about 20 teens.			X	X	Leader.
2.	I am the Sports Editor of the Cougar Chronicle high school newspaper.				X	Sports Editor
3.	I have traveled with my mother, a nationally known speaker, to homeschool conventions and seminars to man her book tables. Also, by the end of the 2001 summer, I will have spoken in four different cities about homeschooling in high school as part of the seminar High School at Home. Cities I have been to or will be going to include Indianapolis, Phoenix, Denver, Gaithersburg, Lancaster, and Richmond.	X	X	X	X	
4.	Football player and captain	X	X	X	X	4 Varsity letters and 4-year starter. Patriot News 3-time All-Conference player, and Lebanon Daily All-County player.

399

	ACTIVITY	9	10	11	12	POSITION/OFFICE
5.	Scholastic wrestler and co-captain of the team.	X	X	X	X	3 varsity letters, County All-Star, Sectional Champion, two-time District Qualifier, co-MVP
6.	Member of church youth band	X	X	X	X	Bass player.
7.	Member of church worship band		X	X	X	Bass player
8.	Leader of church youth group			X	X	Leader
9.	Member of the Learning Center (a home-school cooperative)	X	X			
10.	Organized and taught a football class of 9-12 year-old boys		X			Leader
11.	Organized and led a worship band class		X			Leader
12.	Hosted French exchange student in our home for 3 weeks			X	X	We are field reps for an exchange program. Our family will host an additional student in April.
13.	Volunteered at the Dauphin County Republican Headquarters				X	
14.	Member of the church sound team	X	X	X	X	
15.	Worker at Pennsylvania Family Institute					
16.	Featured on NBC Nightly News as an example of homeschool students who also participate in public school sports			X		Susan Malveaux and a crew spent 8 hours at our home, public school, and football game.

	ACTIVITY	9	10	11	12	POSITION/ OFFICE
17.	I produced a 20-minute video of the 2000 football season for the football banquet where more than 300 people viewed it.				X	
18.	I am the Chair for the 2001 CHESS home-school graduation ceremony.				X	Chairman
19.	I attended the Pennsylvania Scholastic Press Association's journalism conference this year.				X	
20.	I received a Certificate of Merit for a journalism piece I submitted into the 2001 Patriot News Scholastic Awards.				X	Certificate of Merit.

NAME
Address and Phone

BUSINESS EXPERIENCE

OWNER, J&J PROPERTIES (December 2004 - present)
- Purchase and remodel houses for rental income. (Currently own two properties.)

OWNER/MANAGER: GREEN ACRES FAMILY FARM (2000 - present)
- Wrote business plan and started a business selling chemical-free produce and eggs from free-ranging chickens privately and at local farmers' markets.
- Expanded business to include broiler chickens.

AUTHOR, "YOUTH ENTREPRENEURSHIP" BOOK (2003 - 2004)
- Book being revised and expanded; to be published soon.

PIONEER HI-BRED (2001 - 2004)
- Corn pollination (part time — summers 2001, 2002, 2003)
- Full-time staff (June/July 2004)

GOVERNMENT EXPERIENCE/ TRAINING

PLATFORM COMMITTEE MEMBER, REPUBLICAN COUNTY, DISTRICT AND STATE (spring/summer 2006)

DELEGATE, REPUBLICAN COUNTY, DISTRICT AND STATE CONVENTIONS (spring/summer 2006)
- Introduced Parental Rights Amendment plank at state convention; it passed.

VOLUNTEER, IOWA FAMILY POLICY CENTER (2005 - 2006)
- Lobbying at the Iowa Legislature
- Research and writing

POLK COUNTY REPUBLICAN CENTRAL COMMITTEE (member)

PATRIOT ACADEMY, AUSTIN TEXAS — Candidate for Lt. Gov. (June 2005)

TEEN-PACT NATIONAL CONVENTION, ATLANTA (June 2005)

REPUBLICAN NATIONAL COMMITTEE STAFF — IOWA FIELD REPRESENTATIVE in 2004 PRESIDENTIAL CAMPAIGN (Summer/Fall 2004)
- One of two full-time RNC staff for Iowa (my territory covered western half of Iowa)
  - Worked with social conservatives in more than 140 churches
  - Coordinated church voter registration drives/citizenship Sundays
  - Coordinated voter guide distribution in churches prior to election day
  - Trained workers and coordinated 72-hour victory drive in northwestern Iowa
  - Attended private White House reception with President Bush for RNC employees

PAGE, REPUBLICAN NATIONAL CONVENTION, NYC (August/Sept. 2004)
- One of three pages from Iowa at the Republican National Convention)

VOLUNTEER INTERN, BUSH/CHENEY '04 (Early summer 2004)

PAGE, IOWA HOUSE OF REPRESENTATIVES (spring 2004)

LEADERSHIP INSTITUTE: YOUTH LEADERSHIP SCHOOL (March 2004 — Iowa)

NATIONAL HOMESCHOOL LEADERSHIP CONFERENCES (2002 and 2003)
- Youth training in government/worldview by faculty of Patrick Henry College, Purcellville, Va. (2002 training in Rapid City, S.D.; 2003 training in Virginia Beach, Va.)

JUNIOR DELEGATE, POLK COUNTY CONVENTION (2000)

CAUCUS / STRAW POLL INVOLVEMENTS

EDUCATION

PATRICK HENRY COLLEGE, PURCELLVILLE, VIRGINIA (2005 - present)
- Online distance learning (2004 - 2007)
- Campus student (enrolled for Aug. 2007)

DES MOINES AREA COMMUNITY COLLEGE (2001-2004)
- Various Business and Science courses for college credit during high school

HOMESCHOOLED K-12 (graduated June 2004)

DRAKE UNIVERSITY (2000)
- "Growing Your Small-Market Farm": Business planning course

VOLUNTEER

HOOVER UNCOMMON STUDENT ALUMNI (June 2005)
- Co-Chair, Development Committee

ESL TEACHER (spring 2004)
- Taught ESL classes to Hispanics

GUEST SPEAKING (2002 - present)
- University of Iowa's Papajohn Entrepreneurial Camp (July 2005 and 2006)
- Network of Iowa Christian Home Educators (2004 and 2005)
- Business Camp, Simpson College, Indianola, IA (2003)
- Iowa State University Entrepreneur Club (2003)
- Farms, Food & the Future State Conference (2001)

MENTOR (2002)
- 8-year-old boy who moved from country to city and wanted to learn gardening: Gave him a 100-foot row in my 1/2-acre garden and taught him horticultural techniques.

CHILD EVANGELISM FELLOWSHIP OF IOWA (2001)
- Summer Missionary (taught children's Bible clubs in homes)

CHURCH
- Teacher's assistant, 3-year-old Sunday School (1999-2002)

AWARDS

HOOVER UNCOMMON STUDENT (2003)
- $750 scholarship for book writing project

YOUTH ENTREPRENEUR OF THE YEAR NATIONAL WINNER (2003)
- Sponsored by the National Foundation for Teaching Entrepreneurship (NFTE): $1,000 scholarship, plus expense-paid trip to NYC for awards banquet.

YOUNG ENTREPRENEUR OF THE YEAR HONORABLE MENTION (2002)
- Sponsored by the National Coalition for Empowering Youth Entrepreneurs (NCEYE): $300 cash award, plus expense-paid day in Kansas City for awards banquet.

BIZ CAMP FIRST-PLACE AWARD (2002)
- First place award of $500 for business plan writing following week-long business training at the University of Iowa's John Pappajohn Entrepreneurial Center.

FUTURE FARMERS OF AMERICA (FFA) (2001-2003)
- Various awards in Extemporaneous Speaking, Ag Sales and Ag Issues.
- Broiler chicken team project: Helped raise and market 200 broiler chickens.
- Science Fair Project: "Manures as Fertilizers"

IOWA STATE FAIR (2001-2003)
- Various ribbons for vegetables
- Artwork (pastel and colored pencil) selected for youth exhibit

DAUGHTERS OF THE AMERICAN REVOLUTION CONTEST (1993)
- Awarded second place in the nation (2nd-grade division) for essay and model of Fort McHenry. Portfolio displayed in Washington, D.C.

COMMUNITY LEADERSHIP/ PROF. ASSNS.

FUTURE FARMERS OF AMERICA (FFA)
- Vice President, Des Moines, IA chapter

PRACTICAL FARMERS OF IOWA

WORLD FOOD PRIZE YOUTH INSTITUTE (2002)
- Selected as a delegate and presented research paper

ADDITIONAL INVOLVEMENTS

ULTIMATE FRISBEE (2005 - present)
- Competed in the "Iowa Games" (mini olympics) 2005 and 2006

TAE KWON DO (1998 - present)
- Received first-degree Black Belt 2003

SOFTBALL (1998 - present)

PIANO (1994 - 2006)

ART (2002 - 2005): pencil, colored pencil, pastel, charcoal, watercolor

AWANA CLUBS (1989 - 2004)
- Various awards

SPANISH (1998 - 2004)

DRAMA (1997 - 2003)
- "Sherlock Holmes Trilogy," "Arsenic & Old Lace," "Little Women" and others.

SAMPLE ANNOTATED
RÉSUMÉ

An annotated résumé may be submitted when your student is invited to include additional documentation.

KAYTE BELL
Planned Course of Study:
French Major/International Studies/Arabic

EXTRACURRICULAR ACTIVITIES

Lebanon County Quilt Guild, 1994–2003

There are eighty members in our guild and I am the youngest active member. I joined at my own initiative; my mom is not a quilter. I participate in fabric exchanges, quilting conventions and our yearly charity projects. We have made quilts for battered women and veterans, as well as abused children. All in all I have made five quilts for charity. Last year our guild made 150 quilts for the local veteran's hospital and we were featured for this effort in the local press and *Quilt* magazine. Our guild participates in international block exchanges; and I have swapped with several international quilters. I've also made several quilts for my family, including a 2000-plus-piece millennium quilt compiled from swaps with quilters from all fifty states, D.C. and several foreign countries.

**International Business Day, October 2001,
Christchurch College**

I was the guest of my neighbor, Dr. William Nolan, chair, International Business, Troy College. He is an original Peace Corps member who has visited fifty countries and lived in seven. Knowing of my interest in International Studies, he invited me to attend this event with him. I attended several panels on trends in Int'l business, a class on cultural differences, and a luncheon with area executives in international business.

Drama, grades 9–12

My friends and I desired to be in a full-scale production and regretted the fact that, as homeschoolers, we did not have this opportunity. In our freshmen year we took matters into our own hands and started a drama club. In our first production, I helped design and sew costumes and also had a leading role. In the following years, our program grew until we were able to hire a professional director and eventually turn a profit on annual performances. This year we will perform Thornton Wilder's *The Matchmaker*.

Basketball, grades 9–12

I have been a starter and a captain on a homeschool basketball team all four years of high school. We play other homeschool and private school teams.

Volleyball, grades 9–11

I played as a setter on a homeschool volleyball team from seventh through eleventh grades. Our team often placed or won the biannual tournaments.

Yearbook, grades 11–12

The Tuesday co-op I attend began produces an annual yearbook last year. I worked throughout the year to improve the layout and design. Our staff has been able to increase the size and reorganize the spreads in order to be more efficient. This year we will introduce our first full-color senior section.

Business Internship, 1998 to present

I work for my mom's home business, The Home School Resource Center. At this point I can handle most duties related to sales, customer service, and data entry. This has also allowed me to travel much of the country when we do curriculum fairs. Throughout this experience I have observed many different approaches to home education.

Current Events and Government, grade 10

During the 2000 presidential elections, I took a government class taught by a former district attorney. I volunteered twice at a phone bank, participated in a get-out-the-vote campaign, and held a very big election-night party at our house. Supporters for both candidates were well represented, and it became the party that never really ended.

COMMUNITY SERVICE

Center for Champions, grades 11–12

I tutor at-risk students in the Harrisburg school district every Thursday. I've also recruited several friends to attend regularly with me. We are some of their most reliable volunteers and this year I often run a classroom of fourth- and fifth-graders by myself. Our group also cooks and serves the program's monthly dinners for parents and students.

Compassion International, grades 9–12

This is a charity that provides food and schooling for underprivileged children around the world. I organized a group of my friends, and we split the monthly support check so that we could participate. First, we supported Victoria from Rwanda. We are now supporting Jesus from the Dominican Republic. In both instances I learned about the student's country and the social issues there from their letters and the background material sent to us.

Math Tutoring, grade 11

I tutored a fifth grader in math to help her catch up before she got into algebra. It was a great opportunity to learn how to explain things clearly.

CHURCH

I am very involved in my church and serve monthly as a greeter and Sunday school teacher. I help organize and put on youth activities and am active at our bimonthly meetings.

Homeless Shelters grades 11–12

I have donated food to the shelters in our area. Also, our drama team put on performances at two shelters as well as serving dinner. This year I participated in the Stamp Out Hunger program and Taste of Central PA fundraiser for the Harrisburg Food Bank.

AP COURSES

AP American History (score: 5), grade 10
AP European History (score: 5), grade 11
AP French, grade 12
AP Psychology, grade 12
AP English Literature, grade 12

FRENCH

French Club, grade 10

I organized a group of my friends, and we met weekly. I assigned homework and helped them correct it. We watched the French in Action videos and took a trip to Montréal to practice our French. During this year and the following summer, I completed all of the French In Action video coursework.

College French, grade 11

I was permitted to take French 201 and 202 at Lebanon Valley College. It was wonderful finally having an actual French instructor!

French Class, grade 12

For my PGSIS senior project I offered to teach a high school French class at my homeschool co-op. Twelve students, grades 8–12, attend my weekly French 1 and cultures class. I teach part of the class completely in French and then go over grammar and culture lessons with them. This has been my favorite opportunity of my senior year because I am able to try out different teaching techniques. I am utilizing the knowledge I have of immersion methods and witness the results first-hand. This, as well as the joy I find in tutoring at Center for Champions, has clarified my future goals.

French exchange students, grades 10–12

My family has hosted two French exchange students to date. Clemence stayed with us for three weeks during the summer, and Jean-Charles stayed for two weeks over Easter. We will host another student this April.

Organized French Exchange Groups, grades 10 and 12

When my mom volunteered as a field director for another

exchange group, I helped her find homes for twelve students and basically planned the itinerary. During our family's first exchange experience, I had noticed the segregation of Americans and French. The host families and students rarely mixed at any of the social activities. This time I decided it would be different, so I attempted a butchered conversation on day one. By the end of two weeks, the Americans and French were inseparable, and we all cried when the students had to leave. When I went to Paris this summer, I was able to meet up with three of them. I was recently successful in setting up another exchange for this April through Sejours Homestay in Versailles. We will again make arrangements for ten to twelve students to stay with host families for two weeks in April 2003.

INTERNATIONAL TRIPS

Paris, France, Summer 2001

After we hosted Clemence at our house for three weeks, she invited my friend and me to stay with her for two weeks. We flew alone as 16-year-olds and met her family for the first time at Charles de Gaulle airport. In two weeks we toured all of Paris, learned a great deal about French culture, and improved exponentially our French comprehension. We also stayed with a family aiding Algerian refugees for a couple of days, and I was able to talk with several Algerians. This sparked my interests in Europe's immigration problems and the francophone world.

Lyon, France, September 2002

Seeking to improve my French, I made contact with an American family living in Lyon. I went alone and stayed with them for two weeks, using my French daily and touring the city. They were able to offer many insights as foreigners into cross-cultural communication. The mother is a quilter, and I helped her teach many classes to French women. Upon my return to the United States, I organized an international exchange between our guild and the French quilters. During my stay I also stayed with a native French family for five days. I attended lycée with their daughter and observed family customs.

Juarez, Mexico, Summer 2000

When I was 14, my church went on a missions trip to Juarez, a border town across from El Paso, Texas. It was for 15 to 18 year olds, but I begged to go along. It was my first international experience, and I thrived on the novelty of it all. I started picking up Spanish wherever I could (mainly from little kids) and plunged into the culture, even trying their hot salsa. I stayed with a Mexican family for the ten days and felt that I got an accurate glimpse into the culture.

Tijuana, Mexico, August 2001

I went to Tijuana for ten days. I stayed with a Mexican family who spoke very little English. I learned Spanish because I had to and I soon fell in love with the sound of it. By the end of the first week I was able to converse. During the day, I did community outreach with other Mexicans. I still keep in touch with many of the friends I made there. Because Tijuana is right on the border with California, I also learned quickly about the problems of the drug trade and illegal immigration. My experiences with the impoverished Mexicans made me rethink my staunch closed-door immigration position.

Pennsylvania Governor's School for International Studies (PGSIS), Summer 2002

I was accepted as one of 100 students to attend this five-week summer camp at the University of Pittsburgh campus. While taking courses in Portuguese, anthropology, global issues, political science, community involvement, and much more, I was able to grasp the broader picture of international affairs and relations. I came away from the camp not only with a much larger knowledge base, but more importantly with sharpened learning skills. With classes from 9:00 a.m. to 9:00 p.m., I learned how to study efficiently and focus my energies on the most important materials. The friendships I forged there also played a key part in my education. Living for five weeks with a refugee from Croatia, an immigrant from Albania, and a dozen Japanese exchange students stretched me while forcing me to rethink many of my assumptions about different cultures.

HONORS

Commended National Merit Scholar
Pennsylvania Governor's School for International Studies,
        University of Pittsburgh, Summer 2002
Scholastic Writing Awards: Gold Key winner, Silver Key
        winner (2), Honorable Mention (2)

QUESTIONS TO ASK DURING A COLLEGE VISIT

Try to ask these questions of admissions staff, students, and professors, where possible.

Academics

What are your best-known programs?

Are professors required to hold office hours?

Do you accept AP and/or transfer credits?

How difficult is it to enroll in the courses needed for graduation?

Are freshman assigned an advisor? What does the school or department do to help students stay on track?

What percentage of students study abroad? Is there a study abroad office?

When do I have to declare a major?

What kind of general education credits are required?

What access to computers do students have? Do I need to bring my own laptop?

What kind of workload is typical for a class in this department?

What percentage of students do not return for the second year? What are some of the more common reasons?

Student Life

Is housing guaranteed?

Are the dorms co-ed? What is the visitation policy for dorms?

What percentage of students are commuters?

What clubs and activities are most popular on campus?

What is the process of selecting a roommate? What is the process for changing roommates?

What kinds of campus security measures are provided?

What is the process for resolving a complaint about a professor? Or another student?

Finances

Am I automatically considered for any merit-based college scholarship when I apply?

What types of jobs are available on campus? What are the qualifications required for these positions?

Are additional scholarships available for upper classmen?

If accepted, does the college meet 100% of financial need?

How can my parents stay abreast of my academic progress and financial accounts?

What must a student do to maintain scholarships and aid?

SAMPLE QUESTIONS TO PREPARE FOR A COLLEGE INTERVIEW

Why are you considering this college? (Know a lot about the school if you want in or want a scholarship.)

What are you looking for in a college? How do you anticipate being involved here?

Why did you homeschool? (Be prepared to explain your family's philosophy of education and the opportunities this provided.)

What did you do last summer?

What classes did you enjoy most/least in high school?

How have you challenged yourself academically?

Describe a challenge you have faced and how you overcame it.

What are you passionate about? Why?

What three things do you want us to know about you?

What do you want your life to look like in ten years?

Tell us a bit about your personal and professional life.

What have been the pivotal experiences that shaped your future ambitions? (Anticipate questions that allow you to evaluate your past experiences in light of your future goals.)

How did ____ experience shape your future goals or change you? What did you learn about yourself through this opportunity?

What are your chief strengths and chief weaknesses? (Talk

414

about steps you take to compensate for your weaknesses.)

Tell us about your volunteer service in high school.

Tell us about leadership opportunities you've had.

Do you have a job?

Talk about your homeschool experience. How does it set you apart from your peers?

What do you think about (current issue or global problem)?

Why do you want to study (name of major)?

Where else have you applied? What offers have you received?

SAMPLE RUBRICS

SIX TRAITS RUBRIC

	10/9	8	7/6	5
Ideas & Content	• The writing conveys ideas in a controlled and interesting manner. • The focus is stated clearly and meets requirements • Clear, relevant details, directions, examples, and/or anecdotes develop and enrich the central focus. • Primary and secondary ideas are developed in proportion to their significance; the writing is balanced.	• The writing presents important information about a specific topic by providing facts or directions, explaining ideas or defining terms. • The focus is stated clearly and meets requirements. • Primary and secondary ideas are developed in proportion to their significance; the writing has a sense of balance.	• The writing presents information about a specific topic by providing facts or directions, explaining ideas or terms. • The focus is unclear. • An attempt is made to develop primary and secondary ideas. • The writing has a limited sense of balance.	• The writing presents information about a topic by providing facts or directions, explaining ideas or defining terms. • The focus is unclear. • Specific requirements have been ignored or misunderstood. • Primary and secondary ideas lack a sense of development and/or balance.
Organization	• The writing is organized in a way that enhances meaning or helps to develop the central idea. • Each developmental paragraph addresses a specific aspect of the topic. • The sequence is effective and moves the reader through the paper—the order may or may not be conventional. • Transitions work well.	• The writing is clearly organized in a way that enhances meaning or helps to develop the central idea. • Each developmental paragraph addresses a specific aspect of the topic. • Transitions work well.	• The writing is fairly organized. • Each developmental paragraph attempts to address a specific aspect of the topic. • Transitions are limited.	• The writing needs more structure. • Developmental paragraphs are limited in focus and may be confusing. • Transitions need improvement.
Word Choice	• Well-chosen words convey the intended message in an interesting, precise, and natural way. • Lively, powerful verbs provide energy. (Be verbs are limited). • Specific nouns add color and clarity. • Modifiers work to provide strong imagery. • Expression is fresh and appealing: original or unusual phrasing adds to meaning. Figurative language, if used, is effective. Vocabulary is striking but not overdone. Technical terms and notations are effective.	• Well-chosen words convey the intended message in an interesting, precise, and natural way. • Powerful verbs, specific nouns, and descriptive modifiers enhance meaning. • Expression attempts to be fresh and appealing. Original or unusual phrasing adds to the meaning. Figurative language, if used, is generally effective. Vocabulary is striking but, at times, overdone. Technical terms and notations are effective.	• Words are reasonable accurate and convey the intended message in a general manner. • Some verbs provide energy, and some simply link one point to another. • Some nouns are specific, which other nouns are fairly general. • Modifiers attempt to be descriptive. • Expression is limited. Figurative language, if used, may or may not be effective. Vocabulary is either common or slangy, or attempts to be uncommon and leads to confusion. Technical terms and notations are limited in their effectiveness.	• Word choice limits the clarity of the intended message. • Verbs, nouns, and/or modifiers lack the ability to convey an image. • Expression is lacking. Vocabulary is limited and restricting or too technical.
Sentence Fluency	• Strong and varied sentence structure clearly conveys meaning and invites expressive reading. • Sentences are appropriately concise. • The writing has a natural flow and rhythm when read aloud.	• Strong and varied sentence beginnings, length, and structure help to convey meaning and invite expressive reading. • Sentences are appropriately concise. • The writing sounds smooth and rhythmic when read aloud.	• Varied sentence beginnings, length, and structure help to convey meaning. • Sentences are sometimes concise and sometimes wordy. • The writing sounds businesslike or mechanical when read aloud.	• Sentence beginnings, length, and structure lack variation. • The writing lacks fluency when read aloud.

Voice	• The personality of the writer is evident in the writing. • The writer's enthusiasm and/or interest brings the topic to life. • The writing is natural and compelling. • The tone is appropriate and consistently controlled. • The overall effect is individualistic, expressive, and engaging.	• Personality, confidence and feeling are expressed throughout the writing. • A commitment to the topic is obvious. • The writer connects to the audience and clearly indicates a purpose for the writing. • The tone is sincere, pleasant and generally appropriate. • The writing evokes emotion in the reader.	• Personality, confidence and feeling weave in and out of the writing. • Commitment to the topic is limited. • Connection to the audience and purpose for the writing are unclear. • The tone is generally appropriate. • The writing evokes some emotion in the reader.	• The writing lacks commitment to the topic. • Connection to the audience and purpose for the writing are unclear. • The tone is flat or inappropriate. • The writing evokes little emotion in the reader.
Conventions	• A strong grasp of standard writing conventions is apparent: capitalization is accurate; punctuation is smooth and enhances meaning; spelling is correct even on more difficult words; grammar is essentially correct; usage is correct; paragraphing (indenting) enhances the organization of the paper. • Specialized conventions (title, subtitles, in-text notes, table of contents, works cited) are used accurately enhance the text.	• A good grasp of standard writing conventions is apparent: capitalization is correct; punctuation is smooth and enhances meaning; spelling of common words is accurate, and more difficult words are generally correct; grammar is essentially correct; usage is generally correct; paragraphing (indenting) works with the organization of the paper. • Specialized conventions (title, subtitles, in-text notes, table of contents, works cited) generally enhance the text.	• A basic grasp of standard writing conventions is apparent. • Errors in conventions may impair readability. • Specialized conventions (title, subtitles, in-text notes, table of contents, works cited) are disruptive or confusing.	• A minimal grasp of standard writing conventions is apparent. • Numerous errors in conventions distract and/or confuse the reader. • Specialized conventions (title, subtitles, in-text notes, table of contents, works cited) are disruptive or confusing.
Presentation	Follows Falcon Skills & Style Handbook:	Deviates slightly from expectations.	Deviates significantly from expectations.	No attempt to follow style for presentation is apparent.
	• 12 pt. Type • no script or bold fonts • double-spaced • standard margins • choose indent or block style for paragraphs		• name, date, class in upper right corner or title page is correct if required • title is descriptive and centered • number multiple pages beginning with two • staple multiple pages in upper left corner	
Insight	• Discussion acknowledges complexities, ambiguity and contradictions • Essay reveals a sophisticated understanding of the passage/reading	• Has all of the above, but is less thorough, sophisticated or powerful.	• Discussion is simplistic, obvious, or dualistic.	• The passage was misread.
Support CSE: Claim/Support/ Explanation (Warrant)	• Support is detailed, specific, correct and embedded. Level of support is consistent throughout. • CSE is clear.	• Support is less detailed, less specific, awkwardly embedded or less consistent.	• Support is mostly paraphrase rather than direct. Some quoted passages are too long and then not developed. (CSE weak).	• There is little or no support. The writer rambles and doesn't follow CSE.
Introduction & Conclusion	• Introduction is powerful and insightful and presents the thesis in a compelling way. • Appropriately introduces author and work. • The conclusion is graceful and leads to a powerful abstraction (insight).	• Introduction is interesting, meaningful and presents the thesis/main purpose clearly. • Appropriately introduces author and work. • The conclusion brings the essay to a close, but does so less powerfully or memorably.	• Introduction is adequate and presents thesis in a general way. • Conclusion goes nowhere, simply repeats the introduction.	• Introduction is empty of meaning. • Thesis may not be evident or clearly understood. • The conclusion is empty of meaning.

417

AP ESSAY RUBRIC

AP Essay Rubric   Score: _____   Student Name: _____

Traits	9–10	8	6–7	5
Introduction & Conclusion Score _____	➢ Introduction is powerful and insightful and presents the thesis in clear response to the prompt. ➢ Appropriately introduces author and work. ➢ The conclusion is graceful and leads to powerful abstractions (insight).	➢ Introduction is interesting, meaningful and presents the thesis/main purpose clearly. ➢ Appropriately introduces author and work. ➢ The conclusion brings the essay to a close, but does so less powerfully or memorably.	➢ Introduction is adequate and presents thesis in a general way. ➢ Thesis indirectly addresses the prompt. ➢ Conclusion goes nowhere, simply repeats the introduction	➢ Introduction is empty of meaning. ➢ Thesis does not address the prompt. ➢ Thesis may not be evident or clearly understood. ➢ The conclusion is empty of meaning or missing.
Ideas & Content Score _____	➢ The writing conveys ideas in a controlled and interesting manner. ➢ The focus is clearly stated and maintained throughout. ➢ Clear, relevant details, directions, examples, and/or anecdotes develop and enrich the central focus. Unpack the thesis. ➢ Primary and secondary ideas are developed in proportion to their significance; the writing is balanced.	➢ The writing presents important information about a specific focus by providing facts and examples. ➢ The focus is stated and maintained throughout. ➢ Primary and secondary ideas are developed in proportion to their significance; the writing has a sense of balance.	➢ The writing presents information about a specific focus by providing a few facts and examples from the text. ➢ The focus is stated and sometimes maintained ➢ An attempt is made to develop primary and secondary ideas. ➢ The writing has a limited sense of balance	➢ The writing presents information about a topic by providing facts or examples from the text. ➢ The focus remains unclear. ➢ Primary and secondary ideas lack a sense of development and/or balance.
Organization Score _____	➢ Writing is organized in a way that enhances meaning or helps to develop the central idea. (thesis) ➢ Each developmental paragraph addresses a specific aspect of the topic. ➢ The sequence is effective and moves the reader through the paper – the order may or may not be conventional. ➢ Transitions work well and help support the logical inter-connection of ideas	➢ Writing is clearly organized in a way that enhances meaning or helps to develop the central idea. (thesis) ➢ Each developmental paragraph addresses a specific aspect of the topic. ➢ Transitions work well.	➢ The writing is fairly organized. ➢ Each developmental paragraph attempts to address a specific aspect of the thesis. ➢ Transitions are limited.	➢ The writing needs more structure. ➢ Developmental paragraphs are limited in focus and may be confusing. ➢ Transitions need improvement.
Sentence Fluency Score _____	➢ Strong and varied sentence structure (syntax) clearly conveys meaning and invites expressive reading. ➢ Sentences are appropriately concise. ➢ The writing has a natural flow and rhythm when read aloud.	➢ Strong and varied sentence beginnings, lengths and structure help to convey meaning and invite expressive reading. ➢ Sentences are appropriately concise. ➢ The writing sounds smooth and rhythmic when read aloud.	➢ Varied sentence beginnings, length, and structure help to convey meaning. ➢ Sentences are sometimes concise and sometimes wordy. ➢ The writing sounds businesslike or mechanical when read aloud.	➢ Sentences beginnings, length and, structure lack variation. ➢ The writing lacks fluency when read aloud.
Word Choice Score _____	➢ Well-chosen words convey the intended message in an interesting, precise and natural way. ➢ Expression is fresh and appealing; original or unusual phrasing adds to meaning. Figurative language, if used, is effective. ➢ Vocabulary is striking but not overdone. Technical terms and notations are accurate and effective. ➢ Lively, powerful verbs provide energy. (To be verbs are very limited) ➢ Specific nouns add color and clarity. ➢ Modifiers work to provide strong imagery.	➢ Well-chosen words convey the intended message in an interesting, precise and natural way. ➢ Expressions attempt to be fresh and appealing. Original or unusual phrasing adds to the meaning. Figurative language, if used, is generally effective. ➢ Vocabulary is striking but, at times, overdone. Technical terms and notations are accurate and effective. ➢ Powerful verbs, specific nouns, and descriptive modifiers enhance meaning.	➢ Words are reasonably accurate and convey the intended message in a general manner. ➢ Expression is limited. Figurative language, if used, may or may not be effective. Vocabulary is either common or slang, or attempts to be uncommon and leads to confusion. ➢ Technical terms and notations are limited, or inaccurate and limited in effectiveness.	➢ Word choice limits the clarity of the intended message. ➢ Expression is lacking. Vocabulary is limited and restricted. ➢ Technical terms used to write about literature are absent.
Support CSE: Claim/Support/Explanation (Warrant) Score _____	➢ Support is detailed, specific, correct and incorporated into writer's own sentences. Level of support is consistent throughout. ➢ CSE is clear and convincingly proves thesis. ➢ CSE is pulled exclusively from the text and/or background knowledge from the literary canon. ➢ CSE is not derived from personal experience, generalization, over-reaching, conjecture, or personal beliefs.	➢ Support is less detailed, less specific, awkwardly embedded or less consistent. ➢ Support from the text only partially prove thesis. ➢ Evidence from the canon is not significantly relevant.	➢ Support is mostly paraphrased rather than direct. Some quoted passages are too long and then not developed (CSE is weak). ➢ Support is from a mix of sources, including personal experience or beliefs.	➢ There is little or no support. ➢ The writer rambles and doesn't follow CSE
Insight Score _____	➢ Discussion shows grasp of complexities, ambiguities and contradictions. ➢ Discussion shows grasp of inference, nuance and connotation. ➢ Discussion shows understanding of how the author's tone, and use of allusion, figurative language or irony creates meaning. ➢ Essay reveals a sophisticated understanding of the passage/reading	➢ Shows some grasp of complexities, ambiguities and contradictions. ➢ Shows some grasp of inference, nuance and connotation. ➢ Recognizes the presence of irony, and artistry. ➢ Is somewhat sophisticated in understanding of the passage/reading.	➢ Discussion is simplistic, obvious or dualistic.	➢ The passage was misread.

418

Powerful — I am looking for commitment, not wishy-washy stance. Power is associated with confident positioning. Use words that carry this meaning. They say, "Mrs. Bell, I've thought long and hard about the question raised by the prompt, I've considered the possibility, and now I've chosen a position which I am prepared to defend until the "last, full measure of my reasoning powers are spilt out in ink upon this page."

Insightful — The writer's ability to read literature sensitively, perceptively and analytically are evidenced by the insight they have into the text.

Controlled — The writer is not rambling, un-directed, or confused. The language used conveys logical thought and orderly progression of ideas.

Focus — another way of saying *thesis*. This is the controlling idea. In AP writing, it is the position you seek to prove.

Thesis — provides the focus. It is the defensible position you take, much as a general might position his troops along a ridge in battle. You then prove your position is wise and defendable with the artillery of your support from the text.

Expressive — denotes emphasis. As I read your essay aloud, I recognize through the organization of a particular sentence which words should be stressed and which words support the emphasis. The word order helps to signal to the reader what ideas in the sentence are important and most closely related to the thesis being supported.

Dualistic — boiling down the meaning to a black-and-white, either/or interpretation. It strips the passage of any complexity or subtleties ("This character is good" or "evil"); theme is over-generalized ("The author shows slavery is wrong"); tone is simplistic ("The author likes this character and dislikes this one").

SCIENCE FAIR RUBRIC

Project Name _____ Project # _____

SCIENCE FAIR
Judge's Evaluation Form

CRITERIA		Total
I. Creative Ability	Maximum points = 13	

	Possible	Earned
How original is the idea or approach? (Very Original – 3; Been done before but has a new idea or angle – 2; Typical fair project, done frequently – 1)	3	
Was equipment properly used or created? (Yes or N/A – 3; Equipment was used but should have been modified to obtain best results – 2; Equipment was used but not properly – 1; Equipment not used but needed- 0)	3	
Is there evidence of proper planning & orderly execution? (Yes – 2; Some planning is evident and execution is orderly – 21 Slipshod planning and execution – 0)	2	
Is the analysis of data creatively displayed? (Charts &/or graphs show excellent data analysis – 3; Some data analysis is displayed – 2; Very little data analysis is displayed – 1; No data analysis is displayed – 0)	3	
Is the display board neat and orderly? (Yes, all parts are easy to find and information flows easily – 2; Board is neat but information isn't organized effectively – 1; Board lacks neatness & organization – 0)	2	

	Possible	Earned
II. Scientific Method and Thought	Maximum points = 30	

	Possible	Earned
Is the problem/purpose stated clearly and unambiguously? (Yes – 3; P/P is stated but not enough detail is given to be clear – 2; P/P is stated but is very vague – 1; No P/P is stated – 0)	3	
Is the hypothesis stated clearly and unambiguously? (Yes – 3; H is stated but results are not predicted in measurable terms – 2; H is stated but not in the form of a prediction – 1; No H is stated – 0)	3	
Is the procedural plan for obtaining a solution detailed and specific? (Yes – 3; Procedure lacks some detail – 2; Procedure lacks some detail and isn't specific about measurements – 1; No procedure – 0)	3	
Are the experimental variables recognized in the procedure & controlled? (Yes – 3; Experimental variables are recognized but no control was designed – 2; EV vaguely mentioned – 1; No recognition of variables – 0)	3	
Is there adequate data to support the conclusions? (Yes as evidenced in the data journal – 3; Experiment needed to be replicated again to provide more data – 2; Very little data gathered – 1)	3	
Has the data been adequately analyzed and explained? (Yes as evidenced by graphs, charts, diagrams and paragraphs – 3; Some analysis and explanation is evident – 2; Very little analysis is evident – 1; None – 0)	3	
Are the interpretation of results and the significance of knowledge gained shown in discussion /conclusion? (Yes – 3; Significance of project not covered – 2; P/P statement is not answered – 1; No conclusion – 0)	3	
Are further recommended studies or changes to existing study discussed in conclusion/discussion? (Yes – 3; Some – 2; Very little – 1; Not at all – 0)	3	
Is related research discussed in conclusion/discussion as it ties to the project? Or is need for further research noted? (Yes – 3; Some discussion – 2; Very little discussion – 1; No discussion – 0)	3	
Is scientific literature used for research cited in bibliography? (Yes –1; No – 0)	1	
Is Abstract present and well written? (Yes or N/A-2; Abstract present but not well written–1; No Abstract–0)	2	

	Possible	Earned
III. Thoroughness, Skill and Clarity	Maximum points = 7	

	Possible	Earned
Is the purpose completed within the scope of original intent? (Yes – 1; No – 0)	1	
Does the experiment require skill commensurate with the division entered (Junior/Senior)? (Yes – 1; No – 0)	1	
Are complete project notes displayed? (Yes – 1; No – 0)	1	
Was time spent on the project adequate? (Yes – 1; No – 0)	1	
Does the display adequately explain the project? (Yes – 1; No – 0)	1	
Does the written material reflect understanding of the research? (Yes – 1; No – 0)	1	
Is awareness of other approaches or theories shown? (Yes – 1; No – 0)	1	

	Possible	Earned
VI. Teamwork	Maximum points = 3	

	Possible	Earned
Are the tasks and contributions of each team member clearly outlined? (Yes – 1; No – 0)	1	
Was each team member fully involved with the project? (Yes – 1; No – 0)	1	
Does the final work reflect the coordinated efforts of all team members? (Yes – 1; No – 0)	1	

Project Name _____ Project # _____

TOTAL SCORE	
TOTAL SCORE X 2 (X .94 for Team Projects)	

MIDDLE SCHOOL
READING LIST

This list has been compiled from several sources and represents a suitable range of subject matter and leading writers of literary merit for this age group.

Lloyd Alexander
The Arkadians
Three Arkadians wander through a fantasy land from one misadventure to another. An out-of-work bean counter, a young woman of mysterious talents, and a poet try to escape the wicked King Bromios and his crooked soothsayers.

Jennifer Armstrong
Steal Away
Two women, one white and one black, tell the story of their escape from a southern farm during the 1850s and of their difficult journey north to freedom.

James L. and Christopher Collier
With Every Drop of Blood
Although Johnny promises his dying father he will not desert the family to fight for the rebel cause, the lure of adventure and financial gain are strong. The book realistically focuses on the reasons the Civil War was fought as well as the enormity of the suffering of soldiers and civilians.

Christopher Paul Curtis

The Watsons Go to Birmingham—1963

A family story, both comic and moving, touches on the frightening times of the early civil rights movement.

Karen Cushman

The Midwife's Apprentice

A homeless girl in Medieval England finds a place when she becomes a midwife's apprentice.

Russell Freedman

Eleanor Roosevelt: A Life of Discovery

A biography of one of this century's most outstanding, inspirational women.

Jean Craighead George

Julie

A terrific sequel to *Julie of the Wolves*. When Julie returns to her father's Eskimo village, she struggles to find a way to save her beloved wolves in a changing Arctic world.

Joy Hakim

A History of Us, Volumes 1–10

Ernest Hemingway

The Old Man and the Sea

This beautiful novella should be one's first introduction to Hemingway and a basis for beginning the study of literary fiction.

Karen Hesse

Letters from Rifka

In a series of letters to her cousin, a young Jewish girl reveals the struggles of her family's flight from Russia in 1919.

Irene Hunt

Across Five Aprils

Presents a heartfelt and moving narrative of the personal cost to families on both sides of the conflict during the Civil War.

Brian Jacques

Redwall

The first in the series set in the mythical animal world created by Jacques in the vein of Tolkein and Lewis.

Madeleine L'Engle

A Wrinkle in Time

The standard bearer in science fiction for young adults.

Katherine Paterson

Lyddie

In an effort to gain independence, a poor girl from a Vermont farm leaves home and becomes a factory worker in Lowell, Massachusetts during the 1840s.

Gary Paulsen

Brian's Winter

What would have happened if Brian Robeson, the subject of *Hatchet*, had not been rescued when he had? Brian must confront the Canadian winter; he scrambles to reinforce his shelter and make animal skin clothing and arrowhead tools to help him improve hunting techniques.

Gary Paulsen

Call Me Francis Tucket

In this sequel to Mr. Tucket, Francis feels he can handle himself in the wild. The story relates his many mishaps as he attempts to conquer the wilderness.

Robert Newton Peck

A Part of the Sky

A sequel to *A Day No Pigs Would Die*. Robert's coming-of-age story continues as the Peck family struggles to keep the family farm during the Depression.

Wilson Rawls

Where the Red Fern Grows

A young boy living in the Ozarks works hard to fulfill his dream of purchasing two redbone hound dogs and training them to be champions.

Rosemary Sutcliff

Black Ships Before Troy

A great introduction to the Iliad.

Michael Shaara

The Killer Angels

A compelling retelling and analysis of the Battle of Gettysburg.

Mildred Taylor

The Well: David's Story

Despite the racial prejudice and injustice of the South in the early 1900s, the Logans share their well water.

Theodore Taylor

The Cay (and its prequel *Timothy of the Cay*)

When the ship Phillip is traveling on is torpedoed during WWII, the twelve-year-old boy becomes stranded on a small island in the Caribbean, where he must rely on Timothy, an elderly island man.

T. H. White

The Once and Future King

The best introduction for young people to Arthurian Legend.

COLLEGE-BOUND
READING LIST

This list was compiled by the Arrowhead Library System and modified by the author.

AMERICAN LITERATURE

James Agee
A Death in the Family
Story of loss and heartbreak felt when a young father dies.

Sherwood Anderson
Winesburg, Ohio
A collection of short stories lays bare the life of a small town in the Midwest.

James Baldwin
Go Tell It On the Mountain
Semi-autobiographical novel about a fourteen-year-old black youth's religious conversion.

Edward Bellamy
Looking Backward: 2000–1887
Written in 1887 about a young man who travels in time to a utopian year 2000, where economic security and a healthy moral environment have reduced crime.

Saul Bellow

Seize the Day

A son grapples with his love and hate for an unworthy father.

Ray Bradbury

Fahrenheit 451

Reading is a crime and firemen burn books in this futuristic society.

Willa Cather

My Antonia

Immigrant pioneers strive to adapt to the Nebraska prairies.

Kate Chopin

The Awakening

The story of a New Orleans woman who abandons her husband and children to search for love and self-understanding.

Walter Van Tilburg Clark

The Ox-Bow Incident

When a group of citizens discovers cattle rustlers have murdered one of their members, they form an illegal posse, pursue the murderers, and lynch them.

Robert Cormier

The Chocolate War

Jerry Renault challenges the power structure of his school when he refuses to sell chocolates for the annual fundraiser.

Stephen Crane

The Red Badge of Courage

During the Civil War, Henry Fleming joins the army full of romantic visions of battle, which are shattered by combat.

Michael Dorris

A Yellow Raft in Blue Water

Three generations of Native American women recount their searches for identity and love.

Ralph Ellison

Invisible Man

A black man's search for himself as an individual and as a member of his race and his society.

William Faulkner

As I Lay Dying

The Bundren family takes the ripening corpse of Addie, wife and mother, on a gruesomely comic journey.

F. Scott Fitzgerald

The Great Gatsby

A young man corrupts himself and the American Dream to regain a lost love.

Ernest Gaines

The Autobiography of Miss Jane Pittman

In her 100 years, Miss Jane Pittman experiences it all, from slavery to the civil rights movement.

Nathaniel Hawthorne

The Scarlet Letter

An adulterous Puritan woman keeps secret the identity of the father of her illegitimate child.

Joseph Heller

Catch-22

A broad comedy about a WWII bombardier based in Italy and

his efforts to avoid bombing missions.

Ernest Hemingway

A Farewell to Arms

During World War I, an American lieutenant runs away with the woman who nurses him back to health.

Zora Neale Hurston

Their Eyes Were Watching God

Janie repudiates many roles in her quest for self-fulfillment.

Ken Kesey

One Flew Over the Cuckoo's Nest

A novel about a power struggle between the head nurse and one of the male patients in a mental institution.

Harper Lee

To Kill a Mockingbird

At great peril to himself and his children, lawyer Atticus Finch defends an African-American man accused of raping a white woman in a small Alabama town.

Sinclair Lewis

Main Street

A young doctor's wife tries to change the ugliness, dullness, and ignorance that prevail in Gopher Prairie, Minn.

429

Jack London

Call of the Wild

Buck is a loyal pet dog until cruel men make him a pawn in their search for Klondike gold.

Carson McCullers
The Member of the Wedding
A young southern girl is determined to be the third party on a honeymoon, despite all the advice against it from friends and family.

Herman Melville
Moby-Dick
A complex novel about a mad sea captain's pursuit of the White Whale.

Toni Morrison
Sula
The lifelong friendship of two women becomes strained when one causes the other's husband to abandon her.

Flannery O'Connor
A Good Man is Hard to Find and Other Stories
Social awareness, the grotesque, and the need for faith characterize these stories of the contemporary South.

Gordon Parks
The Learning Tree
A fictional study of a black family in a small Kansas town in the 1920s.

Sylvia Plath
The Bell Jar
The heartbreaking story of a talented young woman's descent into madness.

Edgar Allan Poe
Great Tales and Poems

Poe is considered the father of detective stories and a master of supernatural tales.

Chaim Potok

The Chosen

Friendship between two Jewish boys, one Hasidic and the other Orthodox, begins at a baseball game and flourishes despite their different backgrounds and beliefs.

Upton Sinclair

The Jungle

The deplorable conditions of the Chicago stockyards are exposed in this turn-of-the-century novel.

John Steinbeck

The Grapes of Wrath

The desperate flight of tenant farmers from Oklahoma during the Depression.

Harriet Beecher Stowe

Uncle Tom's Cabin

The classic tale that awakened a nation about the slave system.

Mark Twain

The Adventures of Huckleberry Finn

Huck and Jim, a runaway slave, travel down the Mississippi in search of freedom.

431

H. G. Wells

The Time Machine

A scientist invents a machine that transports him into the future.

Eudora Welty

Thirteen Stories

A collection of short stories about people and life in the deep South.

Thomas Wolfe

Look Homeward, Angel

A novel depicting the coming of age of Eugene Gant and his passion to experience life.

Richard Wright

Native Son

Bigger Thomas, a young man from the Chicago slums, lashes out against a hostile society by committing two murders.

WORLD LITERATURE

Chinua Achebe

Things Fall Apart

Okonkwo, a proud village leader, is driven to murder and suicide by European changes to his traditional Ibo society.

Isabel Allende

House of the Spirits

The story of the Trueba family in Chile, from the turn of the century to the violent days of the overthrow of the Salvador Allende government in 1973.

Jane Austen

Pride and Prejudice

Love and marriage among the English country gentry of Austen's day.

Honore de Balzac

Père Goriot

A father is reduced to poverty after giving money to his daughters.

Jorge Luis Borges

Labyrinths: Selected Stories & Other Writings

An anthology of literary fireworks based on Borges' favorite symbol.

Charlotte Brontë

Jane Eyre

An intelligent and passionate governess falls in love with a strange, moody man tormented by dark secrets.

Emily Brontë

Wuthering Heights

One of the masterpieces of English romanticism, this is a novel of Heathcliff and Catherine, love and revenge.

Albert Camus

The Stranger

A man who is virtually unknown to both himself and others commits a pointless murder for which he has no explanation.

Lewis Carroll

Alice's Adventures in Wonderland

A fantasy in which Alice follows the White Rabbit to a dream world.

Miguel de Cervantes

Don Quixote

An eccentric old gentleman sets out as a knight "tilting at

windmills" to right the wrongs of the world.

Joseph Conrad

Heart of Darkness

The novel's narrator journeys into the Congo where he discovers the extent to which greed can corrupt a good man.

Daniel Defoe

Robinson Crusoe

The adventures of a man who spends twenty-four years on an isolated island.

Charles Dickens

Great Expectations

The moving story of the rise, fall, and rise again of a humbly born young orphan.

Fyodor Dostoevsky

Crime and Punishment

A psychological novel about a poor student who murders an old woman pawnbroker and her sister.

George Eliot

The Mill on the Floss

Maggie is miserable because her brother disapproves of her choices of romances.

Carlos Fuentes

The Death of Artemio Cruz

A powerful Mexican newspaper publisher recalls his life as he is dying.

Gabriel Garcia Marquez

One Hundred Years of Solitude

A technique called magical realism is used in this portrait of seven generations in the lives of the Buendía family.

Nikolai Gogol

The Overcoat

Russian tales of good and evil.

William Golding

Lord of the Flies

English schoolboys marooned on an uninhabited island test the values of civilization when they attempt to set up a society of their own.

Günter Grass

The Tin Drum

Oskar describes the amoral conditions through which he has lived in Germany, both during and after the Hitler regime.

Thomas Hardy

Tess of the D'Urbervilles

The happiness of Tess and her husband is destroyed when she confesses that she bore a child as the result of a forced sexual relationship with her employer's son.

435

Hermann Hesse

Siddhartha

Emerging from a kaleidoscope of experiences and pleasures, a young Brahmin ascends to a state of peace and mystic holiness.

Aldous Huxley

Brave New World

A bitter satire of the future, in which advances in science and social changes control the world.

James Joyce

A Portrait of the Artist as a Young Man

A novel about a young man growing up in Ireland and rebelling against family, country, and religion.

Franz Kafka

The Trial

A man is tried for a crime he knows nothing about, yet for which he feels guilt.

Jhumpa Lahiri

The Namesake

Specifically captures the nuances of the Indian-American immigrant experience; but speaks for the sorrows and joys of all immigrants adjusting to a new country as well.

D. H. Lawrence

Sons and Lovers

An autobiographical novel about a youth torn between a dominant working-class father and a possessive genteel mother.

Thomas Mann

Death in Venice

In this novella, an author becomes aware of a darker side of himself when he visits Venice.

George Orwell

Animal Farm

Animals turn the tables on their masters.

Boris Pasternak

Doctor Zhivago

An epic novel of Russia before and after the Bolshevik revolution.

Alan Paton

Cry, the Beloved Country

A country Zulu pastor searches for his sick sister in Johannesburg, and discovers that she has become a prostitute and his son a murderer.

Erich Maria Remarque

All Quiet on the Western Front

A young German soldier in World War I experiences pounding shellfire, hunger, sickness, and death.

Sir Walter Scott

Ivanhoe

Tale of Ivanhoe, the disinherited knight, Lady Rowena, Richard the Lion-Hearted, and Robin Hood at the time of the Crusades.

Mary W. Shelley

Frankenstein

A gothic tale of terror in which Frankenstein creates a monster from corpses.

Alexander Solzhenitsyn

One Day in the Life of Ivan Denisovich

Ivan Denisovich Shukhov endures one more day in a Siberian prison camp and finds joy in survival.

Jonathan Swift

Gulliver's Travels

Gulliver encounters dwarfs and giants and has other strange adventures when his ship is wrecked in distant lands.

Amy Tan

The Joy Luck Club

After her mother's death, a young Chinese-American woman learns of her mother's tragic early life in China.

Leo Tolstoy

Anna Karenina

Anna forsakes her husband for the dashing Count Vronsky and brief happiness.

Elie Wiesel

Night

A searing account of the Holocaust as experienced by a 15-year-old boy.

BIOGRAPHY/HISTORY

Maya Angelou

I Know Why the Caged Bird Sings

An African-American writer traces her coming of age.

Arthur Ashe and Arnold Rampersad

Days of Grace

Biography of a highly respected tennis star and citizen of the world who dies of AIDS.

Russell Baker

Growing Up

A columnist with a sense of humor takes a gentle look at his childhood in Baltimore during the Depression.

Michael Berenbaum
The World Must Know: The History of the Holocaust as told in the United States Holocaust Memorial Museum.

Dee Brown
Bury My Heart at Wounded Knee
A narrative of the white man's conquest of the American land as the Indian victims experienced it.

Alistair Cooke
Alistair Cooke's America
A history of the continent, with anecdotes and insight into what makes America work.

JoAn D. Criddle and Teeda Butt Mam
To Destroy You Is No Loss: The Odyssey of a Cambodian Family
After the 1975 Communist takeover of Cambodia, Teeda's upper-class life is reduced to surviving impossible conditions.

Mary Crow Dog and Richard Erdoes
Lakota Woman
Mary Crow Dog stands with 2,000 other Native Americans at the site of the Wounded Knee massacre, demonstrating for Native American rights.

Eve Curie
Madame Curie
In sharing personal papers and her own memories, a daughter pays tribute to her mother, a scientific genius.

Sara and A. Elizabeth Delany, with Amy Hill Hearth
Having Our Say: The Delany Sisters' First 100 Years
Two daughters of former slaves tell their stories of fighting racial and gender prejudice during the twentieth century.

Norrie Epstein
The Friendly Shakespeare: A Thoroughly Painless Guide to the Best of the Bard
Gain a perspective on Shakespeare's works through these sidelights, interpretations, anecdotes, and historical insights.

Anne Frank
The Diary of a Young Girl
The story of a Jewish family forced by encroaching Nazis to live in hiding.

Benjamin Franklin
The Autobiography of Benjamin Franklin
Considered one of the most interesting autobiographies in English.

Alex Haley
Roots
Traces Haley's search for the history of his family, from Africa through the era of slavery to the twentieth century.

John Hersey
Hiroshima
Six Hiroshima survivors reflect on the aftermath of the first atomic bomb.

Helen Keller
The Story of My Life

The story of Helen Keller, who was both blind and deaf, and her relationship with her devoted teacher Anne Sullivan.

John F. Kennedy

Profiles in Courage

A series of profiles of Americans who took courageous stands in public life.

Martin Luther King, Jr.

A Testament of Hope: The Essential Writings and Speeches of Martin Luther King, Jr.

King's most important writings are gathered together in one source.

Ron Kovic

Born on the Fourth of July

Paralyzed in the Vietnam War, Ron Kovic received little support from his country and its government.

Niccolò Machiavelli

The Prince

A treatise giving the absolute ruler practical advice on ways to maintain a strong central government.

Malcolm X, with Alex Haley

The Autobiography of Malcolm X

Traces the transformation of a controversial Black Muslim figure from street hustler to religious and national leader.

Karl Marx

The Communist Manifesto

Expresses Marx's belief in the inevitability of conflict between social classes and calls on the workers of the world to unite and revolt.

Mark Mathabane

Kaffir Boy: The True Story of a Black Youth's Coming of Age in Apartheid South Africa

A tennis player breaks down racial barriers and escape to a better life in America.

David Maybury-Lewis

Millennium: Tribal Wisdom and the Modern World

Profiles members of several tribal cultures.

James McPherson

Battle Cry of Freedom: The Civil War Era

From the Mexican War to Appomattox, aspects of the Civil War are examined.

Kay Mills

This Little Light of Mine: The Life of Fannie Lou Hamer

Fannie, a sharecropper's daughter, uses her considerable courage and singing talent to become a leader in the civil rights movement.

Plato

The Republic

Plato creates an ideal society where justice is equated with health and happiness in the state and the individual.

Donn Rogosin

Invisible Men: Life in Baseball's Negro Leagues

Negro League players finally gain recognition for their contributions to baseball.

Henry David Thoreau

Walden

In the mid-nineteenth century, Thoreau spends 26 months alone in the woods to "front the essential facts of life."

Alexis de Tocqueville

Democracy in America

This classic in political literature examines American society from the viewpoint of a leading French magistrate who visited the U.S. in 1831.

Barbara Tuchman

A Distant Mirror: The Calamitous Fourteenth Century

Tuchman uses the example of a single feudal lord to trace the history of the 14th century.

Juan Williams

Eyes on the Prize: America's Civil Rights Years, 1954–65

From Brown vs. the Board of Education to the Voting Rights Act, Williams outlines the social and political gains of African-Americans

Jane Yolen

Favorite Folktales from Around the World

Yolen frames these powerful tales with explanations of historical and literary significance.

SCIENCE

David Attenborough

The Living Planet: A Portrait of the Earth

Various habitats expand the vision of Planet Earth.

Jacob Bronowski

The Ascent of Man

A scientist's history of the human mind and the human condition.

Rachel Carson

Silent Spring

Carson's original clarion call to environmental action sets the stage for saving our planet.

Charles Darwin

On the Origin of Species

The classic exposition of the theory of evolution by natural selection.

Stephen Hawking

A Brief History of Time: From the Big Bang to Black Holes

Cosmology becomes understandable as the author discusses the origin, evolution, and fate of our universe.

Aldo Leopold

A Sand County Almanac: And Sketches Here and There

Leopold shares his present and future visions of a natural world.

Stephen Meyer

Signature in the Cell

The best defense of intelligent design to date.

SOCIAL SCIENCE

Joseph Campbell

The Power of Myth

Explores themes and symbols from world religions and their

relevance to humankind's spiritual journey today.

Edith Hamilton

Mythology

Gods and heroes, their clashes and adventures, come alive in this splendid retelling of the Greek, Roman and Norse myths.

Alex Kotlowitz

There Are No Children Here: The Story of Two Boys Growing Up in the Other America

Lafayette and Pharoah Rivers and their family struggle to survive in one of Chicago's worst housing projects.

Jonathan Kozol

Savage Inequalities: Children in America's Schools

Kozol's indictment of the public school system advocates equalizing per-pupil school expenditures.

Studs Terkel

Race: How Blacks and Whites Think and Feel About the American Obsession

This kaleidoscope covers the full range of America's views on racial issues.

DRAMA

Samuel Beckett

Waiting for Godot

Powerful, symbolic portrayal of the human condition.

Bertolt Brecht

Mother Courage and Her Children

A product of the Nazi era, Mother Courage is a feminine "Everyman" in a play on the futility of war.

Anton Chekhov

The Cherry Orchard

The orchard evokes different meanings for the impoverished aristocrat and the merchant who buys it.

Henrik Ibsen

A Doll's House

A woman leaves her family to pursue personal freedom.

Christopher Marlowe

Doctor Faustus

First dramatization of the medieval legend of a man who sold his soul to the devil.

Arthur Miller

Death of a Salesman

The tragedy of a typical American who, at age sixty-three, is faced with what he cannot face: defeat and disillusionment.

Eugene O'Neill

Long Day's Journey Into Night

A tragedy set in 1912 in the summer home of an isolated, theatrical family.

Jean-Paul Sartre

No Exit

A modern morality play in which three persons are condemned to hell because of crimes against humanity.

William Shakespeare

Romeo and Juliet, Hamlet, Macbeth, Twelfth Night, others

George Bernard Shaw

Man and Superman, Saint Joan, Pygmalion, others

Sophocles

Oedipus Rex

Classical tragedy of Oedipus, who unwittingly killed his father, married his mother and brought the plague to Thebes.

Oscar Wilde

The Importance of Being Earnest

Comedy exposing quirks and foibles of Victorian society.

Thornton Wilder

Our Town

The dead of a New Hampshire village of the early 1900s appreciate life more than the living.

Tennessee Williams

A Streetcar Named Desire

Blanche Dubois's fantasies of refinement and grandeur are brutally destroyed by her brother-in-law.

August Wilson

The Piano Lesson

Drama set in 1936 Pittsburgh chronicles black experience in America.

POETRY

Maya Angelou

And Still I Rise

Poems reflecting themes from her autobiography.

447

Gwendolyn Brooks

Selected Poems

Poetry focusing on the lives of African American residents of Northern urban ghettos, particularly women.

E. E. Cummings

Complete Poems, 1904–1962

Prepared directly from the original manuscripts, preserving the original typography and format.

Emily Dickinson

The Complete Poems of Emily Dickinson

A chronological arrangement of all known Dickinson poems and fragments.

John Donne

The Complete Poetry of John Donne

Poems distinguished by wit, profundity of thought, passion and subtlety.

T. S. Eliot

The Waste Land

A poem of despair by one of the most important modern poets in English.

448

Robert Frost

The Poetry of Robert Frost

Collected works reflecting both flashing insight and practical wisdom.

Allen Ginsberg

Howl and Other Poems

Works from the leading poet of the "beat generation."

Nikki Giovanni

My House

The poems in this collection deal with love, family, nature, friends, music, aloneness, blackness, and Africa.

Langston Hughes

Selected Poems

Poems selected by Hughes shortly before his death in 1967, representing work from his entire career.

John Keats

The Complete Poems

Among the greatest odes in English, written by a genius who died young.

Henry Wadsworth Longfellow

The Poetical Works of Longfellow

Includes "The Song of Hiawatha" and "The Courtship of Miles Standish."

Carl Sandburg

The Complete Poems

Sandburg celebrates industrial and agricultural America and the common people.

Dylan Thomas

Poems of Dylan Thomas

Poetry by a "word magician" with a powerful imagination.

449

William Carlos Williams

Selected Poems

Williams' poetry is firmly rooted in the commonplace details of American life.

William Wordsworth

Poems

Poetry revealing the extraordinary beauty and significance of simple things.

William Butler Yeats

The Collected Poems

Leading poet of the Irish Renaissance.

RECOMMENDED CHRISTIAN LITERATURE

This is the suggested reading list for a course of study in the best of Christian literature.

AUTOBIOGRAPHY

Saint Augustine of Hippo (*Confessions*)

C. S. Lewis (*Surprised by Joy*)

Lauren Winner (*Girl Meets God: A Memoir*)

AUTHORS & POETS

Dante Alighieri (*The Divine Comedy*)

John Milton (*Paradise Lost*)

Edmund Spenser (*The Faerie Queene*)

John Donne

George Herbert

Gerard Manley Hopkins

John Bunyan (*Pilgrim's Progress*)

C. S. Lewis (*Mere Christianity, The Screwtape Letters*)

G. K. Chesterton (*Orthodoxy*)

Flannery O'Connor

Jonathan Swift (*A Modest Proposal*)

T. S. Eliot (*Four Quartets*)

Leif Enger (*Peace Like a River*)

Charles Spurgeon

Walter Wangerin (*Miz Lil and the Chronicles of Grace*)

Marilynne Robinson (*Home, Gilead*)

N. D. Wilson (*Notes from the Tilt-A-Whirl*)

451

ACADEMIC COMPETITIONS

24 Challenge Math Program
First in Math
Suntex International Inc.
3311 Fox Hill Road
Easton, PA 18045
800-242-4542; 610-253-5255 info
www.math24.com

American Society of Mechanical Engineers
www.asme.org/students/competitions/
This site maintains up-to-date database of science competitions.

AoPS Incorporated
P. O. Box 2185
Alpine, CA 91903-2185
www.artofproblemsolving.com
Art of Problem Solving prepares students through online classes and
textbooks for the major math competitions.

452

CTY Talent Search
Center for Talented Youth
Johns Hopkins University
McAuley Hall
5801 Smith Avenue, Suite 400
Baltimore, MD 21209
410-735-6277 or 6278
cty.jhu.edu
For second-through eighth-graders who score in the 97th percentile
or above on standardized achievement test

Education Program for Gifted Youth (EPGY)
Ventura Hall
220 Panama Street
Stanford University
Stanford, CA 94305-4101
800-372-EPGY
http://epgy.stanford.edu
Expensive but prestigious courses online

Freedoms Foundation's National Awards Program for Youth
Freedoms Foundation at Valley Forge
P.O. Box 706
1601 Valley Forge Road
Valley Forge, PA 19482-0706
610-933-8825
www.ffvf.org

Future Problem Solving Program International
2015 Grant Place
Melbourne, FL 32901
800-256-1499

HSLDA Home School Contests
Home School Legal Defense Association
P.O. Box 3000
Purcellville, VA 20134-9000
(540) 338-5600
www.hslda.org/contests/
Art, essay, photo and poetry contests for homeschooled students
    judged by elementary, middle school and high school age
    groups.

HSLDA Homeschooling Thru High School
www.hslda.org/highschool/docs/Competitions.asp
An extensive and up-to-date listing of competitions and scholarships
    opportunities for teens

Intel International Science and Engineering Fair
Society for Science & the Public
1719 N Street NW
Washington, DC 20036
202-785-2255
www.societyforscience.org/isef
National organization that sets standards for locally and regionally
juried science and engineering fairs.

Invent America
www.inventamerica.org
Teaches creative problem-solving skills through inventions

Knowledge Open Academic Competition
Academic Hallmarks
P.O. Box 998
Durango, CO 81302
800-321-9218
www.greatauk.com
Competition comes on CD-ROM

Make a Difference Day
USA WEEKEND/Make a Difference Day
800-416-3824
www.makeadifferenceday.com
For all ages; group volunteer project

Math Olympiad
2154 Bellmore Avenue
Bellmore, NY 11710-5645
516-781-2400
www.moems.org
Registration deadline September 30, $75 per team of up to 35 stu-
dents

Mathcounts
MathCounts Foundation
1420 King Street

Alexandria, VA 22314
703-299-9006
www.mathcounts.org

National Association of Secondary School Principals
NASSP Contests and Activities Advisory List
1904 Association Drive
Reston, VA 20191-1537
703-860-0200
Booklet of recommended academic contests. Updated regularly.

National Christian Forensics and Communications Association
NCFCA Corporate Office
P.O. Box 212
Mountlake Terrace, WA 98043-0212
505-516-5580
www.ncfca.org
HSLDA started a national debate tournament years ago to foster
    forensics. When the movement took off, this organization was
    formed to oversee the activities. Chapters are now located in
    most states.

National Energy Education Development Project (NEED)
The NEED Project
8408 Kao Circle
Manassas, VA 20110
703-257-1117; 703-257-0037 fax
www.need.org
K–12 group project

National Geography Bee
National Geographic Society
1145 17th Street NW
Washington, DC 20036-4688
www.nationalgeographic.com/geographybee

National History Day
0119 Cecil Hall
University of Maryland
College Park, MD 20742
301-314-9739
www.nationalhistoryday.org

National Spelling Bee
Scripps Howard National Spelling Bee
312 Walnut Street, 28th Floor
Cincinnati, OH 45202
513-977-3040
www.spellingbee.com

Odyssey of the Mind Program
c/o Creative Competitions, Inc.
406 Ganttown Road
Sewell, NJ 08080
856-256-2797
www.odysseyofthemind.org

Online Math League
269-795-9680
www.onlinemathleague.com

The President's Challenge
501 N. Morton, Suite 203
Bloomington, IN 47404
800-258-8146
www.presidentschallenge.com

Quill & Scroll Society
University of Iowa
School of Journalism and Mass Communication
100 Adler Journalism Building
Iowa City, IA 52242
319-335-3457
319-335-3989 fax

www.uiowa.edu/~quill-sc
Writing and photography contest
Scholastic Art and Writing Awards
Alliance for Young Artists & Writers
557 Broadway
New York, NY 10012
212-343-6100
www.scholastic.com/artandwritingawards

Science Olympiad
2 Trans Am Plaza Drive, Suite 415
Oakbrook Terrace, IL 60181
630-792-1251
630-792-1287 fax
www.soinc.org
Science tournaments for K–12 on regional, state, and national levels

The Stock Market Game
120 Broadway, 35th Floor
New York, NY 10271-0080
212-313-1350
212-313-1324 fax
www.smgww.org

Stone Soup Magazine
P.O. Box 83
Santa Cruz, CA 95063
800-447-4569
www.stonesoup.com
Publishes the creative work of children ages 8-13

ThinkQuest
www.thinkquest.org
Cooperative teams of students build websites related to specified
    topic

Young America Horticulture Contests
National Junior Horticultural Association
15 Railroad Avenue
Homer City, PA 15748-1378
724-479-3254
www.njha.org
For ages 8-14; group/individual projects

RESOURCE
GUIDE

SPECIAL-INTEREST ORGANIZATIONS

African-American

National Black Home Educators
13434 Plank Road, PMB 110
Baker, LA 70714
www.nbhe.net

Catholic

Catholic Homeschool Support
www.catholichomeschool.org

Keeping It Catholic
604 S. Main St.
Suite 224
Lapeer, MI 48446
www.keepingitcatholic.org

Love 2 Learn
Alicia Van Hecke, FRCH
P.O. Box 61
Hartland, WI 53029
www.love2learn.net

Classical Christian

Classical Christian Homeschooling
www.classical-homeschooling.org
Christine Miller, webmaster

Trivium Pursuit
525 120th Avenue
New Boston, IL 61272
309-537-3641
www.triviumpursuit.com
Harvey and Laurie Bluedorn, owners
Magazine; online catalog, seminars, speech and debate,
    discussion loop, links

The Well-Trained Mind
Peace Hill Farm
18021 The Glebe Lane
Charles City, VA 23030
www.welltrainedmind.com
www.peacehillpress.com
Susan Wise Bauer and Jessie Wise, editors
Book, newsletter, discussion groups, information, resources,
    links

Missionaries

Sonlight Curriculum
8042 South Grant Way
Littleton, CO 80122
303-730-6292
www.sonlight.com
John and Sarita Holzmann, owners
Literature-based curriculum created to provide homeschool
    supplies to missionaries living abroad; mission emphasis
    to curriculum, experienced in shipping overseas

Special Needs

Almaden Valley Christian School
Sharon Hensley
16465 Carlson Drive
Morgan Hill, CA 95037
408-776-6691
www.almadenvalleychristianschool.com
Book, information packet, program planning

Child Diagnostics

Dianne Craft, MA, CNHP

6562 S. Cook Court

Littleton, CO 80121

303-694-0532

www.diannecraft.org

Seminars, private consultations, Right Brain Teaching
    Products

Exceptional Diagnostics

5 Jericho Court

Simpsonville, SC 29681

864-967-4729

www.edtesting.com

Dr. Joe Sutton, director

Strategies for Struggling Learners, testing service,
    evaluations

National Challenged Homeschoolers Associated Network
(NATHHAN)

P.O. Box 310

Moyie Springs, ID 83845

208-267-6246

www.nathhan.com

Membership fee of $25 per year

Support organization for parents who are homeschooling
    special needs children. Publishes *Nathhan News* and a
    catalog of recommended resources. Provides a network
    of ten thousand contact people in the homeschool com
    munity—some providing professional services to
    families

Timberdoodle

1510 E. Spencer Lake Road

Shelton, WA 98584

800-478-0672 or 360-426-0672

360-427-5625 fax

www.timberdoodle.com

461

Dan and Deb Diffinbaugh, owners

Homeschool supplier, in recent years beginning to
specialize in support and educational resources for
autistic children

Worldview Resources

Apologia Press
1106 Meridian Plaza, Suite 220/340
Anderson, IN 46016
888-524-4724
765-608-3290 fax
www.apologia.com
Publishers of the What We Believe series of textbooks, created in
partnership with Summit Ministries; also, Apologia Academy
offers Internet courses on worldview, apologetics, and Bible.

Discovery Institute
208 Columbia Street
Seattle, WA 98104
206-292-0401
206-682-5320 fax
www.discovery.org
Intelligent design think-tank; leading scientists and
thinkers collaborate here

Probe Ministries
972-480-0240
www.probe.org
Kerby Anderson, president
Radio show, Mind Games, College Survival Seminar,
resources, links

Stand to Reason
1438 East 33rd Street
Signal Hill, CA 90755
800-2-REASON
www.str.org
Resources to equip Christians to make an intelligent defense

of the gospel, particularly on college campuses, and to graciously defend Christian values in the public square

Summit Ministries
P.O. Box 207
Manitou Springs, CO 80829
866-786-6483
www.summit.org
Creators of *Understanding the Times* video curriculum and
    summer leadership seminars

Worldview Academy
P.O. Box 2918
Midland, TX 79702
800-241-1123
www.worldview.org
Weekend seminars and camps for teens

Periodicals

God's World Publications
P.O. Box 20001
Asheville, NC 28802-8201
800-951-5437 subscription to *God's World* newspapers
800-951-6397 subscription to *World* magazine for teens/adults
www.gwnews.com
www.worldmag.com
Weekly news and current events publications for school-
    aged children through adults

Home Educating Family
P.O. Box 190451
Nashville, TN 37219
615-957-7411
www.homeeducatingfamily.com

Homeschooling Today
P.O. Box 244
Abingdon, VA 24212
866-804-4478
www.homeschooltoday.com
Classical Christian flavor, high school forum,
    Understanding the Arts, ready-to-use lessons, worldview
    articles

The Old Schoolhouse Magazine
P.O. Box 8426
Gray, TN 37615
888-718-HOME
www.thehomeschoolmagazine.com
Biblical encouragement, a wide array of articles, "Laughable
    Lines," product reviews, and more

Practical Homeschooling
Home Life
P.O. Box 1190
Fenton, MO 63026-1190
800-346-6322
www.home-school.com
Bill and Mary Pride, publishers

Homeschool Digest
Wisdom Gate
P.O. Box 374
Covert, MI 49043
269-764-1910
www.homeschooldigest.com

General Publishers and Suppliers

The companies listed below publish or supply homeschool products in many subject areas. A list of specialized publishers follows this listing.

A Beka Books
P.O. Box 19100
Pensacola, FL 32523-9100
877-223-5226
www.abeka.com
Christian publisher of a traditional line of textbooks with a patriotic emphasis, secure online ordering after an account is established

Apologia Educational Ministries
1106 Meridian Plaza, Suite 220/340
Anderson, IN 46016
888-524-4724
765-608-3290 fax
www.apologia.com
Known for its excellent homeschool K-12 science curriculum, Apologia is now branching out into other areas, including biblical worldview. Visit the website to find out the new product offerings, as well as information on its annual homeschool moms' conference and encouraging e-newsletter, its online catalog with secure ordering, and its academic scholarship programs.

Alpha Omega Publications
804 N. Second Ave. E.
Rock Rapids, IA 51246
800-682-7391
www.aop.com
Christian publisher of inexpensive work texts and software program; online catalog; secure ordering

American Home-School Publishing
P.O. Box 570
Cameron, MO 64429
800-684-2121
800-557-0234 fax
www.ahsp.com
Supplier with a classical emphasis offering an extensive selection
in all subject areas. Especially good for high school, print catalog

Bob Jones University Press
Greenville, SC 29614-0062
800-845-5731
800-525-8398 fax
www.bjup.com
Christian publisher of traditional textbooks, including
    teacher's manuals that are very helpful; online catalog
    and secure ordering after an account is established

Book Peddler
www.bookpeddler.us
Supplier of primarily literature-based curriculum, well-de
    signed website, print and online catalog with secure
    ordering

Christian Book Distributors CBD
140 Summit Street
Peabody, MA 01960
800-247-4784
www.christianbook.com
Supplier of Christian products at a discount, including
    popular homeschool titles; print and online catalog with
    secure ordering

Christian Liberty Press
502 W. Euclid Ave.
Arlington Heights, IL 60004
847-259-4444
www.christianlibertypress.com

Christian publisher and satellite school for homeschoolers. Uses a mix of resources from various other Christian publishers as well. Print and online catalog with secure ordering

Cornerstone Curriculum Project
2006 Flat Creek
Richardson, TX 75080
972-235-5149
www.cornerstonecurriculum.com
David and Shirley Quine, publishers
Popular, integrated, curriculum based on the work of Francis Schaeffer—math, science, music, art, literature; high school worldview course of study; online catalog

Debra Bell's Home School Resource Center
P.O. Box 67
Palmyra, PA 17078
717-473-8059 fax
www.debrabell.com
Scoring High test preparation program, Professor Wise's Discovery Corps Expedition Guides

Farm Country General Store
800-551-3276
www.homeschoolfcgs.com
Supplier, wide selection of resources, most at discount pricing; request catalog online

467

Library & Educational Services
P.O. Box 288
Berrien Springs, MI 49103
269-695-1800
269-695-8500 fax
www.libraryanded.com
School supplier and source of *Your Story Hour* tapes, great discounts on select items, primarily Christian fiction

Lifetime Books and Gifts
18755 SW 272 Street
Homestead, Fl 33031
305-248-1271
www.shoplbg.com
Gus and Shirley Solis, owners
Homeschool supplier emphasizing "living books"; founded
by Bob and Tina Farewell

Living Learning Books
110 Heather Ridge Drive
Pelham, AL 35124
205-620-3365
www.livinglearningbooks.com
Excellent source of curriculum guides paired with
activity books and top-notch nonfiction for children, as
well as award-winning science curriculum.

Modern Curriculum Press
Pearson Learning
800-848-9500
www.pearsonschool.com

Mott Media
1130 Fenway Circle
Fenton, MI 48430
800-421-6645
www.mottmedia.com
Publisher and supplier, source of Ruth Beechick's titles,
specializing in reprints of classic curricula such as *McGuffey's
Readers* and *Harvey's Grammar*

My Father's World
P.O. Box 2140
Rolla, MO 65402
573-426-4600
www.mfwbooks.com
David and Marie Hazell, publishers

K–8 curriculum; distinctions include integrated Bible,
    phonics-based reading program, and literature-based
    unit studies; mission is to fund Bible translation projects
    around the world

Pennsylvania Homeschoolers
105 Richman Lane
Kittanning, PA 16201
724-783-6512
www.pahomeschoolers.com
Howard and Susan Richman, owners
Carries a select line of products you will not find elsewhere,
    including video courses for purchase or rental, used
    textbooks, and Advanced Placement and test-prep
    materials; specializes in high school resources; online
    catalog and secure ordering

Rainbow Resource Center
Route 1, Box 159A
Toulon, IL 61483
888-841-3456
www.rainbowresource.com
Supplier, discounts; online catalog and secure ordering

Rod and Staff Publishers
Box 3, Highway 172
Crockett, KY 41413
606-522-4348
800-643-1244 fax
www.rodstaff.com
Site operated by Anabaptist Bookstore, not by Rod and Staff;
    publishers of Anabaptist curriculum and readers popular
    with many homeschoolers

School Specialty Publishing
3195 Wilson Drive NW
Grand Rapids, MI 49534
800-417-3261

888-203-9361 fax
www.schoolspecialtypublishing.com
Primarily for the school market, but with a successful
    division for homeschoolers; workbooks and
    reproducibles in every subject area

Shekinah Curriculum Cellar
1815 Whittington Road
Kilgore, TX 75662
903-643-2760
903-643-2796 fax
www.shekinahcc.com
Supplier offering more than three thousand titles and
    guaranteed low pricing; warehouse open to public

Sonlight Curriculum
8042 S. Grant Way
Littleton, CO 80122-2705
303-730-6292
www.sonlight.com
Publisher and supplier, source of international homeschool
    curriculum that may be purchased complete or in parts;
    very heavy concentration on reading excellent books

Sycamore Tree
2179 Meyer Place
Costa Mesa, CA 92627
888-334-6711 info
800-779-6750 orders
714-668-1344 fax
www.sycamoretree.com
Supplier offering an extensive line of resources in all subject
    areas; school, online school, printed and online catalog,
    warehouse with hours open to the public

Timberdoodle
1510 E. Spencer Lake Road
Shelton, WA 98584

800-478-0672 or 360-426-0672

360-427-5625 fax

www.timberdoodle.com

Dan and Deb Diffinbaugh, owners

Longtime supplier with unique selection of supplies, very
informative catalog

WinterPromise

10 Folsom Harbor Road

Grand Isle, VT 05458

802-372-9200

www.winterpromise.com

Charlotte Mason-inspired curriculum with living books and
activities

SPECIALIZED PUBLISHERS AND SUPPLIERS

Art

Artistic Pursuits

10142 W. 69th Avenue

Arvada, CO 80004

303-467-0504

208-567-4269 fax

www.artisticpursuits.com

How Great Thou Art

P.O. Box 48

McFarlan, NC 28102

800-982-3729

www.howgreatthouart.com

Christian program

Audio

Greathall Productions
Jim Weiss, storyteller
P.O. Box 5061
Charlottesville, VA 22905-5061
800-477-6234
www.greathall.com
Publisher of Jim Weiss's award-winning storytelling CDs;
excellent selection of children's classics and folklore

Your Story Hour
P.O. Box 15
Berrien Springs, MI 49103
269-471-3701
www.yourstoryhour.org

Catholic Suppliers

Bethlehem Books
10194 Garfield Street South
Bathgate, ND 58216
800-757-6831
www.bethlehembooks.com
Reprints of classic children's literature from the Catholic
tradition, many books of interest to homeschoolers

Catholic Heritage Curricula
P.O. Box 579090
Modesto, CA 95357
800-490-7713 orders
209-551-1781 fax
www.chcweb.com
Curriculum supplemented with additional resources

Ignatius Press
P.O. Box 1339
Fort Collins, CO 80522
800-651-1531
www.ignatius.com

Publisher of Catholic homeschooling books by Laura
    Berquist

Charlotte Mason

Charlotte Mason Research & Supply Company
P.O. Box 296
Quarryville, PA 17566
www.charlottemason.com
Dean and Karen Andreola, owners
Publishers of the Charlotte Mason Companion and articles
    on Mason's philosophy

Queen Homeschool Supply
168 Plantz Ridge Road
New Freeport, PA 15352
888-695-2777
www.queenhomeschool.com
Specializes in the living books popular with a Charlotte
    Mason approach

WinterPromise
10 Folsom Harbor Road
Grand Isle, VT 05458
802-372-9200
www.winterpromise.com
Charlotte Mason-inspired curriculum with living books and
    activities

473

Children's Books

Dorling Kindersley Family Learning
375 Hudson St
New York, NY 10014
800-788-6262 orders
www.dk.com
Publisher of informative and innovative books for adults
    and children; print and online catalog with secure
    ordering

Scholastic Book Clubs
800-724-6527
www.scholastic.com
Discounted software and children's books

Usborne Books at Home
Educational Development Co.
P.O. Box 470663
Tulsa, OK 74147-0663
800-475-4522
www.edcpub.com
Publisher of informative and lavishly illustrated books for
    children

Classical Christian

Canon Press & Book Service
P.O. Box 8729
Moscow, ID 83843
800-488-2034
www.canonpress.org
Publisher of curricula for classical schools, including books
    by Douglas Wilson; print and online catalog

Tapestry of Grace
Lampstand Press
8077 Snouffer School Road
Gaithersburg, MD 20879
800-705-7487
www.tapestryofgrace.com
Publishers of Marcia Somerville's hefty curriculum for high
    school; lovely integration of traditional curricula and
    the providential hand of God through time

Veritas Press
1829 William Penn Way
Lancaster, PA 17601
800-922-5082
717-519-1978 fax

www.veritaspress.com
Publisher and supplier of classical Christian resources and one of
the most beautiful catalogs you are ever likely to see

Well Trained Mind
Peace Hill Press
18021 The Glebe Lane
Charles City, VA 23030
877-322-3445
www.welltrainedmind.com
www.peacehillpress.com

Creation Science

Answers in Genesis
P.O. Box 510
Hebron, KY 41048
800-778-3390
www.answersingenesis.org

Apologia Educational Ministries
1106 Meridian Plaza, Suite 220/340
Anderson, IN 46016
888-524-4724
765-608-3290 fax
www.apologia.com
Christian publisher of excellent middle school and high
     school science curriculum written by Dr. Jay Wile,
     biblical worldview curriculum, and excellent elementary
     material using a Charlotte Mason approach; online
     catalog; secure ordering

Media Angels
www.mediaangels.com
Felice Gerwitz and Jill Whitlock, publishers
Publisher of science study guides for geology, astronomy,
     and anatomy, primarily for elementary students; online
     catalog

Creative Writing

Brave Writer
7723 Tyler's Place Boulevard, #165
West Chester, OH 45069
513-307-1405
www.bravewriter.com
An approach to writing and homeschooling inspired by
    Charlotte Mason

Institute for Excellence in Writing
P.O. Box 6065
Atascadero CA 93423
800-856-5815
www.excellenceinwriting.com
Andrew Pudewa's brainchild for improving writing,
    spelling, and thinking

WriteAtHome
www.writeathome.com
Internet-based writing courses for teens directed by Brian
    Wasko, former high school teacher and homeschool
    father. All coaches are professional writers or educators.

WriteGuide.com
43 Wood Road
Barrington, NH 03825
603-905-9039
www.writeguide.com
Online individualized writing courses for homeschoolers

Driver Education

National Driver Training Institute
4432 Austin Bluffs Parkway
Colorado Springs, CO 80918
800-942-2050
www.nationaldrivertraining.com
Publishers of a certified driver-training course that parents

can conduct; accepted by many states and insurance companies; secure online registration

Financial Management

Crown Financial Concepts
P.O. Box 100
Gainesville, GA 30503-0100
800-722-1976
www.crown.org
Larry Burkett's ministry. Money-management and career-exploration tools for teens. Online catalog and secure ordering

Dave Ramsey
The Lampo Group
1749 Mallory Lane
Brentwood, TN 37027
888.227.3223
Daveramsey.com
Financial Peace University and other excellent resources for responsible money management.

Geography

Bright Idea Press
P.O. Box 333
Cheswold, DE 19936
877-492-8081
www.brightideaspress.com
Maggie Hogan, proprietor
Specializing in geography; also publishes history curricula and timelines

Educational Insights
152 W. Walnut Street, Suite 201
Gardena, CA 90248
888-591-9334
www.educationalinsights.com
School supplier; distributor of GeoSafari Electronic Game

Geography Matters
P.O. Box 92
Nancy, KY 42544
800-426-4650
www.geomatters.com
Cindy and Josh Wiggers, owner
Publisher and supplier of geography curriculum, maps,
    other resources; great links for history and geography;
    online catalog

Knowledge Quest
P.O. Box 789
Boring, OR 97009
877-697-8611
www.knowledgequestmaps.com
Excellent geography program and blackline maps

National Council for Geographic Education
1710 16th Street NW
Washington, DC 20009-3198
202-360-4237
www.ncge.org
Publisher of *Geography for Life* national standards; online
    catalog; secure ordering

History

Beautiful Feet Books
1306 Mill Street
San Luis Obispo, CA 93401
800-889-1978 orders
805-542-9847
www.bfbooks.com
Russ and Rea Berg, publishers
Also suppliers offering great study guides for history using
    classic and quality children's literature

Christian History Institute
P.O. Box 540
Worcester, PA 19490
800-468-0458
www.chitorch.org
Publishers of excellent bulletin inserts on church history;
    many archived online

Cobblestone Publishing
30 Grove Street, Suite C
Peterborough, NH 03458
800-821-0115
603-924-7380 fax
www.cobblestonepub.com
Publishes several history and culture magazines, including
    Cobblestone American history magazine

Diana Waring Presents!
621 State Route 9 NE, PMB B-14
Lake Stevens, WA 98258
425-397-0631
www.dianawaring.com
Bill and Diana Waring, publishers and entertainers
Hilarious presentations; Diana is a popular speaker who has
    produced, among other things, a great history course;
    also a passionate Christian with a heart for missions;
    print and online catalog with secure ordering

Drive Thru History with Dave Stotts
Coldwater Media
P.O. Box 470
Palmer Lake, CO 80133
719-488-8670
www.coldwatermedia.com
Produces exceptional and entertaining DVDs on history
    and other topics

Greenleaf Press
3761 Highway 109 North
Lebanon, TN 37087
615-449-1617
www.greenleafpress.com
Rob and Cyndy Shearer, publishers
Also suppliers; beautiful catalog majoring in history re
    sources and the Greenleaf Press study guides

Home School in the Woods
3997 Roosevelt Highway
Holley, NY 14470
585-964-8188
www.homeschoolinthewoods.com
Specializes in timelines, timeline figures and unit studies

Jackdaw Publications
P.O. Box 503
Amawalk, NY 10501
800-789-0022
www.jackdaws.com
Hands-on primary sources for grades 5–12

Social Studies School Service
10200 Jefferson Boulevard, Box 802
Culver City, CA 90232
800-421-4246
800-944-5432 fax
socialstudies.com
School supplier offering a vast array of resources for high school
    history, cultures, government, civics, and economics courses;
    Advanced Placement resources as well

Veritas Press
1829 William Penn Way
Lancaster, PA 17601
800-922-5082
www.veritaspress.com

Publisher of an exquisite, history-based classical Christian curriculum

Foreign Languages

Greek 'n' Stuff
P.O. Box 882
Moline, IL 61266-0882
309-796-2707
309-796-2706 fax
www.greeknstuff.com
Karen Mohs, owner
Latin and Greek curricula plus great links to the classical world; online catalog

Rosetta Stone
135 W. Market Street
Harrisonburg, VA 22801
800-767-3882
www.rosettastone.com
Excellent language courses used by the Peace Corps, the diplomatic community, and many homeschoolers

Language Arts

Educators Publishing Service (EPS)
P.O. Box 9031
Cambridge, MA 02139-9031
800-225-5750
888-440-2665 fax
www.epsbooks.com
Publisher of *Explode the Code, Wordly Wise,* and other popular resources

Great Source Books
P.O. Box 7050
Wilmington, MA 01887
800-289-4490
www.greatsource.com
Source of Write Source curriculum

481

Total Language Plus
P.O. Box 12622
Olympia, WA 98508
360-754-3660
www.totallanguageplus.com
Publisher of a curriculum that teaches thinking and
communication skills using literature as a base

Literature

Five in a Row
P.O. Box 707
Grandview, MO 64030-0707
816-246-9252
www.fiveinarow.com
Literature-based unit study program for early elementary

Progeny Press
P.O. Box 100
Fall Creek, WI 54742
877-776-4369
715-877-9953 fax
www.progenypress.com
Bible-based study guides to the classics and popular
children's literature; online catalog

Math

Art of Problem-Solving Incorporated
P.O. Box 2185
Alpine, CA 91903-2185
(619) 659-1612
www.artofproblemsolving.com
ETA/Cuisenaire
500 Greenview Court
Vernon Hills, IL 60061
800-445-5985
800-875-9643 fax
www.etacuisenaire.com
Distributor of Cuisenaire products

Boxer Math

www.boxermath.com

Interactive and self-paced math tutorial for students in
grades 3–12; lessons cover fundamentals of arithmetic
through trigonometry

Chalk Dust Company

PMB 256, 16107 Kensington Drive

Sugar Land, TX 77479-4401

800-588-7564

www.chalkdust.com

Dana Mosely, instructor

DVD courses including algebra, algebra II, trigonometry,
pre-calculus, calculus, and SAT review; online product
descriptions

Common Sense Press

Educators Publishing Service

8786 Highway 21

Melrose, FL 32666

352-475-5757

www.commonsensepress.com

Publisher of *Grocery Cart Math*

Curriculum Associates

153 Rangeway Road

North Billerica, MA 01862

800-225-0248

www.curriculumassociates.com

Source of *Figure It Out* workbooks

 Dale Seymour Publications / Pearson Learning

800-848-9500

www.pearsonlearning.com

School supplier of resources for elementary level; online
catalog; secure ordering

Equals
Lawrence Hall of Science
University of California Berkeley
Centennial Drive
Berkeley, CA 94720-5200
510-642-5132
www.lawrencehallofscience.org/equals
Publisher of *Family Math* and several other engaging
    programs for children

Key Curriculum Press
1150 65th Street
Emeryville, CA 94608
800-995-6284
800-541-2442 fax
www.keycurriculumpress.com
Publishers of *Miquon Math* and the Keys to... series; online
    catalog; secure ordering

Learning Wrap-Ups
1660 W. Gordon Avenue #4
Layton, UT 84041
800-992-4966
801-497-0063 fax
www.learningwrapups.com
Deftly simple and hand-held learning aid for teaching basic
    arithmetic facts

Math-U-See
888-854-6284
www.mathusee.com
Innovative and hands-on math program by Steve Demme;
    must be ordered through area representatives; ordering
    information available online

Muggins Math
Old Fashioned Products
4860 Burnt Mountain Road

Ellijay, GA 30536
800-962-8849
706-635-7611 fax
www.mugginsmath.com
Math games; online catalog; secure ordering

Providence Project
14566 NW 110th Street
Whitewater, KS 67154
888-776-8776
www.providenceproject.com
Sequential drills; online catalog; secure ordering

RightStart Math
Activities for Learning
321 Hill Street
P.O. Box 468
Hazelton, ND 58544
888-272-3291
www.alabacus.com

Saxon Publishers
HMH Supplemental Publishers
181 Ballardvale Street
Wilmington, MA 01887
800-289-4490
800-289-3994 fax
www.saxonpub.com
Publisher of a traditional program widely available from
    homeschool suppliers

Singapore Math
404 Beavercreek Road #225
Oregon City, OR 97045
503-557-8100 no phone orders
503-557-8103 fax
www.singaporemath.com
An import gaining broad appeal in the U.S. market against the

485

face of declining math scores; K–12 program, emphasizing problem solving and concepts instead of rote learning; disciplines integrated and introduced much earlier than traditionally taught

Teaching Textbooks
P.O. Box 60529
Oklahoma City, OK 73146-0529
866-867-6284
405-525-3605 fax
www.teachingtextbooks.com
Curriculum for grades 4–7 and from pre-algebra through pre-calculus; companion CDs include a graphic demonstration of all lessons plus steps to correctly solve all problems; students can complete courses with little help from parents

Twenty-Four Math Game
Suntex International
3311 Fox Hill Road
Easton, PA 18045
610-253-5255
www.math24.com
Publisher of games that teach critical thinking using math facts and algebra

VideoText Interactive
800-254-3272
www.videotext.com
Lavishly produced DVD courses for algebra and geometry by master teacher Tom Clark, who is passionate about teaching math from a conceptual level, devoting ample time to the "why" undergirding the steps taken to solve a math problem; well-thought-out animations illustrate each lesson; program builds sequentially on students' prior knowledge

Wide World Publishing/Math Products Plus
P.O. Box 476
San Carlos, CA 94070
650-593-2839
650-595-0802 fax
www.mathproductsplus.com
Publisher of Theoni Pappas's excellent books; online catalog

Parenting Resources
Shepherd Press
800-338-1445
www.shepherdpress.com
Publisher of Tedd Tripp's *Shepherding a Child's Heart* and
    its sequel on parenting teens, *Age of Opportunity* by
    Paul Tripp

Sovereign Grace Ministries
7505 Muncaster Mill Road
Gaithersburg, MD 20877
800-736-2202
www.sovereigngraceministries.com
Publisher of Bible studies and teaching recordings for
    families and small groups; parent organization for
    Joshua Harris's teaching ministry

Whole Heart Ministries
P.O. Box 3445
Monument, CO 80132
800-311-2146 orders
719-488-4466 info
www.wholeheart.org
Clay and Sally Clarkson, owners

Planners
Edu-Track Home School Software
ConTECH Solutions
5517 N. Farmer Branch Road, PMB 130
Ozark, MO 65721866-682-3025

www.contechsolutions.net

High-tech solution to planning lessons and organizing
records; customizable

Ferg N Us Services
P.O. Box 350
Richville, NY 13681
315-287-9131
www.fergnusservices.com

Publisher of the popular Homeschool Journal daily
planners for moms and teens

Homeschool Tracker
TGHomeSoft
4521 Ross Lanier Lane
Kissimmee, FL 34758
www.homeschooltracker.com

Managers of Their Homes
1504 Santa Fe Street
Leavenworth, KS 66048-4141
913-772-0392
www.titus2.com

Publisher of *A Practical Guide to Daily Scheduling for
Christian Home-School Families* by Steve and Teri
Maxwell

Public Speaking

Myers Institute for Leadership & Communication
P.O. Box 7
Dayton, TN 37321
423-570-1000
www.myersinstitute.com

Reading

Educators Publishing Service (EPS)
P.O. Box 9031
Cambridge, MA 02139-9031

800-435-7728
888-440-2665 fax
www.epsbooks.com
Publisher of *Explode the Code* and other phonics-based
workbooks

Pearson Learning Group
800-526-9907
800-393-3156
www.pearsonlearning.com
Publisher of *Sing, Spell, Read and Write* and *Winning*
reading programs

Teach 4 Mastery
800-745-8212
www.teach4mastery.com
Joyce Herzog's *Scaredy Cat Reading* program; use the
website to find your area representative

Also see My Father's World under General Publishers and
Suppliers.

Science
See also Creation Science

American Chemical Society
1155 Sixteenth Street NW
Washington, DC 20036
800-227-5558
www.chemistry.org
Publisher of *The Best of WonderScience*

Apologia Educational Ministries
1106 Meridian Plaza, Suite 220/340
Anderson, IN 46016
888-524-4724; 765-608-3290 fax
www.apologia.com
Christian publisher of excellent middle and high school

science curriculum by Dr. Jay Wile and colorful
elementary science texts by Jeannie Fulbright

Carolina Biological Supply
2700 York Road
Burlington, NC 27215-3398
800-334-5551
www.carolina.com
Large supplier of science resources, lab equipment, and
    supplies; online catalog; secure ordering

Castle Heights Press
200 E. Iowa Avenue
Berthoud, CO 80513
970-532-2209
www.castleheightspress.com
Kathleen and Mark Julicher, publishers
Science programs for high school; online catalog

Delta Education
80 Northwest Blvd.
Nashua, NH 03061-3000
800-258-1302
www.delta-education.com
Hands-on manipulatives for science and math for grades K–8

Home Science Tools
665 Carbon Street
Billings, MT 59102
800-860-6272; 888-860-2344 fax
www.hometrainingtools.com
Supplier of science equipment and labs designed to match
    BJU, A Beka, and other programs

Insect Lore
P.O. Box 1535
Shafter, CA 93263-1535
800-LIVE-BUG

www.insectlore.com
Source of exploratory kits and supplies for life sciences

Lyrical Life Science
8008 Cardwell Hill
Corvallis, OR 97330
800-761-0906
www.lyricallearning.com
Publishers of an excellent upper elementary/junior high
    science program especially suited to auditory learners

National Wildlife Federation
11100 Wildlife Center Drive
Reston, VA 20190
800-822-9919
www.nwf.org
Publishers of Your Big Backyard and other nature magazines
    for kids

Tobin's Lab
P.O. Box 725
Culpeper, VA 22701
540-829-6906
www.tobinslab.com
Homeschool supplier of science resources organized around
    the six days of creation

Tops Learning Systems
10970 S. Mulino Road
Canby, OR 97013
503-266-5200 fax (preferred to calling for orders)
503-263-2040
www.topscience.org
Innovative, low-cost science—and now math—labs designed for
    schools on small budgets; uses many house
    hold items for excellent labs

Wild Goose Science Company
888-621-1040
www.carsondellosa.com
www.wildgoosescience.com

Scope and Sequence

Core Knowledge Foundation
801 E. High Street
Charlottesville, VA 22902
800-238-3233
www.coreknowledge.org
Source of "core knowledge sequence," the scope and sequence
    recommended in E. D. Hirsch's books

World Book Educational Division
233 N. Michigan Avenue, Suite 2000
Chicago, IL 60601
312-729-5800
www.worldbook.com
Scope and sequence "Kindergarten Through Grade Twelve:
    A Typical Course of Study" is published free online

Software

Academic Superstore
2101 E. Saint Elmo Road, Suite 360
Austin, TX 787444
800-817-2347
www.academicsuperstore.com

Barnum Software
1910 Lyon Avenue
Belmont, CA 94002
800-553-9155
800-553-9156 fax
www.thequartermile.com
Broderbund/Edmark/Learning Company
800-395-0277
www.broderbund.com

Broderbund publishes a wide range of popular software. Edmark specializes in software for remediation and rein forcement of skill areas. The Learning Company publishes the Carmen Sandiego software.

Grammar Key
P.O. Box 33230
Tulsa, OK 74153
www.grammarkey.com

Harmonic Vision
210 S. 5th Street, Suite 12
Saint Charles, IL 60174
800-474-0903
www.harmonicvision.com
Publisher of *Music Ace* software

Knowledge Adventure School
800-871-2969
www.knowledgeadventureschool.com
Distributor of *Blaster, Jump Start, Dr. Brain series*, and *Spell It Deluxe* software

Testing Services

College Board
45 Columbus Avenue
New York, NY 10023-6917
212-713-8000
www.collegeboard.com
Publisher of many books to assist students in preparing for College Board-administered tests and for college

Bayside School Services
P.O. Box 250
Kill Devil Hills, NC 27948
800-723-3057
www.baysideschoolservices.com

Bob Jones University Press
Customer Service
1700 Wade Hampton Blvd.
Greenville, SC 29614-0062
800-845-5731
www.bjup.com/services/testing

Family Learning Organization
P.O. Box 1750
Mead, WA 99021-1750
800-405-8378
www.familylearning.org

Piedmont Education Services
1629 Turfwood Drive
Pfafftown, NC 27040
336-924-2494
www.pesdirect.com

Seton Testing Services
1350 Progress Drive
Front Royal, VA 22630
800-542-1066
www.setontesting.com

Sycamore Tree
2179 Meyer Place
Costa Mesa, CA 92627
800-779-6750
www.sycamoretree.com

Unit Studies

Amanda Bennett's Unit Study Adventures
423-243-4748
www.unitstudy.com

Design-A-Study
408 Victoria Avenue
Wilmington, DE 19804-2124
800-965-2719
www.designastudy.com
Kathryn and Richard Stout, publishers
Study guides for language arts, science, math, and social
    studies; online catalog

KONOS
P.O. Box 250
Anna, TX 75409
972-924-2712
www.konos.com
Jessica and Wade Hulcy, publishers
One of the earliest unit study programs, redesigned for ease
    of use; online catalog; secure ordering

Video Instruction

Annenberg Media
P.O. Box 55742
Indianapolis, IN 46205-0742
800-532-7637
317-579-0402 fax
www.learner.org
Distributor of high school- and college-level video courses;
    online catalog; secure ordering

The Teaching Company
4840 Westfields Blvd., Suite 500
Chantilly, VA 20151
800-832-2412
703-378-3819 fax
www.teach12.com
Producer of audio and video courses featuring top-rated lecturers

Used-Curriculum Suppliers

The Back Pack
P.O. Box 125
Ernul, NC 28527
252-244-0728
www.thebackpack.com

Educator's Exchange
10755 Midlothian Turnpike, Suite 308
Richmond, VA 23235
804-794-6994 info
888-257-4159 orders
www.edexbooks.com
Jim and Glenda Chiarello, owners

Follett Educational Services
Home Education Division
1433 International Parkway
Woodbridge, IL 60517-4941
800-621-4272
800-638-4424 fax
www.fes.follett.com
Supplier of used and refurbished textbooks; good source of
    the Chicago Math (UCSMP) student texts, although
    support material must typically be purchased from the
    publisher

Homeschooler's Curriculum Swap
P.O. Box 645
The Dalles, OR 97058
www.theswap.com
Well-organized site with lots of other areas of interest,
    including moderated forums

Moore Expressions
6070 Indiana River Road, Suites 106-112
Virginia Beach, VA 23464
757-523-4965

www.mooreexpressions.com
Cherie Moore, owner
Store and mail order business

CONTACT THE AUTHOR

Debra Bell's Home School Resource Center
P.O. Box 67
Palmyra, PA 17078
E-mail: debraabell@gmail.com
www.debrabell.com

Debra loves to travel and is available to speak at conventions and seminars. These are just a few of her most requested topics:

Twenty-First Century Homeschooling
Homeschooling from a Foundation of Grace
Cultivating a Love for Learning in our Homes
Motivating the Reluctant Learner
Raising an Independent Learner
Developing Creative and Critical Thinking Skills
Choosing and Using Children's Literature
Homeschooling Teens
Determining Your Child's Learning Style
Raising a Writer
Designing a College-Prep High School Program

For a description of these and many other seminar topics, visit www.debrabell.com.

INDEX

NOTES

NOTES

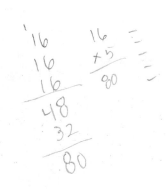